WASTELAND WITH WORDS

Wasteland with Words

A Social History of Iceland

Sigurður Gylfi Magnússon

REAKTION BOOKS

A book for Tinna Laufey and Pétur Bjarni

Published by Reaktion Books Ltd
33 Great Sutton Street
London EC1V 0DX, UK
www.reaktionbooks.co.uk

First published 2010

Printed and bound in Great Britain by
Cromwell Press Group, Trowbridge, Wiltshire

British Library Cataloguing in Publication Data
Magnusson, Sigurdur Gylfi.
Wasteland with words: a social history of Iceland.
1. Social evolution — Iceland.
2. Iceland — Civilization.
3. Iceland — Intellectual life.
4. Learning and scholarship — Iceland — History.
I. Title
949.1'2-DC22

ISBN: 978 1 86189 661 2

Contents

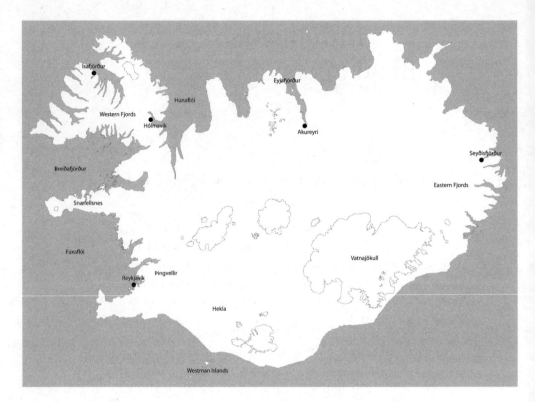

Iceland

Introduction:
Blind Spots in History

There are moments so beautiful, so rich in delight, that the tongue has no words, and the heart as it were shuts itself off against the articulation of emotion, and one of these has always come over me when I have been with you. I know well that you have gone through a baptism of fire of your innermost desires, and now look forward full of hope towards the future of our youths, now that we love each other through real experience and times of danger. But childhood love and the ardour of youth is the hottest of loves, the saying goes. So you will be my strongest spur, and a good woman makes the man steadfast, and the best wages I can have for my labour are if what I do may meet your approval. I would pray to God fervently and from the depths of my soul that he turn our plans to happiness, and strengthen us both on our way along the treacherous path of life.

This is the ending of a love letter that Níels Jónsson, farm labourer from Strandasýsla in the remote north-west of Iceland, wrote to his betrothed, Guðrún Bjarnadóttir, of Gjögur in the same county, during their courtship in the final decade of the nineteenth century. Twenty-two letters of this type have been preserved, all of them long and elaborate, and almost without parallel. Níels was a prolific writer of diaries, letters and copier of texts, like his brother Halldór Jónsson of Miðdalsgröf. Over the last years I have researched the papers of both these men in detail. The material they left behind is vast in quantity and will be described specially later in this book.

The language and imagery and Níels's outpourings of emotion remain strikingly similar from one letter to another. There is also a striking similarity between the letters and his diary entries. In both he speaks with great warmth of 'my lower sweethart' as he is apt to call her, turning to English, which he was learning at the time on his own initiative. In the distance that separated them he often let his mind stray to Gjögur and the home of Guðrún's parents: 'All I can do is to promise my mind the indulgence of flying across the mountains to where it desires to rest the night.'[1] Typical entries in his diary from the time he was in labouring work in the farming districts of Strandasýsla read like this: 'Ah! Dearest friend of my heart! God give you good night! I kiss you with a kiss in the spirit of love, and cleave to your heart, which is in my breast. My mind and my heart are ever with you, my purest and keenest feelings are dedicated to you, while my heart beats, and not unworthily.'[2] It makes one wonder whether he was really talking to himself, maybe rehearsing lines, or perhaps intending his beloved to read the diary when they next met. There is no way of knowing, but the similarities between the diary entries and the language of the love letters are inescapable.

The letters are a powerful testament to Níels's feelings for his beloved. He usually opens them with somewhat formulaic phrases such as: 'My dear-heart beloved Guðrún Bjarnadóttir, may your lot be fortune and happiness! So prays he who loves you.'[3] In this letter from 1892 the salutation is set apart within a special border that forms part of a drawing that decorates the top of the page. Then follows a poem and the beginning of the text, that sounds thus: 'My ardently adored, dearest beloved, may God make all your hours full of joy and fortune. A tender kiss on this letter to carry to you from your loving friend, and more for the letters that you have written me, which have brought me inexpressible pleasure.' The closing words of this particular letter are in similar style to the opening: 'I say farewell to you in spirit, most dearly beloved of my heart, even as you read these lines, and so much more fervently than words can express. I kiss you now and clasp you to me, and ask the good Lord to care for you and bless you, and to lead you on the path of happiness, my unforgettable Guðrún Bjarnadóttir. Your ever-loving Níels Jónsson.'

The letters are strongly individualized by their ornamentation, a feature that must presumably be very rare in declarations of love. A great amount of work has gone into the draughtsmanship of some of them. This interplay of words and form creates a highly effective tool for communicating the intended message, that this was a man speaking from the depths of his heart. Níels was quite aware of this power and on one occasion was unable to resist alluding to it. In a footnote at the end of one letter he writes: 'The rose is ugly and small. I had no time to produce this kind of thing, but, for all that, I felt better about it being different from other letters of the kind you more usually see, for there can be few people that write like this, at least, none that I know or have heard of. It is now past 2 o'clock in the night. I kiss you

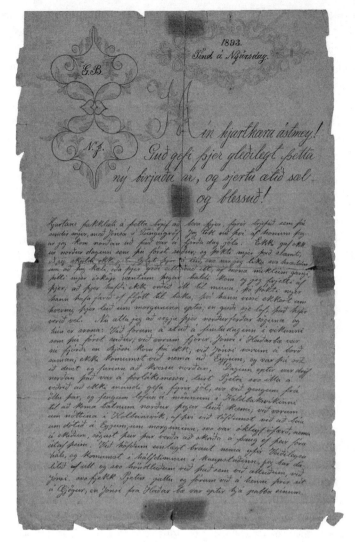

Love and marriage were bound by class in traditional Icelandic rural society. Farmers used the opportunity to secure their own social positions by marrying their sons and daughters into suitable families. Things changed in the nineteenth century as social boundaries began to break down. The opportunities open to young couples increased markedly with the growth of urban centres and the emigrations to America, making it possible for them to move away and start a new life for themselves as independent individuals. Couples could now set their own terms, as we find expressed in the love letters that Níels Jónsson wrote to his betrothed Guðrún Bjarnadóttir. Love was still subject to conditions – it was far from being blind – but it could now have a much greater personal element, as exemplified in the intense language and pictorial decoration of Níels's letter.

more passionately than your heart can imagine. And may you dream sweet angels that carry you to your loving friend.' The rose Níels is referring to is beautifully done – green and red in colour, held up by a hand in flesh tints. His assessment of the drawing serves to underline the seriousness with which the letter was written: as Níels says, nobody else writes letters like this.

In 1997 I published a book based on my research on the brothers Níels and Halldór Jónsson and the people that came into their lives. In this research I made use of a great quantity of personal records from them and others who were alive at the time. In my work I applied a methodology known as 'microhistory' – the historian takes on a smaller unit for study than those that historians customarily deal with and attempts to present and explain it in the greatest depth possible, making use of all available sources that touch on the subject in question. The book came out in Icelandic, published by the University of Iceland Press, under a title that translates as *Education, Love and Grief: A Microhistorical Analysis of Nineteenth- and Twentieth-century Peasant Society in Iceland*.[4]

A year after the book came out I received a letter from a farmer in Strandasýsla, the same county where Níels and Halldór had lived their entire lives. The writer talked about various aspects of my book and appeared largely in favour of most of what it said. But on one point he was in strong disagreement, and that was how I had portrayed the emotional lives of Níels Jónsson and Guðrún Bjarnadóttir. What he had to say suggested that events had occurred that had cast a shadow on their life together, a shadow so long that he could not imagine that relations between these people had been as profoundly loving as the letters led one to believe. This was all he said about it. He thanked me for the book and with that closed his letter of over twenty handwritten sheets.

I was naturally extremely curious to know more. When someone has spent years of his life working on a particular collection of diaries, letters and notebooks, he is liable to form a kind of emotional attachment to his subject. At least, that was how it was with me. After all this time I felt I knew these people almost as well as I knew myself and my own family. My correspondent was however suggesting that I had missed something important. I wrote back to him and asked him to give me the whole story, tell me everything he knew about what had come up in the couple's relations. Some while later, in the summer of 1998, an answer arrived. The writer was a long time bringing himself round to the main issue; it was plainly something he found it difficult to talk about. Finally, however, the story emerged:

I now come to the matter you ask me for clearer information about and that I touched on in my previous letter to you. I was clumsy enough to allude to what I believe turned into a long-standing anguish in the lives of the pair of them. It seems that Níels and Guðrún had not been married and living together long when signs of discord began to appear. Perhaps Níels failed to find in Guðrún the woman he had built up in his imagination while they were courting. There are no reports that one can take as being entirely reliable but I heard two stories on the subject. It was not long before jealousy raised its head and began to come between them. – Níels accused his wife of being unfaithful to him and she the same of him. So far as Guðrún was concerned, I do not think there was anything in this. But I think, and I take it as true, that Níels started going behind his wife's back and got into an affair with a young girl there at Gjögur. This led to arguments, as will happen in such cases, and these became worse and worse.

One time, many years after the death of both the couple, I asked Valdimar Thorarensen of Gjögur about it. Valdimar was a year older than me, born in 1904. So he was not born when this happened, but he was very close to it and all the talk about it. He maintained that Níels had formed an attraction for this young girl that I mentioned. As a result, Guðrún accused Níels of cheating on her. Níels accused Guðrún of the same, without any real grounds. Níels became vehement and heated. To cut a long story short, at this point all hell broke loose.

During these years their daughter Elísabet had been born and she was probably then 2–3 years old. Somehow the child became mixed up in this quarrel of theirs. In one of their bouts of recrimination things got so heated that Níels stormed out with threats aimed at Guðrún, including that she would not need to have any more children bearing his name or they need to argue about other children. He rushed off in furious temper. A long time passed and Níels did not return. People went out to look for him. He was found somewhere a fair way off, racked by torment and helpless with pain, so that they feared for his life.

In his rage he had drawn a cord tight around his testicles and torn them off.

I was dumbstruck and had no idea how to react. The farmer's account of how Níels had castrated himself affected me so deeply that I could never bring myself to answer his letter and thank him. Shortly afterwards my correspondent died at a ripe old age, in his late nineties, without my ever having found myself able to write back to him. He ended his letter by describing what had been done with Níels and the epilogue to this sorry affair:

> He was carried home and they tried to nurse him inasmuch as it was possible. The wound went badly and a doctor was called. At the time Oddur Jónsson was the doctor on Strandir and he lived at Smáhamrar in Tungusveit. – Oddur was a coarse and foul-mouthed man and a heavy drinker (though I do not know whether he had been drinking on this occasion). It was said that he hauled Níels over the coals. – Oddur treated his wounds and said it was a miracle that Níels had not killed himself.
>
> As things happened, Níels began to recover and survived and got back to health and work. But there was a great change. It was said that Níels looked very different afterwards, as a result of his maiming.

My acquaintance with Níels and his people was such that the whole thing seemed inconceivable. I immediately started asking myself whether the sources I had been working with were, by their very nature, simply not to be trusted. I told myself that these events fell outside the scope of my research, since the subject I had actually been interested in was courtship and I had only followed the lives of Níels and Guðrún through this period of their relationship. I tried to take the attitude that what became of them after they got married simply did not matter: I was not writing their biography; my book was about the interplay between education and emotional life (love and grief), and to this extent the emphasis was not directly on these two people and their lives. But even so I was filled with an uncomfortable sense that I had failed to recognize these extreme and violent tendencies in Níels's character. For many years I had pored over the writings of this man and his brother, wondered at their fortitude and perseverance, tried to put myself in their shoes and understand all the intricacies of their thoughts and deeds. And yet despite this I had managed to miss such a profound defect of character as the one that had manifested itself here in so macabre a fashion. How could such a thing happen?

One thing I considered long and hard was whether these events did not call into question the ability of personal sources to shed light on the past. In the end, I came to the conclusion that this was not so. It was simply not possible to assume that a limited collection of texts might tell us everything. It was a bit like someone nowadays waking up one day to discover that the man who lives in the house next door is some monstrous serial killer. The horror and disgust prevents people from putting what has happened into any kind of coherent context. They even blame themselves for failing to realize what was going on when the perpetrator had stood before their eyes every day of the year.

This book is built first and foremost upon personal writings and other contemporary records of people's experience of their own times – records such as newspaper articles and other public commentary on life and human existence. Sources like these, it seems to me, provide us with our best chance to present past conditions and events in the way I am seeking, that is, in so far as they impinged on people's personal lives. The intention here is not to 'magic up' the past as it was but to try to tell an interesting story, a story of people set against the background of their country's cultural history. This story has significant differences from what happened in most other Western countries and perhaps casts an interesting light on how Iceland and its people went on to develop in the twentieth century.

As has already become clear, these sources – personal sources – just like any other sources, are far from perfect. They present illuminating momentary images from the past, but they tell only a fragment of what actually happened. What they do above all is allow us to look at the aspects of human existence that touch individuals closest, the most personal things in people's lives. The approach taken here directs our sight at matters outside those that customarily lie at the centre of general works of history. The focus is particularly on cultural history, how culture and education shaped the lives of individuals and provided them with opportunities for personal development in a society that, for most of the period we are looking at, remained unsophisticated and almost entirely devoid of the formal institutions that had developed in other Western nations. To appreciate the unique character of this society it is necessary to present the individual and his position in it in as clear a light as possible. While most of the book concentrates on conditions and changes in the eighteenth, nineteenth and early twentieth centuries, the time when Iceland was taken its first steps towards Western forms of administration and production, it also looks back to earlier periods in the country's history when necessary, to explain the roots of the culture on which the later history rested. Despite its emphasis on the early modern age, the book therefore provides a broad overview of Iceland's cultural history during the last 1,100 years.

As fortune would have it, Iceland preserves a rich variety of sources from the hands of ordinary working people – both in manuscript form, such as diaries, letters, autobiographies or other biographical material, and contributions to public media such as newspapers and journals. This fund of material allows us to approach the past in a quite different way from that taken in conventional economic and political history. This does not mean that economic and political developments can be ignored; simply that they will set within the context of the lives of real people at all levels of society.

The book builds upon a quarter of a century's research into personal sources and popular culture in Iceland. The fruits of this research have appeared in many books and articles published both in Iceland and abroad. The path taken here – the concentration of personal sources and the microhistorical method – is somewhat unusual in general overviews of history, but I write in the belief that a fresh approach may open up new ways of understanding the past.

I have long held reservations about the validity of 'broad-brush' overviews of history as a medium for presenting and explaining events from the past. History is a relatively young field of higher study in Iceland, and this has perhaps encouraged Icelanders to produce more of this kind of work than one finds in most other countries; many areas of Icelandic history have been little researched, and some not at all, and in order to provide some kind of understanding of the structure of Icelandic society many academic historians have felt obliged to produce wide-ranging syntheses of the country's history aimed at illustrating long-term trends and developments. It is largely a question of demand. Meanwhile, outside Iceland academic attitudes have moved on: the value of historical overviews has been called into serious question, in particular in their implicit claim that the author knows more than is credible about what actually happened, that he or she is capable of putting themselves into the shoes of many different groups of people at different times and giving each of them equal prominence.

This is of course not to say that summary overviews have no place in the writing of history. For instance, historians writing about remote or exotic regions inevitably have to rely on more or less universally acknowledged 'facts' from the area in question – at least, this is the approach usually taken. Like other works of general history, the present book aims to provide the reader with a solid overview of the general development of Icelandic society. But, as noted earlier, the primary focus is on cultural and educational history, with the centre of attention on the individual and an attempt to present the narrative from his or her point of view. This, I hope, will give readers a sense of kinship and involvement with the material and enable them to draw comparisons between what is special to Icelandic culture and what one finds equally in the histories of other countries.

A number of points are worth noting at the outset.

Throughout this book I use the Icelandic system of naming when referring to Icelanders: 'Sigurður writes . . .', for instance. Personal names in Iceland still follow the ancient Germanic system of given name plus patronymic. Thus the leader of the earliest recorded European attempt to settle mainland North America, Leifur Eiríksson, was called Leifur but *was* Eiríksson, that is, the son of Eiríkur (the Red). Eiríksson is not considered a name but a fact, and was not passed on to Leifur's children. The same is true for women: the singer Björk Guðmundsdóttir is named Björk and she is the daughter of Guðmundur. Since most Icelanders have no surnames, women cannot take their husband's names on marriage. Similarly, the use of first names does not imply familiarity: the former president, Vigdís Finnbogadóttir, is referred to as 'Vigdís forseti' (President Vigdís), or just Vigdís, never President Finnbogadóttir or the like. Familiarity is usually indicated by using a pet form of the given name, for example, Halldór Jónsson refers to his brother Níels as Nilli. Something like ten to fifteen per cent of Icelanders have surnames. These can be recognized by their not ending in -son or -dóttir, for example the writer and Nobel prize winner Halldór Laxness. But the principle of first-name use still applies.

The vast majority of the sources used in this book are of course written in Icelandic. Much of what they say deals with a world which is very different from modern Icelandic society and putting it into English has proved a difficult and complex task. Wherever possible I have tried to stay as close to the originals as I could. But in many cases literal translation would have made the text barely comprehensible and I have compromised for the sake of clarity and, at times, to give what I hope is a better idea of the style or 'feel' of the original. The translations, and much else in the book, are the result of co-operation between me and my editorial assistant, the grammarian and translator Nicholas Jones.

The Icelandic language is descended from the Old Norse spoken by the original Viking settlers in the ninth and tenth centuries. However, while the other Scandinavian languages (Danish, Norwegian and Swedish) have changed considerably over the centuries, in part due to influence from other European languages, Icelandic has remained remarkably conservative – at least in matters of grammar and vocabulary. The thirteenth-century sagas, for instance, are readily readable by modern Icelanders. By the late Middle Ages, Icelandic would have been incomprehensible to other Scandinavians, and the language formed, and forms, an important element in Icelanders' sense of national identity.

Icelandic uses a number of characters not found in English. There are various systems of transliteration but I decided, in the interests of consistency, to keep to the Icelandic forms of names and other words cited. I hope this gives the reader a sense of closer contact and involvement with the text and the cultural world it describes.

This is not the place for a detailed account of the pronunciation of modern Icelandic but the following hints may prove helpful.

Stress

All words are stressed on the first syllable. So the name *Guðmundur Ólafsson* has the same stress pattern as *Jonathan Robinson*.

Vowels

All Icelandic vowels have long and short variants – short before two or more consonants, long before no or one consonant. This is not easy to show in English, but where two closest equivalents are given, the first is short and the second long.

vowel	closest equivalent
a	*shut, calm*
á	*now*
e	*bed,* Br.E. *Mary*
é	*yes*
i, y	*bid*
í, ý	*need*
o	Br.E. *pod,* Br.E. *law*
ó	Am.E. *load*
u	*put* (or, better, between *put* and *pit*)
ú	*boot*
æ	*ride*
ö	Br.E. *word*
ei, ey	*day*
au	French *feuille.* Say *early* and miss out the 'l'

Consonants

All consonants are pronounced. Consonants written double are pronounced long: so, for instance, the -dd- in *Edda* is like the -d d- in *I did do!*

ð (Ð)	*with, mother.* Called 'eth'
g	many variants. The best bet is *good, big.* Never as in *ginger*
h	also pronounced in 'hl', 'hn', 'hr'

hv	/kv/, or /hw/ as in Am.E., Irish *where*
j	*yes, m*[y]*usic*
s	*sauce*, never *rose*
þ (Þ)	*think*. Called 'thorn'

The book is made up of an Introduction and eighteen chapters of approximately equal length, covering areas such as changes within society, the family and the opportunities open to individuals for personal growth and development. As noted, the emphasis is primarily on the last three hundred years, but with discussion of earlier times where appropriate. In particular, this includes the medieval period, and especially the literary heritage that was created at the time – the Icelandic sagas – and that has had, and continues to have, an enormous influence on Icelandic concepts of culture and education. I have tried to keep the chapters fairly short and self-contained, as much as possible without depending on direct knowledge of the material in the chapters before or after. However, the material is intended to build up to present a coherent and integrated story that can be followed throughout the book.

I have tried to keep the number of references in check, though with mixed success. The emphasis is on the individual and his or her place in history, and I have therefore chosen to let the sources speak for themselves, to present readers with people's own accounts of their experience of the various events and circumstances in which they were involved. The list of sources is largely limited to works in English and that are fairly readily accessible to readers interested in extending their knowledge of Icelandic history and society further.

I

Modern Times: Society, Work and Demography

After long years of poverty and stagnation, Icelandic society underwent huge changes in the eighteenth, nineteenth and twentieth centuries – changes that touched people at all levels of society. Some of these changes had their roots in contemporary political upheavals, both elsewhere in Europe and at home in Iceland, around the struggle for independence. Doubtless more important, however, were the new social and cultural opportunities that were opening up to people for the first time in the country's history. The propertied classes' fear of any kind of social disruption was hardly a particularly Icelandic phenomenon; it existed in equal measure throughout Europe and in America. The political changes of the nineteenth century threatened the entire social and economic fabric of the Western world and promised to undermine the power of the moneyed classes in Iceland and elsewhere. New groups within society were demanding their say, while others found themselves more downtrodden than ever before as capitalist modes of agriculture began to take root.

The most obvious characteristic of Icelandic society in the eighteenth and nineteenth centuries was the sparse and scattered nature of its settlement. The local farming districts and their culture reigned supreme, dwarfing in influence the little pockets of urban settlement that started to coalesce during the period. The land was poor and its inhabitants were entirely dependent on the vagaries of the weather. For much of the country the eighteenth century was a time of difficult farming conditions and things only started to improve around 1820. Thereafter the changes in living conditions, working practices and culture began to gather pace. The new conditions that appeared in most areas of human life in the nineteenth century laid the foundations for the even greater changes that were to occur in Iceland in the following century.

The island and the people who lived there

Iceland is an island of about 103,000 square kilometres located in the North Atlantic Ocean. It was colonized in the ninth century, mostly by farmers of Norwegian extraction, as part of the Viking migrations. By the eleventh century the population had reached 70,000, around a third of that of Norway at the time.[1] Iceland was incorporated into the kingdom of Norway in the latter half of the thirteenth century, and subsequently, in 1383, it followed Norway when Norway was merged with Denmark. From then up until the twentieth century, the Icelanders were subjects of the Danish crown. Despite this, the people retained a distinct culture shaped by their harsh and isolated island environment. Notably, the Icelanders spoke their own language, which by the later Middle Ages was incomprehensible to speakers of the continental Scandinavian languages: Icelandic remained close to the Old Norse brought by the original settlers, while Norwegian, Danish and Swedish diverged considerably under the influence of other European tongues.[2]

Iceland's isolation was somewhat alleviated in the eighteenth and the nineteenth centuries. The country became a focus of interest for a sizeable group of educated European aristocrats interested in the folk cultures of remote European societies.[3] In his study of nineteenth-century political developments in Iceland, the historian Guðmundur Hálfdanarson tries to explain the attraction the place exerted over these foreign travellers, and what they might expect to see once they got there:

> Drawn to this northern country by their hunger for exploring the exotic, the upper-class travellers certainly got what they were looking for. The landscape of the desolate island was unlike any they had experienced; scars of an unceasing struggle between the natural elements abounded and made large parts of the country a wasteland. Extensive tracts of lava, where only moss seemed to grow, black sand-deserts, hills eroded of all soil, and snow-capped mountains, served as constant reminders of the ever-present ice and fire. Furthermore, the harsh climatic conditions set their distinctive mark on the cultural landscape. Long winters and cool summers, strong winds and incessant rains rendered commercial grain growing impossible in Iceland and severely restricted all arboreal vegetation. Thus, the countryside lacked the familiar and comforting sight of fields or trees, further emphasizing the country's desolation.[4]

A Swede called Uno von Troil, who accompanied Sir Joseph Banks on his expedition to Iceland in the summer of 1772, described his impressions of the country in the following terms:

> We seemed here to be in another world; instead of the fine prospects with which we had fed our eyes, we now saw only the horrid remains of many devastations. Imagine to yourself a country, which from one end to the other presents to your view only barren mountains, whole summits are covered with eternal snow, and between them fields divided by vitrified cliffs, whole high and sharp points seem to vie with each other, to deprive you of the sight of a little grass that springs up scantily among them. These same dreary rocks likewise conceal the few scattered habitations of the natives, and a single tree does no where appear that may afford shelter to friendship and innocence. I suppose, Sir, this will not inspire you with any great inclination of becoming an inhabitant of Iceland; and indeed at first sight of such a country one is tempted to believe it impossible to be inhabited by any human creature, if the sea, near the shores, was not every where covered with boats.[5]

It was not only the landscape and scenery that struck the many foreign travellers from the upper ranks of European society that visited the country as disconcerting and alien; the people too often seemed strange and outlandish. In the summer of 1789 the English baronet Sir John Stanley of Alderley led a party to Iceland which included a young man of West Indian origin named Isaac S. Benners, who was studying chemistry in Edinburgh at the time. Benners's diary entry for Friday, 17 July, records his observations of the Icelanders he encountered on his journey around the Snæfellsnes peninsula in the west:

> The people are very far from being bright, they appear the most stupid wretches I have seen, they are not so well made both here & at Harnefjord [Hafnafjörður] & in short all those we saw from the Inland Country, as the Inhabitants of the Fero Isles, neither are the Women so handsome & well made, but neither of them can boast of beauties, at least I have seen no alluring Objects in neither. We soon had reason to be disgusted with the behaviour of the Icelanders in every part we visited, they shew no marks of obliging, and when they attempt to render one any Service, it is so much clothed in lucrative views, that a penetration of no great depth may soon discover how far their attention leads them to self interest & that with conniving

& mean Cunningness & in this they excel. The Icelanders are very indolent, upon fish alone they daily wants depend, happy for them, that this their only support affords them not much trouble, otherwise they would inevitably fall a sacrifice to their own laziness, rather than undergo the least exertion, there are many farms, but far from being in the highest state of Culti-vation, Grain, they have not much of, nor have they but a very scanty allowance of Greens, the Inhabitants are most of them afflicted with Scrophulous Ringworms, Itch &c. they all kiss one another upon taking leave, & are not satisfied with one but 3 or 4 kisses.[6]

Given the size of the country and its tiny population, Iceland indeed created a very different impression from anywhere else in Europe. The country was almost entirely rural, with farmsteads scattered usually with long distances between them throughout the lower lying areas. Isolation was the norm rather than the exception. Communication was extremely difficult due to the complete absence of roads and the frequent obstacles presented by glaciers and fast-flowing rivers. Each farm was in this sense an island of its own, often with minimal contact with the outside world, especially during the long, cold, dark months of winter. In addition, the frequency and unpredictability of earthquakes and volcanic eruptions, which repeatedly led to the destruction of grazing land and ensuing famine, made all life in Iceland uncertain and problematic. It is against this background, a background of a constant challenge to survive everyday conditions, that we have to consider the individual participants whose lives are described in this book.

During the eighteenth and nineteenth centuries Europe went through a period of significant population growth – significant in various respects and with repercussions that were felt at all levels of society. This increase in population has been cited as one of the major causes of the chain of events that led to the Industrial Revolution and the introduction of capitalist modes of agriculture, as well as being an impetus behind the emigration from European countries to the New World. These changes occurred in Iceland in much the same way as else-where in Europe and the emigrations of the nineteenth and early twentieth centuries form the material for later chapters in this book.

It is worth taking a brief look at the demography of Iceland in the relevant period. The eighteenth century was a time of immense hard-ship: in the first decades of the century the population fell below 50,000 and did not rise back past this figure again until the second decade of the nineteenth century.[7] During the century the country suffered repeated catastrophes in the form of epidemics, earthquakes and eruptions. In the eruptions much of the farming land was poisoned by layers of volcanic ash that led to virulent cattle diseases, leading in turn to famines in which a substantial part of the population starved, with mortality particularly high among the most productive members of society. By the last quarter of the eighteenth century the country was unable to support more than a little over 40,000 people. Between 1787 and the end of the century the population recovered rapidly, but then remained stable until 1830. This number of people, however, was barely sufficient to maintain normal life in the country and in many places it became difficult to effect even the most essential tasks.[8] For most Icelanders life remained very hard for the first two decades of the nineteenth century. Thereafter things began to improve somewhat and the population increased steadily as agriculture, the fisheries and trade began to develop.

A balance was restored in the nineteenth century as the average age of marriage fell, the birth rate increased, and more children survived into adulthood. But as time went on resources became increasingly stretched; young people found it more difficult to obtain land to set up on their own and support a family and the average age of marriage rose again, to about thirty for both sexes, consigning ever more Icelanders to a lifetime of bound service. A further factor in these developments was that for much of the nineteenth century climatic conditions in Iceland were tolerable and at times relatively good. There was little disruption to farming from natural disasters. Infant mortality fell sharply in the second half of the nineteenth century, largely as a result of improved diet and, probably, new ideas about breastfeeding and childrearing.[9] As a result there was a considerable increase in population in the second half of the nineteenth century, a development that had a wide range of consequences for society.

One such consequence was the increased importance acquired by fishing as a source of employment and income in the nineteenth century. The growth of fisheries put great pressure on the existing form of society, based as it was on the pre-eminence of the farming communities, with rural households forming the backbone of the nation. This old system presented few openings for people interested in making their living in any other way. By law, every person had to have a fixed place of abode and, if not an independent farmer, to have a place within the system of tied service. Viable farming land being limited, rural society was hard pressed to accommodate the increase in population. Existing farms were divided into smaller units and new farms were set up on marginal upland. The shortage of land led to an increase in the size of households. Farmworkers, most of whom under normal conditions would have eventually established themselves as independent farmers, were constrained to remain in service. Fewer and fewer got the chance to set up on their own and live independently. The structure of society was thus put into a state of flux and for many the solution lay in the urban areas that were beginning to develop along the coasts of the country, or away from Iceland altogether. It was under these conditions that the emigrations to North America got under way around 1870. It is not unreasonable to suppose that one of the main motives was an attempt by ordinary people to break free of the stranglehold of those who controlled society, the landowning farmers. People who found their options severely limited in the rural areas of Iceland chose to move out and settle either on the coast or try their luck even farther away in the New World – in the land of the free and the brave, the USA and Canada.[10]

Despite the degree of tension and upheaval within rural society in the second half of the nineteenth century, ordinary people remained fettered within the system of tied service.[11] Only a small proportion of farmers owned the land they lived on; the rest were tenants who worked the land armed only with the sweat of their brow and without any but the most rudimentary tools and equipment. Most were sheep farmers and running a farm was a labour-intensive business, with production based on hand power alone. There were a number of months a year during which work went on more or less day and night. In between, the use of manpower was patchy, making production levels throughout society very low. The working year was divided broadly between three different areas: first, there was the work on the land – cultivation, haymaking and other matters relating to the upkeep of buildings and meadows – second, there was the animal husbandry and the accumulation of various kinds of supplies for the household; and third, there was the processing of dairy produce and wool. These jobs were distributed fairly evenly across the year, with one taking over from another without large breaks and often overlapping. This pattern was repeated year after year.

This mode of production depended on the availability of a large and cheap labour force. Working people were obliged to contract themselves to a farm for one year at a time. This system of bonded service put severe constraints on people's freedom and extended to between 35 and 40 per cent of the entire population of Iceland through most of the nineteenth century. Its primary function appears to have been to supply farmers with a ready source of cheap labour; in addition, it prevented poor and unlanded people from establishing families, since permission to marry was dependent on control of enough land to be self-sufficient. In its justification, it also served to provide a safety net for the poor, designed to ensure that everyone was able to keep a secure roof over their head and to prevent them from falling into destitution in times of hardship. However, the laws on bonded service were frequently applied with great inflexibility and severity. One significant effect was that the average age of marriage remained very high in Iceland and a large percentage of each generation never managed to achieve the point where it could change its social status, especially as we move further into the nineteenth century.

At the heart of Icelandic society in this period lay agriculture, which was almost the only source of income and sustenance for the vast majority of the people. Farming in Iceland revolved entirely around livestock and the production of fodder for winter feed. The majority of farms were small and relatively unproductive. The size of farms differed considerably and was determined by the number of cattle the land could support. The number of farms had not changed for centuries, at around 4,000 'assessed farms', many of which were subdivided into independent or dependent farms. At the beginning of the nineteenth century only ten per cent of farms were operated by the person who owned the land. This changed during the latter part of the nineteenth century and at the beginning of the twentieth, when the church and state started to sell off their landholdings on reasonable terms in an attempt to bolster the underpinning of the peasant society and to prevent the constant drift of workers from one county to another. A further motive behind this move was to encourage farmers to break new lands and improve their farms. By around 1910 the number of those owning their own farms had reached 37.5 per cent; by 1930 it stood at 58.8 per cent.[12]

The commune

The independent farms formed the core of the commune (*hreppur*). Each commune contained at least twenty farms. The total number of farming units in Iceland in the eighteenth and nineteenth centuries was around 6,000, taking in farms of all types – assessed farms (*lögbýli*), independent farms (*heimajörð*) and dependent farms (*hjáleigur*). The distinction between these types depended on their different duties to the commune. The social historian Gísli Ágúst Gunnlaugsson points out that the number of dependent farmers, cottars and tenant farmers stood at around 2,200 at the start of the eighteenth century, in addition to the dependent farmers, but that this figure rose as the nineteenth century progressed. To give an indication of the extent of this expansion in the farming community during the nineteenth century we can compare the number of households in the period in question. In 1703 Iceland contained 8,191 households; by 1861 this number had risen to 9,607, the increase being almost entirely the result of the growing number of dependent farms, cottages and tenant farms. Dependent farms were always part of an independent farm, but with a separate farmhouse

Traditional agriculture was highly labour-intensive. Sheep and cattle rearing required a considerable input of time and effort in tending the livestock and ensuring sufficient food supplies to last over the long winter while the animals were kept inside. When conditions were right for mowing and bringing in the hay in summer, everyone was called on to do their part, young and old alike. The work continued night and day with little rest until the hay was safely under cover. Everything was done by hand with the aid of horses.

and operated by a separate family. The farmers of assessed farms were responsible for paying the tithe for both independent and dependent farms and had to arrange the proportion of the tithe each farmer had to bear. The actual types of work done on the two types of farm were more or less identical: the difference lay in the size of the farms, a difference which undoubtedly 'had far-reaching consequences in a country where a large proportion of the population was constantly struggling on the margins of subsistence.'[13]

The central function of the commune in Icelandic rural society was to administer poor relief and determine if and where individual paupers qualified for it. By law, the provision of poor relief was the duty of a person's home commune, that is, the one where they were born. In practice, this requirement often proved highly problematic. In many cases families and individuals who became destitute were forcibly removed from distant parts of the country back to their home commune. Individuals could, however, earn the right to poor relief in a commune other than their own after living in it for ten consecutive years. As a result, people on the edge of poverty were often forced to move when they approached ten years' residence in a commune because the local authorities were anxious to avoid any liability for new calls on their poor relief.

Poor relief and its administration was one of the most hotly debated issues of the nineteenth century. The law had remained unchanged from 1280 until 1834, when some statutory limitations were introduced on the transportation of paupers, for example, the enforced movement of pregnant women to their commune of origin was made illegal. But these reforms did nothing to change the fundamental principles of the law: that those who needed poor relief should be forcibly removed to their home commune and that those who received it were not allowed to marry until it had been repaid. Parliament tinkered with these laws throughout the nineteenth century but it was not until the start of the twentieth century that any wholesale reform was undertaken. However much sympathy politicians might express for the plight of those thrown back on the commune, the effect of the law remained essentially the same. It was not until 1917 that major changes were introduced, and not until 1934 that those on relief were given the right to vote. The debate divided the nation very much along established lines, with liberal nationalists who wanted to ease restrictions on one side and on the other conservative nationalists set on maintaining things as they were. Huge amounts of ink were spilt over the issue in newspapers and magazines.[14] In essence, the local authorities encouraged the independent farmers to evict their tenants if there appeared any likelihood that they might pose a burden on local resources. In many instances it was very difficult for poor people to establish themselves in a commune other than their own without substantial financial backing, which of course few had.

There was a further aspect to the problem. Farms differed greatly in size and, because of the type of farming practised in Iceland, tended to be spread over large areas. Pasturing demanded space, which was one of the main reasons that village communities never developed in Iceland in the same way as in most other parts of rural Europe. When population pressure increased, as it did markedly in the nineteenth century, the tendency was to divide up the available land and establish new farms in marginal and less productive areas, especially on higher land closer to the interior. When temperatures dropped, as in the 1850s and early 1880s, the consequences could be catastrophic: farmers in these newly established areas and those living on small dependent farms found themselves unable to support themselves and their families and were driven from their land. Many were forced to apply for relief to the local commune and their families were split up. As a result the local authorities were encouraged to regulate the activities of the poorer section of society even more closely.

Poor relief was seen as a great burden on society and the authorities often took draconian measures to expel poor families, often with large numbers of children, from their commune. It should be borne in mind that, when people became recipients of poor relief, they lost all right to participate in society as free members until they had paid back what they had received. In addition, as many autobiographies attest, turning to the community for assistance came at a severe emotional cost of shame and humiliation. Recipients immediately became second-class citizens. A huge stigma attached to the word *sveitalimur*, denoting a person in receipt of poor relief. Writer after writer describes the struggle they or their relatives went through to settle their debts to the local authorities. Their desire to buy their freedom was often motivated simply by pride. But there were also practical considerations for people's often long and bitter struggles for personal independence, such as the desire to marry. One autobiographer, Hafsteinn Sigurbjarnarson (b. 1895), describes in detail the hardships his mother went through to be able to pay off her debts, as well as the satisfaction and relief once they had been paid: 'Now I was no longer called a waif and a pauper, because my mother had repaid what she owed to the commune.'

Paradoxically, the same independent farmers who collectively controlled the local government which often discouraged farm rental were under temptation as individuals to divide up their land and rent it out. This was one of the few ways in which an individual could capitalize on his assets and increase his wealth: it not only provided the owner with money for the land but in many instances the tenant was also forced to rent livestock. The economic historian Magnús S. Magnússon points out that '[t]he practice of cattle hire – sometimes with a rate of interest of 16 per cent – became a widespread means to extract more income (other than land rent) by the landlord providing cattle for the tenant's farm.'[15] This practice continued throughout the nineteenth century and was one of the reasons why farmers fought so vigorously against the spread of independent settlements along the coast, where cottars could manage on much smaller pieces of land by supplementing their farming with fishing.

The class structure and the economy

Despite the low productivity of each farm, the type of agriculture practised in Iceland was highly labour-intensive, largely because of the rudimentary technology available and the generally poor quality of the land. As a result, farming households remained comparatively large throughout the nineteenth century. At times when population growth outstripped the demand for labour, the local authorities were generally ready to turn a blind eye when people with outstanding poor-relief debts married and started farming marginal land. But for most years of the nineteenth century this outlet was unavailable and traditional farming society came under increasing pressure. Towards the end of the century the pressure was relieved somewhat by a mounting exodus of people from the country to the coast. This of course created its own problems for the local authorities in their attempts to control the number of paupers and the activities of unattached wage-earners and to regulate who and under what circumstances people could marry. The disruption caused by the population growth of the nineteenth century convinced the authorities still further of the need for tight controls over family building. As Gísli Ágúst Gunnlaugsson points out, action was taken with the aim of both 'maintaining the unit's highest production efficiency, and at the same time, keeping unemployment as low as possible.'[16] Legislation such as the poor laws and legal definitions of the social classes played a central part within this system of social control, working entirely in the interests of the taxpaying section of society. Farmers' representatives lobbied parliament repeatedly for stricter controls on marriage among the poor in both rural and coastal areas. The liberal government in Denmark, on the other hand, consistently refused to acknowledge the need for such laws as they ran counter to their principles of granting their subjects increased freedoms. In the event, through the whole of the nineteenth century little was done to narrow the great economic divide between those who owned their farms or were successful tenants and those who were at the mercy of the farming community.

Gísli Ágúst Gunnlaugsson identifies ten different groups within nineteenth-century agricultural society in Iceland:

1 – Crown officials (*embættismenn*) (who were often farmers as well). This group can be further divided into several categories according to education, economic, social, and political status. 2 – Landowning farmers (*sjálfseignarbændur*) who were not crown officials. This group can also be subdivided according to the value and size of land owned. 3 – Merchants (*kaupmenn*) and artisans (*handverksmenn*). This was until the turn of the twentieth century a relatively small group, but grew in size during the last decades of the nineteenth century. 4 – Tenant farmers (*leiguliðar*). This group can also be divided into two or three categories according to economic means, size of land, live-stock, terms of tenancy etc. 5–6 – Sub-tenants (*hjáleigumenn*) and cottars (*búðsetumenn*). The position of these differed slightly. Their social and economic position was in most cases weak, but they enjoyed a household situation of their own. 7–8 – Lodgers (*húsmenn*) and boarders

(*lausamenn*). Although their legal status varied slightly, these groups enjoyed in theory, at least, a household status of their own, although (particularly in farming districts) they often resided within households where they worked. They could freely dispose their labour capabilities, live as day laborers in towns and villages or be seasonal workers in farming districts. 9 – Servants (*vinnuhjú*). They did not enjoy a household status of their own and were forced to sign (although probably their contracts were often verbal) a contract with a head of household on an annual basis. 10 – Paupers (*þurfamenn*). This group lacked several personal, political, and economic rights enjoyed by others. Paupers can be divided into sub-groups according to whether or not they lived (with the help of poor relief) in a household of their own or were cared for in the household of taxpaying farmers.[17]

Although agriculture remained by far the main occupation in nineteenth-century Iceland, many farmers who had access to the sea also relied quite heavily on fishing. Most fishing was done from open rowing boats that could be managed with a relatively small crew. Late in the century the industry was revolutionized with the introduction of larger decked vessels powered by sail. The fishing season varied from one part of the country to another as the cod migrated north from the south coast late in spring: in the north and north-west the season lasted from about April to September, with a break in summer

The boat in the picture is typical of those used by Icelandic fishermen over the centuries. Often the boats were even smaller. Open boats of this type were highly unreliable and many Icelandic men were lost at sea every year.

for haymaking; in the south-west, the 'winter season', as it was called, ran from February to mid-May.

Inland farmers too, especially those in the south of the country, often supplemented their incomes with seasonal fishing. They left their homes in February and travelled to the fishing stations along the coast, staying on well into spring. In return for their labour they took an agreed share of the catch, which was dried and taken back to the farm for domestic consumption. Often the farmer was accompanied by his older sons and male servants, leaving his wife and younger children behind to tend the livestock. The fishing was treated as part of servants' normal terms of service at the farm, for which the annual pay was agreed in advance, with the farmer taking a share of the catch. This arrangement had various advantages for inland farmers: it provided employment for surplus workforce during the quietest part of the farming year, and it provided a ready market for some of the goods produced on the farm, such as butter and wool, which were bartered for dried fish. Dried fish came to form an important part of the diet even on inland farms, used to tide families over when food supplies began to run low in spring.

Cottars or the landless poor also depended heavily on fishing. Through most of the nineteenth century the local authorities attempted, with considerable success, to prevent landless cottars from moving out of the farming districts and settling on the coast. Permission to settle depended on control of enough land to support a cow. This land had to be rented from a landowner, and after 1863 landowners were obliged to obtain the permission of the local authority to rent land to cottars. An act of 1887 also required cottars to prove that they had assets of 400 krónur (a considerable sum at the time) and possession of land and household equipment, both measures designed to tie cottars to rural areas. As fishermen, cottars either worked on their own open boats or, more often, in the crews of coastal farmers. If fishing proved insufficient to provide for their needs, they took on work as day labourers in the surrounding areas or moved to farming districts for seasonal work. In general the social and economic situation of cottars remained highly unstable and destitution was never far away: a poor fishing season could force them back onto poor relief, a fate that everyone was anxious to avoid.

The rapid growth of population in Europe in the middle years of the nineteenth century created a boom in markets. The increased demand for food, and particularly for salted cod and shark liver oil, made fishing a much more profitable occupation than it had been up till then. Icelandic and Danish merchants had experimented with decked vessels earlier in the century but it was not until the latter part of the nineteenth century that such ships came into common use. These new, larger vessels could carry more fish and operate further out to sea and so exploit the richer fishing grounds surrounding the country on all sides. The change in actual fishing technology was minimal: work on the new decked vessels was still an individual occupation, with each member of the crew having their own hook and line and the catch being distributed among the crew according to traditional rules, basically the same as those used on the smaller oared boats. Despite this, the change from the rowing boats to decked sailing ships encountered considerable resistance: certain conditions were necessary for the new methods to succeed, as Magnús S. Magnússon points out:

> Fisheries, on a larger scale than the customary rowing-boats could sustain, required a) good knowledge in both ocean navigation and fishing; b) fishermen to man the vessels for longer periods than previously experienced; c) high capital outlets, and d) a minimum of land-based facilities on private coastal land. Often these requirements could only be achieved through a partnership or co-operation of merchants, fishermen (captains) and financiers, which also implied that the risks were spread on many hands. The personal engagement of the Icelandic merchants was presumably a key factor which spurred them to mobilize the available resources into modern fisheries.[18]

The decked vessels had little impact on Icelandic society before around 1880. They remained in use into the first decades of the twentieth century, when there was a further revolution with the introduction of motorboats and mechanized trawlers. A central part in this movement from oared boats to decked sailing ships was played by the Icelandic merchant-entrepreneurs. Several functions were often combined in a single person: as well as running their store and chandlery, they owned the new ships, processed their own fish, bought fish from smaller-scale fishermen, and formed the first stage in the export of fish to markets outside.

Even at this stage, the Icelandic merchant was a comparatively new phenomenon. Until 1787 trade with Iceland had been the monopoly of the Danish Crown, with the king selling licences to his (Danish) subjects. In 1787 the right to trade with Iceland was extended to all subjects of the Danish Crown, including Icelanders. Even so, all business still had to be conducted through Copenhagen, and the few Icelanders who tried to set up in Iceland met with little success. Trade with Iceland continued to be in the hands of Danish merchants, who had better access to finance. Trading stations were scattered along the coast and, in the absence of any competition, merchants were able to fix prices to their own benefit. If the price of Icelandic goods rose merchants simply increased the margins on imported goods like sugar, coffee, wheat and tobacco. As a result, virtually all the profits from trade in Iceland went back to Denmark and very little was reinvested in the country itself.

In 1854 all trade restrictions were lifted and henceforth citizens of all nations were permitted to trade in Iceland. This had two important consequences: first, the growth in the domestic market encouraged more Icelandic merchants to set up in business, including farmers who started to band together in a co-operative movement in the latter half of the nineteenth century; and second, British merchants started coming to Iceland to buy livestock, especially sheep, for export to England. These British merchants paid in hard currency, something that had enormous significance for the development of the Icelandic economy as, up to this time, trade had been largely in the form of barter and the money supply in Iceland had been severely limited. These changes provided the foundation for the expansion of the fishing industry in the late nineteenth century, led by some of the wealthier landowning farmers and the new class of merchant-entrepreneurs.[19]

A crucial step in this occurred in 1886 with the establishment of the first bank in Iceland, the National Bank (Landsbankinn), providing a safe financial conduit for people interested in investing in the further development of the fishing industry. More importantly, the industrialization of fishing provided an outlet for the population pressure in rural society, especially in the last decade of the nineteenth century. From this point on it became a realistic option for people who had previously been trapped in a life of domestic service to move away from the rural areas and settle on the coast, and this in turn provided the pool of labour necessary for the further expansion of the fisheries.

2

People and Politics

Power structure

The political structure of eighteenth- and nineteenth-century Iceland was relatively uncomplicated. There were basically two formal power groups within the country, which were in many ways intertwined: government officials and clergy. The power behind both these groups derived ultimately from the king of Denmark. In 1845 Iceland was still a colony of the Danish Crown, but in that year the ancient Icelandic parliament (*Alþingi*) was reconvened and accorded the status of advisory assembly. Three years later a special bureau for Icelandic affairs was established in Copenhagen, presided over by a government minister. In 1874 the country was granted a constitution and the powers of the Alþingi were extended, although the king of Denmark retained the right to veto proposed new laws. This newly constituted Icelandic parliament included both members elected in Iceland and others nominated by the king – originally 20 representatives from Iceland against 6 nominees from the Crown, later changed to 24 against 12. Initially the vote in Iceland was severely limited – to only males aged over 25, with a stringent property qualification – but voting rights were steadily increased through the final years of the nineteenth century. Women's suffrage came in 1915. In 1904 the Icelanders got their first minister resident in Iceland, and in 1918 the country became a sovereign state with domestic independence but still linked to Denmark by a Treaty of Union. In 1944, while Denmark was under Nazi occupation and Iceland occupied by an Allied defence force, Iceland declared itself an independent republic.

The highest ranking colonial official in Iceland was the Governor (*landshöfðingi*), who had overall control of the administration of the country. Beneath him were district governors (*amtmaður,* pl. *amtmenn*) who, along with the Governor, oversaw the four administrative districts into which the country was divided. These districts were further divided into counties (*sýsla*), twenty in all, each with a sheriff (*sýslumaður*), who also acted as a magistrate and tax-collector. The lowest level of administration was the commune (*hreppur*), of which there were usually about ten to each county, run by an unsalaried communal director (*hreppstjóri*), who was in most cases a prominent local farmer. The position carried considerable prestige but also a great amount of responsibility including, for example, the administration of poor relief. These responsibilities were shared by communal committees (*hreppsnefnd*), generally made up of established farmers and the parish pastor.

Above the local sheriffs' courts was the High Court (court of appeals) in Reykjavík; beyond that appeals had to be directed to the Supreme Court in Copenhagen. As Guðmundur Hálfdanarson points out: 'The administrative system in Iceland was both simple and structurally well organized. Judicial and administrative functions were concentrated in the hands of a small group of officials, who were all connected in one hierarchical structure. The system had a potential for strong centralization, but difficulties in communication limited the flow of information between the different levels of the hierarchy and allowed each official a fairly large range of action in his district. An administrative office was, therefore, a major source of prestige and power in a country with few opportunities for social distinction.'[1] By the late nineteenth century, most of these posts in the administrative system were occupied by native Icelanders.

The second most important power group in Icelandic society was the clergy. The country was divided into 180 parishes, each served by a pastor and the majority with fewer than 500 parishioners.[2] The bishop was the highest ecclesiastical authority in the land and had his seat in Reykjavík. Until 1874, when the right to religious freedom was included in the new constitution, the established Lutheran National Church (*þjóðkirkjan*) had a complete monopoly over religious affairs. Even after this the National Church maintained its position of dominance – a position it still retains. For example, in 1860 the entire population of the country was registered as members of the National Church, barring two Roman Catholics. In 1901 the number belonging to non-established Christian churches was 84, plus 14 unspecified, plus 61 listed as being outside all religious groups.

The clergy had a threefold function in Icelandic society. First, they attended to the religious needs of their parishioners and carried out the official functions of the Lutheran Church. Second, they supervised all primary education in the country, leading up to a test given to children prior to confirmation. Finally, the local pastor was as a rule a member of the communal committee and participated in various informal activities within the parish. This remained true even after 1872, when the committees became democratically elected, and continued well on into the twentieth century. This broad range of activity gave the clergy considerable prestige within their communities and unrivalled leadership in spiritual, social and cultural matters.

The social origins of these two power groups have been the subject of some discussion. Guðmundur Hálfdanarson has argued that, even though in theory all administrative jobs in the country were open to people from all walks of life so long as they met the qualification criteria, in practice it was only members of the elite who had the opportunity to gain the necessary level of education. In support of his argument, Guðmundur pointed out that in 1850 almost 60 per cent of government officials and clergymen were the sons of government officials and clergymen. The chief reason behind this continuity, Guðmundur argued, lay in the structure of the formal educational system: to have any chance of passing the entrance examination to the Latin School, the only school in the country that prepared students for university education, a degree of private tuition was necessary. 'Consequently, those who were able to provide these services (usually the parish pastors) had full discretion in selecting candidates for higher education.'[3] While there is an element of truth in this, it probably does not tell the whole story. It is certainly very likely that the clergy, who were the people chiefly responsible for preparing students for the Latin School, gave their own children priority; but, as is attested in many autobiographies from the nineteenth century, the clergy were often eager to support and promote the education of boys who they thought had exceptional talent, regardless of their parents' social standing.

This seems to be supported by the figures in a table showing the fathers' occupations of nineteenth-century clergymen, lawyers and physicians, prepared by Pétur Pétursson for his book *Church and Social Change*. For the period 1850–1900, 45 per cent of clergymen and 15 per cent of lawyers had fathers who were farmers, against 34 per cent of clergymen and 18 per cent of lawyers who had fathers from the clergy. Only seven per cent of clergymen had fathers who were governmental officials while 42 per cent of lawyers had fathers who were government officials. This is especially significant if we bear in mind that 'for each civil official of higher rank there were about 2 clergymen whereas, at the beginning of the century, there were about 7 clergymen to one civil official.'[4] This increase in the number of civil servants in the second half of the nineteenth century was the result of the increasing importance of Reykjavík as a political and administrative centre. In addition, the number of physicians increased greatly after 1870, from six in 1860 to 47 in 1900. Unquestionably, therefore, farmers enjoyed some opportunities to get their sons educated. On the other hand, it is very likely that the majority of those in this position came from the ranks of the well-to-do landowning farmers.

Guðmundur Hálfdanarson points to an important social consequence of the educational system: the fact that, in general, all students went through the same schools (the Latin School, the Theological Seminary in Reykjavík, and finally the University of Copenhagen), 'contributed to the sense of shared identity among the elite; the common experience was a basis of intra-elite unity, at the same time as it became a criteria of distinction *vis-à-vis* the general public.'[5] There was a high degree of interaction between the clergy and the general public: as noted, the clergy usually enjoyed a position of influence and leadership within their community, but equally they were all also farmers who shared similar experiences with the other farmers of their parish. The pastor's main source of income remained the farm he held as part of his terms of tenure. This income might in places be bolstered by the rents from additional church landholdings and by other perks and economic benefits, depending on the local conditions of the land he occupied, such as the right to collect driftwood. As a result, some individual churches, and their pastors, were considerably better off than others. Nevertheless, the fact that pastors' incomes derived entirely from the farming economy created a strong link between them and the rest of rural society. In addition, the isolation of the Icelandic farming communities and the lack of communications made it very difficult for any exclusively educated and middle-class local groupings to coalesce and almost forced the clergy to interact with the general public in their community. However, the shared experiences of the educated section of society dating from their school years helped them to forge broader, national networks that took on a political importance as the movement for national independence gathered momentum in the second half of the nineteenth century.

While, broadly, all Icelanders supported political autonomy, there were sharply divergent views over economic and social policy, with different visions of the future of society and the direction in which it should develop. The public debate centred around three distinct groups. Firstly there was the old landed elite – the conservative nationalists – the people who essentially owned the country and looked on themselves as the sole representatives of 'true Icelandic values'. Their roots lay firmly within the rural community through their local leadership and their ownership of most of the land. As Guðmundur Hálfdanarson puts it, in their eyes they *were* the 'nation', alone qualified to represent all aspects of Icelandic society and standing as the epitome of the Icelandic experience: 'The nationalist peasant leaders perceived themselves not as a class apart from the peasantry, and never as an elite chosen through some divine selection; in their own view, they spoke as peasants, for the peasants, and, therefore, they spoke for the nation.'[6] Secondly there was the educated elite. The vast majority of these were former students of the University of Copenhagen and were strongly influenced by the nascent ideology of national liberalism that had first surfaced in the French Revolution and subsequently spread across Europe. They constituted the enlightened section of the society and were strong advocates of social change and new approaches within society at large. And thirdly, there was the ordinary peasantry of Iceland, the non-landowning majority, the subject of the discussions on the direction of society, and looked upon as the problem.

These three groups of course differed greatly in size. In particular, the number of national liberals was probably very small, made up largely of a portion of the clergy and government officials. In 1850 this group consisted of only 203 individuals, though their ranks increased as the century progressed. However, we need to remember that many of these people sided with the national conservatives for the simple reason that their interests were identical to those of many of the well-to-do farmers. It is thus almost impossible to gauge the amount of support enjoyed by national liberal thinking. The national conservatives, on the other hand, included the majority of the landowning farmers, those with most to gain from an active enforcement of the social controls that the national liberals wanted to abolish. The third group, the ordinary peasantry, was divided between the two, torn between tradition and the promise of change.[7] However, they lacked the status and influence of the other two groups and were largely denied practicable ways of expressing their opinions and aspirations. Even so, it is essential to make a clear distinction between them and the other two groups: part of the purpose of this book is to compare their story with the general rhetoric in society in the eighteenth, nineteenth and twentieth centuries, that is, to present a contrast between normative behaviour and actual behaviour, through the use of first-hand sources. Even though the general public played little direct part in the formal political debate over national independence and social change, they at times found means to express their views on the social issues that lay behind this debate.

It is important to realize that the political rhetoric was followed closely and broadly accepted by the general public of Iceland – or at least some parts of it. Though Guðmundur Hálfdanarson argues that the struggle for independence was never a mass movement, it is clear that it, and the arguments that went with it, became a part of people's lives and affected their ways of thinking. Elsewhere in this book I shall argue that the ordinary people were what might be called 'passive participants' in the independence movement: they followed the debate with interest and the promises it made led them to view their lives in a new light. The instructional and didactic literature that encouraged people to better themselves and represented 'the normative aspirations' of society went hand in hand with the political developments and was widely read and thoroughly discussed in the cold, isolated farmsteads of Iceland.

What the conservatives and liberals had in common was their demand for full and unconditional independence for the Icelandic people and a total end to foreign domination. In the eighteenth and the nineteenth centuries the idea of the state on which absolute monarchy rested, that all power had its origins in God and that God's power could only be exercised through an all-powerful monarch, was losing its appeal. The concept of the nation state took increasing hold as people from different geographical areas united around values such as freedom and equality, or simply shared language, history or religion. Towards the end of the 1840s these ideas began to make themselves felt with increasing force in the territories governed by the Danish Crown and fuelled a growing movement in Iceland for the Icelanders to be permitted to manage their own affairs. The enemy was Danish colonial power, an enemy that everyone could and should unite together to oppose. For most people, as Guðmundur Hálfdanarson points out, independence 'was some sort of a total solution: poor circumstances in Iceland were only the result of a commercial monopoly or incomprehension of the foreign government and if the power was put into Icelandic hands these obstacles would be overcome and the country's road to progress would automatically open up.'[8]

Especially for the conservative nationalists, independence was seen as necessary to maintain traditional social and cultural structures in the face of foreign domination and ideology. Icelanders alone were capable of understanding the Icelandic experience, the argument went, and without political autonomy the country was doomed to fail to provide for its citizens and lift itself out of poverty and misery. The popular rhetoric was reinforced by appeal to the hardships of previous centuries and a universal popular image of a lost and glorious past, the time of the sagas, when every farmstead was the home of great warriors and noble heroes. The country had to rise up again and improve itself in every area of life. Part of this rhetoric was also shared by the liberal nationalists, often resulting in a blurring of the distinction between the two groups.

The liberal vision for the future of Iceland had its roots in the wider movement towards economic liberalism that became a dominant force in Western societies in the nineteenth century, with its emphasis on free trade and freedom of labour. Behind the consensus over the main issue, independence, the conservatives and liberals were divided by sharp differences of outlook. At the heart of the debate lay the issue of individual rights – how far should they extend? – and the nature of the individual's obligations towards society. The conservative ideology was grounded in the old order of home and piety established in the eighteenth century: that the cornerstone of society was the household and that all social relationships should be based on the same principles as those between masters and servants. A distinction was made between 'verified freedom' and 'unconditional freedom': to merit 'verified freedom', an individual had to show himself capable of governing himself through virtuous behaviour; 'unconditional freedom' was viewed as a threat to the society at large, since individuals were by nature irrational and needed to be trained, disciplined and assigned their place in society according to their mental and physical capacities. The conservatives' guiding principle was the desire to protect and maintain the old order, which was, according to the rhetoric, the thing that made Icelandic culture what it was. This was entirely in line with their perception that peasant society was under threat, tottering under the pressure of population and the steady stream of people to the new urban centres.[9]

This view of a hierarchical and regimented society was viewed by the liberals as authoritarian and reactionary. To them, the fundamental necessity was to lift as many restrictions on individual freedom as possible: only in this way would people have the opportunity to rise up from their backwardness and poverty and use their talents for their own betterment, regardless of their origins and background. An early manifestation of this ideology appeared in the journal *Fjölnir*, published by a small group of intellectuals based in Copenhagen between 1835 and 1847. The writers viewed Iceland very much within the context of contemporary European politics. Much of the material was instructional and didactic, aimed at guiding and encouraging Icelanders to improve their situation.

The driving force behind the independence movement, and for the longest time viewed as the national hero of Iceland, was the scholar and archivist Jón Sigurðsson, also based in Copenhagen. Between 1841 and 1873 Jón published a journal, *Ný félagsrit* (New Society), in which he urged his fellow countrymen to reform themselves both culturally and economically. This group of intellectual liberal nationalists argued unrelentingly for increased economic and social freedom for the country and its people, driven by the idea that each individual citizen had an important part to play. Progress began at the personal level. This meant, for example, an abolition of all restrictions on freedom of labour, and a drastic improvement in general education to enable people to shoulder the responsibilities that came with freedom. Here is not the place to discuss the political history of the independence struggle. It is, however, important to realize that to these campaigners independence always meant more than simply freedom from foreign domination; it meant facing up to and resolving the social and economic dilemmas in which peasant society found itself in the late nineteenth century, and it is on this that this book aims to concentrate.

The family

One of the main factors determining a person's social position was their position within the household. The average family was a unit of production, reproduction and consumption, and typically consisted of a husband and wife, their children, and quite often also foster-children, relatives and servants. Gísli Ágúst Gunnlaugsson has compared household sizes in a number of farming and fishing districts during the period under study here. For 1845, he found that the mean household size (MHS) in five coastal parishes in the south of the country was 5.0, while in five farming parishes also in the south the figure was 7.9. This is much as one would expect, since the need for labour was considerably less in the fishing districts. During the next 30 years, and especially between 1860 and 1880, the population grew rapidly without new farms being established. At the same time the authorities deliberately prevented people from settling on the coast through the strict enforcement of a series of laws aimed at maintaining the pre-eminence of the farming community. This of course led to an increase in MHS, especially in farming parishes. During the period 1880–1930 the MHS fell markedly in farming districts but only slightly in coastal parishes, the result of massive migration from the country to the coast. This change had other significant effects on household composition, most notably a sharp decline in the number of servants.[10]

Forming a household depended almost entirely on whether a couple could obtain land to farm on. Land acquisition could take time; people could spend many years in service to others before they acquired the status and money to set up on their own. As a result, the age of marriage in nineteenth-century Iceland was unusually high. As Gísli Ágúst Gunnlaugsson points out, 'the mean age of bridegrooms was 30.8 years between 1890 and 1895 and the mean age of brides 28.2 during the same years. This was an extremely high average age at marriage by European standards.'[11] The Icelandic household was strongly patriarchal, with the master of the household exercising absolute control over household affairs. He was the face of the home towards the outside world and legally the only member of the household who could participate in

The rural Icelandic household consisted of the farmer and his wife, their children, workers and often their parents. Running the farm covered a wide range of activities. The buildings were often poor and required considerable maintenance. Leisure was a rarity. Church attendance once or twice a summer provided a diversion and the opportunity to dress up in one's finest. The picture shows a couple and their seven children in their traditional Sunday best.

public affairs. In practice, the farmer's wife often shared some – even many – of her husband's responsibilities, but only those that concerned domestic matters.

Children were raised by their parents up to the age of at least thirteen, and more often fifteen or sixteen. Learning how to survive in the harsh realities of everyday life constituted a central element in children's education and they were expected to take an active part in the farm work from an early age. This education continued after they took up positions of service, when, like all people who did not have their own household, they were required to commit themselves to bonded service within a household for a year at a time. Moving away from their parents and entering service did not change a child's legal or moral status. Between the ages of fifteen and thirty most people had very limited rights and they were expected to follow the rules and orders laid down by the master of the household with unquestioning obedience.

The rights and duties of servants were set out in detail in a local ordinance from 1722. This ordinance, among other things, defined the levels of punishment permitted to a master of a household in his dealings with his workers: 'Whensoever the master of a household

The division of Iceland into communes (hreppar) goes back almost unchanged to the earliest days of the settlement. One of the functions of the commune was to organize the round-ups when the sheep were brought down from the mountains in autumn. The sheep were sent up to the highlands as soon as the snows cleared in spring and stayed there until September. The highlands remain common land to this day for the use of all the farmers of the surrounding areas. The autumn round-up was an occasion for socializing, jollity and celebration. People dressed up specially. The sheep were herded into the pens, sorted according to ear-mark, and driven back to their farms by their owners. This was one of highpoints of the year for farmers and workers, high and low, young and old, alike.

disapproves of the deeds of unworthy labourers, and they have in some way done him harm or disobeyed, then the master and mistress of the house is free to strike the labourer, whether with hand, whip, tree root or such object, but not such as to wound or disfigure in any way.' The discipline meted out to servants was thus on a level with what parents were charged to use on their own children:

> Chastise them with stern words (though without swearing and unseemly profanity), or so otherwise with hand or rod according to the nature of the transgression . . . Though shall all blows to the head and blows made in sudden anger be here strictly forbidden . . . If the children make complaint or allow to be seen on themselves a rebellious or wrathful demeanour . . . they should then be punished with the greater seriousness, until they learn to show themselves loving and meek.[12]

People could, however, move from one household to another on the termination of their year of contract. The fixedly hierarchical relationship between masters and servants was a product of the Lutheran Reformation and the centralization of authority that accompanied it. In the eighteenth century the pre-eminent position of the master of the household was further reinforced through the principles of the Pietist movement. For most of the second half of the nineteenth century, servants made up 35–40 per cent of the general population over the age of fifteen. One striking consequence of this social system was that, during the middle years of the nineteenth century, 40 per cent of women aged between 50 and 54 had never married, most of them having spent their entire adult lives in domestic service.

Many Icelandic households included a number of foster-children. Broadly, these can be divided into two very different types, 'genuine foster-children' and 'private paupers'. The first group enjoyed the same status within the household as the children of the head of the household; they were generally relatives taken into the home, either permanently or temporarily, as a result of some family crisis, for instance if their parents had died or were unable to look after them for some other reason. Private paupers occupied a very different world; they came from broken homes and, if the local authorities could not find any relative to care for them, they were often auctioned off to anyone willing to take them on. Since the local authorities were obliged to provide for the maintenance of such children, it was invariably the person who made the lowest bid in the auction that 'won'. Private paupers were expected to work hard and in many instances lacked emotional support of any kind. Children described in the records as 'foster-children' often made up a significant part of the child population of a parish; for instance, in the records cited by Gísli Ágúst Gunnlaugsson from the years between 1801 and 1816, we find variation between two per cent in one parish and 18.3 per cent in another.[13] The records are hard to interpret and it is often difficult to determine exactly how many foster-children there were at any given time: some were fostered for a short period with strangers, while others were registered along with a mother or a father in a household to which they did not belong. In reality, many of these children were effectively on their own.

The number of children living without family support is not surprising when one considers the social predicament of people who were just setting out on their adult careers. This was the most fertile section of society and so tended to have a lot of children. They often started on a small farm, with the hope that, eventually, they might be able to work their way up the social ladder to something more prosperous. But their world was extremely fragile: death of livestock or a bad harvest could have a devastating effect on these people's ability to support themselves and lead to bankruptcy and the break-up of the family. In such cases these families received little sympathy from the local authorities, as Gísli Ágúst explains:

> By splitting up families, the local authorities achieved several objectives: the reproduction function of the poverty-stricken family was cut short, a farm was made vacant for another family, support (and care) was provided for those members of the family who were not fit to work, and the working capacities of those members who were partially able to do so were utilized. Grown up and healthy members of the family were not categorized as paupers, but were required to seek employment as servants. This procedure also provided farmers with cheap labour, since many paupers were still able to perform some tasks within the households in which they were placed. Furthermore, the arrangement helped to maintain social discipline. The fate of the paupers was put entirely into the hands of the local governments. They organized the relief and tried to enforce the law, which among other things, made it illegal for paupers to travel around as vagrant beggars.[14]

Lastly, many Icelandic households included a number of more distant relatives. Gísli Ágúst Gunnlaugsson investigated two parishes, one on the coast, the other in a farming district, in the years 1845, 1860 and 1880. In the farming parish the percentage of households containing relatives was 34.2 in 1845, 12.5 in 1860, and 25.0 in 1880. In the coastal parish the numbers were considerably lower: 8.6 per cent in 1845, 12.1 per cent in 1860, and 18.5 per cent in 1880.[15] These figures indicate that it was generally easier for people to provide for their relatives on farms, where their often limited ability to work could be more effectively utilized. Additionally, it was easier in coastal areas for older people to establish or hold on to their own households or to continue to provide for themselves as fishermen or day labourers. Again, the figures are subject to distortion and hard to interpret. There are, for example, cases of more than one family sharing a single farm where it is difficult to ascertain the nature of the relationship between them. And many people who were classed as lodgers or boarders, and were therefore free to dispose of their own labour, lived with the families with whom they worked, though, theoretically at least, they were deemed to have the status of constituting a separate household.

Contemporary debate may have had much to say about cultural and economic reform and the need for the people of Iceland to strive to improve their conditions. But the truth was that the opportunities open to ordinary people within the farming community were closely limited in all ways. For some a solution lay in the newly emerging urban centres along the coast, but for increasing numbers it was the prospect of a new start in a new continent, America, that captured the imagination. Rural society could no longer support the number of people living in it, and as time went on changes in employment patterns and culture became inevitable.

3

The Feeling of Swallowing a Hunchback: Material Culture

During the latter part of the nineteenth century the social structure of rural Iceland underwent considerable change, especially after 1860, when the farming community came under increasing pressure to support its steadily growing population. These changes came down particularly hard on those who were growing up at the time. Radical changes in the formal structure of society can not only have a deep effect on people's general outlook but also on the directions they choose to take throughout their lives. Up to this point, the transition from one life stage to the next had been governed by tradition, rules and laws that people took as given and did not question. When this path was disrupted, the traditional patterns no longer held; ways of living and looking to the future could no longer be taken for granted and many found themselves in a dilemma. But of course this was not immediately obvious to the people involved, for whom the received image of life and society still held considerable power – especially as the changes in society were masked by the fact that other aspects of life remained unchanged. In the case of Iceland, the demographics may have changed, making traditional views and aspirations untenable for many, but material conditions remained much as they had always been.

This chapter looks at certain aspects of the material conditions under which people lived in eighteenth- and nineteenth-century Iceland and considers how these conditions influenced the general well-being. Conditions such as food shortage, incurable diseases and cold, damp housing have consequences beyond the merely physical; they also affect the way people think and how they view the world and react to everyday life experiences. Thus, before moving on to the individual life course in nineteenth-century rural society, we need to have a clear picture of the problems people faced in their daily lives. Contemporary sources, particularly official reports and autobiographies – contain a great deal of comment on these subjects and allow us considerable insight into the kinds of material (dis)comfort in which people lived at the time.

Before proceeding, it is worth quoting the description of the Icelanders and their living conditions recorded in the diary of John Baine,
a teacher from Scotland who toured the west of Iceland with the
Stanley expedition of 1789:

> The people are just like those we have seen very meagre dirty
> and greedy. Either money is of far less value here than one can
> imagine or else those people are the most avaricious creatures
> that can be. They are seldom pleas'd if they do not receive more
> than the article appears to be worth even in Britain . . . As a
> Specimen of the cleanliness of these people one of them yes-
> terday offer'd Mr. Crawford a chew of Tobacco – out of his
> own mouth – which assuredly is not the cleanest in the world if
> one can judge from the dirtiness of their faces and their beards
> are I believe seldom or never Shaved. I have now seen many of
> them and whatever their faces may be their hands every man
> and Mothers daughter of them appear scabbed partly owing
> perhaps to their living so poorly particulary on Salt fish a great
> part of their time, but one that sees their houses, cloathes, and
> persons must be of the opinion that a great part of their misery
> has originated from their want of cleanliness that great suppor-
> ter of human life and even promoter of human happiness. I
> have heard a great deal and seen too much of the want of this
> virtue in our own countrymen particularly the Highlanders,
> but nothing can equal the misery apparent in the houses of the
> Icelanders . . . That the Icelanders do not enjoy but suffer life is
> an observation that must be clear to the most superstitious
> Spectator, an Air of melancholy and languor hang upon them,
> particularly on the Women. I confess nothing interests me
> more for the Sex than this appearance of sedateness, but when
> we find it to be Characteristic of the whole of a people and
> necessarily arising from their wretched situation our feelings
> are too sensibly affected.

It is perhaps worth noting that John Baine was travelling at what was
probably the lowest point in the entire history of Iceland: for much of the
eighteenth century the country had suffered a succession of volcanic eruptions, crop failures, famines and epidemics, notably smallpox. However,
Baine's description has an undeniable ring of truth about it, especially as
he goes on to consider his own situation in the light of his observations,
passing the following salutary judgement: 'His wants are few and consequently easily satisfied and what appears to us in their manners as evils
may be only the effects of our luxury and false judgement.'[1]

Housing

Perhaps the most striking feature of housing in Iceland during most of the eighteenth and nineteenth centuries, and even well into the twentieth, was its woeful inadequacy. Iceland is entirely lacking in woodland and trade with other countries was expensive and unreliable. Building materials were thus in very short supply and this, together with the near universal poverty, necessitated the use of whatever was obtainable locally. In most instances houses were constructed of turf and stone, sometimes with timber used for part of the interior. This timber was in many cases driftwood carried by ocean currents from Russia or Scandinavia.

The architect and historian Hörður Ágústsson, writing on the technical development of Icelandic architecture, has argued that the quality of the housing occupied by ordinary working people deteriorated steadily in the early modern period and that much of it constituted little more than hovels. While containing a degree of truth, this view requires certain qualification. Hörður's conclusions were based on a limited sample and we simply do not know whether they stand for the majority of houses. He does note that many of the farms owned by wealthier members of society were in much better condition, but even here it seems that the quality of the houses declined during this period. In all events, it is safe to conclude that for most people housing conditions were basic, primitive and severe, and this is reflected in several contemporary autobiographies.[2]

Most farms had only one small living room where people both worked and slept. The only other room of any importance was the kitchen. In 1930 Kristleifur Þorsteinsson wrote an article in one of the newspapers called *Lesbók Morgunblaðsins* in which he described the layout of the houses at the time he had grown up sixty years earlier. In particular he recalled the discomfort of the kitchens on the old farms: 'The smoke and soot were often unbearable. However much care was taken, food was liable to be spoilt by soot and smoke, even when it had been well prepared in all other respects. No woman was so set in the old ways that she did not welcome the change that went with having a stove to replace the old hearth. But the vast majority of people still had to make do with the old kitchen until the end of the century, and many for much longer.'

Writing in a journal called *Eimreiðin* in 1906, Ólöf Sigurðardóttir (b. 1857) left a vivid account of the house in which she grew up in an article called 'Bernskuheimilið mitt' (My Childhood Home). Her reasons for writing were avowedly historical: 'It could be important for people who want to write cultural history that I try to put down what is memorable about our behaviour and customs, so it is not lost. And even if this may reflect poorly on my family and kin, I look on it as my duty to tell the truth and not to embellish the facts.' Ólöf was as good as her word: 'The house was as bad as any dirt shack could be. The living room was small and low with a turf roof, all unwooden except for portable planks fixed above the beds. The beds were made of turf with a wooden frame. No table, no seats except for the beds.'

The appalling condition of this housing is a constantly repeated theme. In the last decade of the nineteenth century the old turf farms started to be replaced by houses of timber or stone construction, mostly in the towns and villages, but to some extent also in the countryside. A doctor called Guðmundur Hannesson produced a series of articles advocating housing improvements. In one, dealing with changes in housing through the centuries, he provides us with an interesting conspectus of the types of buildings in Iceland at the time. He divides houses into three categories according to their material of construction: stone, timber and turf.

YEAR	STONE	%	TIMBER	%	TURF	%
1910	371	3.7	4488	43.9	5354	52.4
1920	1064	9.4	5196	46.1	5004	44.5
1930	3294	24.3	6595	48.7	3665	27.0

Corresponding figures for subsequent decades are given in *Icelandic Historical Statistics*:[3]

YEAR	STONE	%	TIMBER	%	TURF	%
1940	6146	39.8	7570	49	1744	11.3
1950	10481	52.6	8720	43.8	716	3.6
1960	16257	67.3	7656	31.7	249	1.0

As the figures indicate, Icelandic housing underwent a massive change during the first part of the twentieth century. What is interesting, though, is how long turf remained a significant element in the overall housing stock. In many cases the simple division implied by the statistics may be misleading and certain houses might better be classified as 'mixed', especially in the increasing use of timber in turf house construction. But, as a generalization, even until well on into the twentieth century the overwhelming majority of houses remained in relatively poor condition, in spite of the fact that more and more houses were being built of materials other than turf.[4]

In his article from 1930 – 'Sveitasiðir í Borgarfirði fyrir 60 árum' (Rural customs in Borgarfjörður 60 years ago) – Kristleifur Þorsteinsson describes the state of housing in Iceland at the time he was growing up: 'Sixty years ago all farmhouses were made of turf and a very high proportion of them were in extremely poor condition because building materials were in short supply, and this, and for many other reasons, meant that people had to make all buildings last as long as possible.' A little later in the article he notes: 'None of the windows ever had hinges, but instead there was an air pipe up through the roof. The living room, which was built of turf, was usually horribly cold. Stoves were more or less unknown in farmhouses, and people thought that luxury and comfort like this – sitting around in the heat of a stove – was only for government officials. People preferred to put up with the cold than allow themselves this luxury, both richer farmers and poor.' When Kristleifur says that the living room was made of turf, what he means is that the interior of the farmhouse was not insulated by wooden panelling.

In some of the advice literature that was written to urge people to exert themselves to raise their living standards, the authors argued that the nation was making great progress in almost all areas. This, for instance, was the view presented by Þorvaldur Thoroddsen, a professor of natural sciences at the University of Copenhagen and a native Icelander, in a lecture in 1901 comparing Iceland at the beginning of the nineteenth century to Iceland in his own time. As he saw things, he was in no doubt that, where standards had not advanced, the fault lay squarely with the people themselves. Housing conditions had improved greatly, he believed, but there was still a long way to go: 'There is still a great difference between people's houses, and this difference is not the result of good and bad transportation, but rather people's cultural level in the countryside ... . How people live in different communes is not a matter of landscape or soil or climate, but simply a reflection of the industriousness and capability of those who live there, and especially on how many great and able men there are in the commune for the general public to emulate.'[5]

Many of the writers who discussed society and the way it was changing failed to make a clear distinction between social classes when coming to their conclusions. For example, in an article written in the paper *Norðanfari* in 1882, the unnamed author describes conditions before 1840 in terms that seem little different from those in his own time. Nevertheless, the writer claims that the late nineteenth century had seen a marked improvement in living standards, and goes on to say:

> However ugly this description may be, many know it is no exaggeration. Fortunately cleanliness has improved greatly in many places, though it is still inadequate in many others, and I hope that this is the result rather of poverty than negligence, of ignorance than lack of will, of habit than lack of taste. Certainly it is very different to go into farmhouses and see people in their

homes nowadays from what it was 30 or 40 years ago, although unfortunate exceptions still exist. Then, what met people when they arrived at the farmyard was an unbearable stench and other rubbish tipped out right outside the front door, but such things are now largely a thing of the past.

There are of course often problems involved trying to form an accurate picture of the realities of life on the basis of contemporary descriptions. Different people's perceptions of the same conditions or events can differ widely. A good case in point concerns a debate that went on between Þorkell Bjarnason and Ólafur Sigurðsson during the course of the 1890s in the journal of the Icelandic Literary Society. Þorkell wrote an amazingly frank and vivid account of the area he had grown up in, which elicited a response from Ólafur claiming that he had focused only on the worst in people's lives. Ólafur argued that this kind of writing served only as a blemish on the reputation of past generations and that Þorkell would have done better to concentrate more on families of better standing. Þorkell answered this criticism by pointing out that his article was closer to the real truth, since he had grown up in a poor household, while Ólafur came from a comfortable background. To Þorkell, living conditions had improved greatly since his childhood, but Ólafur seemed blind to this improvement.

Kristleifur Þorsteinsson's comments on the wretched quality of the housing and the hardships suffered as a result of poor insulation are echoed in many contemporary autobiographies. Aside from the poverty, it was lack of fuel that made life in a typical Icelandic farmhouse particularly miserable. Peat was the only fuel in reasonable supply, dug from bogs in spring and stacked and dried during the summer. To make some kind of compensation for the lack of heating material, especially in the eighteenth and early nineteenth centuries, the living quarters were often built above the cowshed so that the family benefited from the warmth rising from the livestock. The downside was of course the smell, especially as most houses had little ventilation. Windows were few and small, and opening one meant letting cold air in and the warm air out. People therefore generally preferred to keep their windows shut at all times, preferring foul warm air to fresh cold air. Poverty, allied at times to conservatism and an enforced economy, discouraged people from heating their houses further. Kristleifur recounts a telling example of this mentality: 'Hardly more than fifty years ago now there was a daughter of one of the wealthiest farmers in Borgarfjörður living in one of these old farmhouses. The winter was cold and she was worried for the health of her children because they were still very young. She wrote to her father and asked him to lend her some money so she could buy a

Firewood is in scant supply in Iceland. The woodlands that originally covered much of the lowlands were almost entirely destroyed in the early days of the settlement as a result of sheep grazing, soil erosion and volcanic eruptions. The only ready supply of heating fuel was peat, compacted plant remains that have decomposed over long periods in waterlogged soils starved of oxygen. The peat that builds up is rich in carbon but burns only slowly, producing a poor heat and much smoke. To make it usable it has to be dug up and dried according to special methods that require considerable work, effort and expertise. The picture shows people cutting peat. The peat was dug from pits in lumps that were first stacked up to let the water drain out. Next it was spread over the ground for drying, and then cut into strips and dried further. Finally it was restacked, covered in turf and kept until winter. Then it was fetched in piece by piece and used for heating.

stove for the farm as the cold was killing her and her children. Her father wrote back at once, refusing to lend her the money and saying that he had always found the best way to keep warm was to put in some hard work.'

As noted earlier, the late nineteenth and particularly early twentieth century saw a trend towards improving the living quarters and the increased use of stone and timber for building purposes. But this still left many problems. One was insulation in new houses. Karvel Ögmundsson (b. 1903) describes in his autobiography *Sjómannsævi* (A Life of a Fisherman) an incident from his childhood, when the old farm burnt down and a new one was built to replace it:

Late that autumn the living room was ready and we moved in, I think in November. But then we were faced by a new problem.

This was the terrible cold, because now we no longer had a thick turf roof over our heads as in the old farm, nor the warmth from the cows underneath the living room. This was a problem, and my father borrowed a big stove from his friend Sigurður Jónatansson, who lived in Keflavík by Sandur. The stove was set up at the north end of the living room but did little to help matters as the only thing we had to burn was heather and so the stove was only used while we were cooking because we had to conserve fuel.

As a result, Karvel's father remained sick throughout the winter and the rest of the family suffered swollen hands and feet: frostbite.

Finnur Ó. Thorlacius (b. 1883), who was a carpenter, built a new stone house for his parents early in the twentieth century and describes in his autobiography *Smiður í fjórum löndum* (Carpenter in four countries) the problems they had insulating it. Guðmundur Hannesson notes that in one of the more forward-looking parts in Iceland (Mýra- og Borgarfjarðarsýslur), out of a total of 397 farms in 1931, 79 had a stove, 165 had running water, and eleven had electricity.

Another recurrent problem of the poor housing was water seepage into the living quarters. Given its location in the North Atlantic, the climate of Iceland is very wet. Spring rain and melting snow could be a major problem when the roof over one's head was made only of turf. Again Ólöf Sigurðardóttir gives us an insight into the world in which she grew up. 'If houses leaked when it rained – and they all did – then cow dung was melted and put on the roof to plug the hole, but beyond this no one repaired their houses. When it started to leak on us in bed, all the spare sheepskins were brought in and put over us and we were told not to move so that we did not get puddles under us. We found this highly entertaining.' This kind of situation, it seems safe to assume, was probably a reality of most people's lives during the eighteenth and nineteenth centuries.

Sanitation

Associated with the poor housing was the poor condition of sanitation in the country. As late as the 1920s the Nobel Prize-winning novelist Halldór Laxness wrote two scathingly critical articles about the general state of health and housing in his country. His comments confirm the parlous picture presented above, and Laxness saw the situation as having a woeful influence on his fellow countrymen's lives: 'I have been in counties were every person was a hunchback, or, more correctly, the people looked as if they had swallowed a hunchback. Grind, danger, snowstorms, cold, toil, overcrowding, darkness, stench, ignorance, hopelessness, surrender: this is the lesson that I read over and over again in peoples' faces.'[6]

It hardly needs saying that, with housing so poor and the majority of the public living in direst poverty, keeping things clean and orderly presented enormous problems. Contemporary descriptions and auto-biographies repeatedly present a picture of poor hygiene and voice concerns over its consequences. From the late nineteenth century, and increasingly as we move into the twentieth century, sanitation comes to play a major part in discussions on the state of Iceland. For instance, in 1867 J. A. Hjaltalín, surgeon-general between 1855 and 1881, wrote a book of practical advice on hygiene and sanitation called *Nokkur orð um hreinlæti* (Few words about hygiene) in which he laid out the prob-lems and urged his fellow countrymen to improve their cleanliness and that of their surroundings.

The repeated exhortations in the advice literature to improve san-itary practices make perfect sense when one considers how little care people took about the state of their houses. Ólöf Sigurðardóttir, quoted earlier in this chapter, was born into a poor family which moved to a much better farm when she was twelve. 'When we moved to this farm, the living room had never been cleaned even though it had a wooden interior and was all right. We did not change anything for the first few years, but eventually we got the urge to clean the floor. I remember the day it was done, and I also remember my feeling of triumph that night when the cleaning was over. On the floor the dirt had been so thick that it had been impossible to see that it was made of wood.'

Kristleifur Þorsteinsson, also quoted earlier, notes that in many farms cleaning the floors was not an issue because the floors were simply dirt rather than wood. He recounts a story he had heard from the poet Einar H. Kvaran, who in his youth had moved with his family into a new church farm. This new farm was considered to be a good one. On their arrival they noticed how close the beds appeared to be to the floor, which seemed to be composed of dirt. Einar's father ordered that the floor be cleaned. 'Eventually a wooden floor came into view, but no one remembered so far back as to recall that there was a wooden floor there, so old was the packed filth. Fourteen wheelbarrows of soil were carted away before the floor came to light. This was in a parsonage in 1870.'

In an article written in 1906 in the journal *Eimreiðin* the doctor Steingrímur Mattíasson discussed popular attitudes to cleanliness in Iceland: 'The ordinary people clean themselves far too seldom; bathing is largely unknown and people are almost afraid of water. Bed linen and underwear are not washed, aired and changed often enough.' Later in the article he goes on: 'I know cases of people walking around in the same underwear for months on end, and bed linen only being washed once a year. Bed linen and woollen underwear can conceal a lot of dirt before it becomes obvious to the eye that it needs washing, and when it is washed the only thing that people think will work is boiling it in urine.' Ólöf Sigurðardóttir gives an even more graphic description of people's personal hygiene habits, and their infrequency:

> Washtubs big or small did not exist in our home. Soap or detergent I first saw as a grown woman. All clothes were washed in warm urine – collected urine – and then rinsed out in water. Shirts were changed once a month, but underwear and bed linen very rarely, once or twice each winter, and then it was almost impossible to get them clean. Socks were seldom washed during the winter: they were laid out on a rock if they were wet in the evening and the dirt rubbed off them in the morning. In summer, sandy socks were rinsed in the stream. Urine was usually used to wash hands, but milk, milk whey and milk curds were used for washing the face and considered better than water. Clothes were washed in pots – food pots of course. The chamber pot, which was made of wood, was used for washing hands . . . Everyone ate from a bowl. Twice a year – before Christmas and on the first day of summer – they were washed out using stock from smoked lamb, but otherwise they were licked clean by the dogs after they had been used.

From the advice literature and autobiographies it is clear that this kind of thing was common practice in nineteenth-century Iceland, and that it could have severe consequences for people's health and physical appearance. The conditions and some of the customs that went with them could affect people for the rest of their lives. One such custom, spitting on the floor inside the home, was taken up in an article called 'Hættulegir ósiðir' (Dangerous bad habits) by an unnamed writer in 1897 in the paper *Ísland*. The writer argues that this could lead to tuberculosis, leaving people severely crippled: 'What is needed is to be cleaner, not to spit on the floor, and to have good air in the rooms. But this kind of cleanliness is wanting in many places, especially in the countryside. The bad, old, dangerous habit of spitting on the floor is common on nearly every farm, and is so rooted among the general population that they fail to see how ugly and unhygienic it is.'

Many writers mention the lack of toilet facilities, which were more or less non-existent in rural areas and to some extent also in towns. In urban areas many houses had an outhouse and, in Reykjavík for instance, there were soil men who went around the town periodically and cleaned them out. The situation slowly improved in the twentieth century with the introduction of piped water and the construction of sewer systems, but even in 1928 45 per cent of dwellings in Reykjavík were still without bathrooms. In rural areas people used the cowshed or relieved themselves against an outside wall. In his book on sanitation J. A. Hjaltalín pointed out that the filth outdoors was often intolerable, and little better indoors. He discusses the dung heap and its proximity to the living quarters: 'On some farms it has got so out of control that people have to ride through the midden to get into the farm-yard. This is no exaggeration. It hardly needs saying how unsanitary this is, living in the middle of a dung heap. It seems such a small thing, having to remind people that it is important to have an outhouse on every farm.' Hjaltalín's criticisms are echoed by Steingrímur Mattíasson in 1906. He notes that the lack of toilets and bathroom facilities is one of the things that amaze foreigners who visit the country and they often complain about the inconvenience.

In another article 'Fátæku heimilin í Reykjavík' (The poor homes in Reykjavík) published in the journal *Lögrjetta* the same year Stein-grímur Mattíasson drew attention to the perennial Icelandic problem of lice, pointing out that the incidence of lice in a nation provided a use-ful indication of its standard of hygiene: 'There is something I wish to make clear: the filth and dirt in Reykjavík is appalling. This is true of most poor homes, though of course one encounters exceptions. In this connection, I declare that, to my knowledge, there is no civilized country more lice-ridden than Iceland. And Reykjavík is no exception. Ask the doctors! This is the best measure of cleanliness there is. It is a huge national disgrace that it is the duty of everyone to fight against, and I would ask all good Icelanders to do so.'

Steingrímur provides a graphic description of the harmful effects of lice, which led eventually to a fungal infection of the scalp called favus, in the other article quoted before in this chapter:

So common is favus in Iceland that almost all Icelanders are familiar with it. Most people from their youth have already seen children or adults who, because of this vile disease, keep their hats on when others take theirs off. This is usually poor people who have been neglected by slovenly mothers or foster mothers and so have to pay for it for the rest of their lives . . . Favus appears as a thick, viscous, yellow-green growth which extends over a large part of the scalp. It destroys the hair, which falls out more and more as the disease progresses, until in the end the head becomes bald. Once the favus has set in it is very difficult to keep the head clean, and invariably heads infected

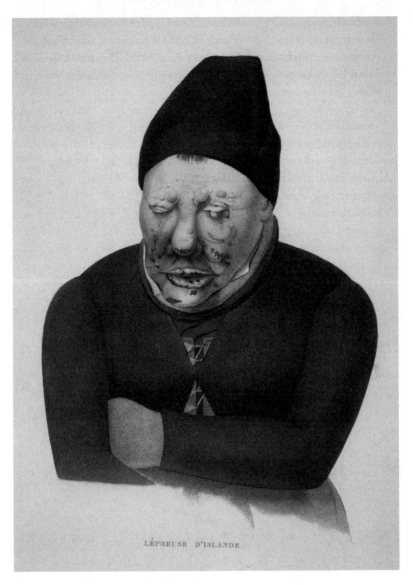

LÉPREUSE D'ISLANDE.

Medicine as a profession dates back in Iceland to the eighteenth century but for the first 150 years the number of doctors was small and many parts of the country had no access to specialized care. A whole range of endemic diseases remained entirely beyond treatment. For most people, living conditions were wretched – bad housing and sanitation, monotonous and poor-quality diet. Most houses were extremely cramped, meaning that the old and sick were forced to share the same cold, leaky quarters as the rest of the household.

with favus attract huge numbers of lice . . . It is a type of growth, not unlike mildew, which lives like other growths except that it grows only on the human head, especially of children and those who fail to keep themselves clean. People who comb their hair every day do not get favus.

Kristján S. Sigurðsson (b. 1875) describes in his autobiography, which was published in the journal *Nýjar kvöldvökur* in the 1960s, the household he entered as a domestic servant at the age of thirteen. He found the filth almost intolerable: 'I had not been there long when I started to notice a rash on both my hands and feet which itched badly. When I complained about this to my masters, they told me that it was just an itch and nothing more was said about it. But then it became apparent that the boy I shared my bed with had been laid low with rashes before I arrived but was now recovering. This had been hidden from me because we were supposed to sleep in the same bed. Then, for the first time, I realized why his hands were always wrapped up tight.' Kristján mentions that he too was soon covered in these rashes and felt very poorly but was still expected to work long hard hours.

In brief, it is hardly an unfair generalization to say that the homes of most people in Iceland exhibited a state of overwhelming squalor. As noted earlier, it was common practice to spit on the floor in people's living rooms and this helped to spread infections from man to man. Jón Blöndal, the district doctor for the Borgarfjörður region, includes the following remarks in his annual report to the surgeon general for 1901: 'It is as if even now people's dwellings have no right to exist free from the expectoration. Most people simply spit wherever they happen to be, and even if there are spittoons to hand people rarely use them, and the Icelander needs to be constantly lectured on this subject.'[7] Lighting and ventilation were limited and baths taken only irregularly. Lice were an unwelcome guest that it was hard to avoid and scalps disfigured with sores and the accompanying rampant bacterial growth were a common sight. Dogs and other domestic animals roamed freely around the house, licking up leftover food from people's plates, and facilities for waste removal and sewerage disposal were few and rudimentary. This, and in fact much else besides, are taken up by Jón Blöndal in his next report for 1902. On the cleanliness and hygiene of Icelandic homes he has this to say:

For instance, far too little care is taken about the cleanliness and sanitation of domestic water supplies. Wells are often dug in the worst possible places, e.g. in rotten bogs where there is so much decay in the soil that that water in them is invariably foul. They are often poorly constructed and inadequately protected against rainwater. Sometimes they are situated unhealthily close to the dung heaps from cattle sheds and other foulness. People generally give insufficient thought to having a special container to lift water with, or if one does exist it is not used. Thus I have more than once seen cowmen sinking the water buckets from the cowshed or the farm down into the well, covered with muck from the floor of the animal shed or kitchen where the dogs sniff about and the men spit as best they can. – Bodily hygiene is woefully inadequate, and it seems to me that those who slop anything off their bodies once a year reckon they are doing a good job, and heaven alone knows the state of the common people out in the country who not once in their lives wash themselves all over after they have reached adulthood . . . In brief, the feeling for cleanliness is to a greater or lesser extent asleep, though there are honourable exceptions and happily many of them, and it will take a great deal of time and effort to awaken it if ever anything starts to be done in earnest. People's dwellings lack light and air. Stoves are far too rare and even where they exist they are little used, so that people have to cluster together in one or two rooms to keep themselves warm. Because of the lack of heating the dwellings lack durability and become unhealthy. They are destroyed by damp in a few years, if they are not by then run down and leaky, and then become uninhabitable again in winter because of the cold.

Jón's account is very much in the same spirit as many, many others found in the district medical officers' reports of this period. These conditions meant that Icelanders generally had little defence against diseases of any kind. On top of this, the care of the sick almost invariably went on inside the home, generally under extremely taxing conditions. As an example we may quote Halldór Jónsson, who appears as a major character later in this book, who recounts in his autobiography having come into contact with a mentally disturbed woman when he was tending sheep at the manse at Fell shortly after confirmation: 'Things did not improve when winter arrived. Then I had to be in the cowshed and for a time there was a madwoman running loose in there. At first I was terribly afraid of her.'[8] Often the only recourse was to isolate such people – 'lock them away', as it was usually expressed. In her autobiography *Gamlar glæður* (Gleams from the Past), Guðbjörg Jónsdóttir (b. 1871) mentions a woman in the commune of Kirkjuból who was suffering derangement and uses these very words, that it was sometimes necessary to 'lock her away'. Sigurður Sigurðsson, regional medical officer for the county of Dalasýsla, describes conditions for the insane in his district as follows in an unpublished report to the surgeon general: 'But as regards *the insane*, there have been and still are the most intractable problems here, people's conditions for looking after them are pitiful, and there is a total lack of accommodation for such people, especially if the illness is very marked. For this reason the mentally ill have generally be kept in outhouses, and so have had to suffer cold in winter, spent most of their time huddled up, with the result that they become bent and doubled up.'[9]

Conditions were often no better for patients with contagious diseases, or for those who attended them. Davíð Scheving Thorsteinsson, the county medical officer for Snæfells- og Hnappadalssýsla, takes this up in his report to the surgeon general for 1899:

> The members of a household are reluctant to give testimony against their masters and so it is difficult to show beyond doubt that the provisions of the law are being followed in all respects. However, one may just imagine what a state of filth you can find in hovels like those where there are two of the lepers living. I measured these shacks and here record the dimensions of one of them for interest's sake.
>
> Height of walls *c*. 1¾ ells. 'Living room' 9 ells in length, 4 ells in breadth, 3½ ells from floor (dirt floor) up to roof ridge. Roof laths and eaves boarding, white with mould and wet with condensation, battens similarly with white patches of mould (this was August). 2 small window openings facing west, *c*. 8 x 12 inches. Inside here there are 5 beds: one across the gable end, and 4 along the side walls, with *c*. 2½ feet = 1¼ ells between the beds. – Here is also a fireplace and so a number of small chests. In this shack there were 8 – eight people . . . Both of these lepers are married and have children, they are not on poor relief and are *absolutely* determined not to go into the leper hospital.[10]

Descriptions such as this occur regularly in the reports of the district medical officers from the second half of the nineteenth century and on into the twentieth. The fact that they come from those best placed of anyone to know about the poverty and squalor of living conditions in the country makes them particularly grim reading.

Health

Public health provision in Iceland in the nineteenth and early twentieth century remained sparse. Among the problems, one of the most pressing was the lack of doctors. Their number increased slowly, from three in

1830, to six in 1860, eleven in 1870, 30 in 1890, 47 in 1900, 65 in 1917, and 120 in 1930. Without question access to doctors and other medical facilities improved significantly during this period. By way of illustration, in 1860 there were 11,000 people per physician; by 1930 this number had fallen to 900. According to Jón Ólafur Ísberg's important study of the history of medicine in Iceland, between 1760 and 1900 a total of 88 medical doctors lived and practised in Iceland.[11]

Given the lack of qualified physicians in the nineteenth century, homeopaths and folk doctors remained active throughout the country and some were actually granted licences to practise. Late in the century the Danish government attempted to outlaw them but this reform was firmly opposed by the Icelandic parliament.

One of the standard reference works on medicine in Iceland includes a list of known folk doctors and laymen involved in the practice of medicine. For the eighteenth, nineteenth and twentieth centuries this list contains approximately 140 names but, as the authors note, it is far from complete; for instance, the lack of sources means that it almost certainly fails to take full account of the number of women involved in healing.[12] Some of these folk doctors retained the right to practise up until 1932, when the parliament introduced laws regulating medical practice. It goes without saying that many people had considerably more faith in homeopaths and folk medicine than in university-trained physicians, and this sentiment, it seems, was shared by a significant number of the members of parliament.

The increase in the number of doctors, especially after 1890, along with advances in medical knowledge, led to significant improvements in public health. One notable manifestation of this was the gradual eradication of major endemic diseases such as leprosy, hydatids and diphtheria in the first decades of the twentieth century. For example, around the turn of the century a leper hospital was established to provide for the 220–30 cases then known in the country; prior to this, patients had lived with friends or relatives where standards of hygiene and sanitation were usually poor.

In 1938 Vilmundur Jónsson, surgeon general from 1931 to 1959, produced a report on the current state of some of the country's endemic diseases: 'Hydatids was until recently one of the commonest diseases treated by Icelandic surgeons; around the year 1880 it was reckoned, at a conservative estimate, that every sixtieth inhabitant of the country was suffering from this condition.'[13] Hydatids is an infestation by a tapeworm which can grow to enormous sizes in the human liver and is carried from sheep to dogs to humans. In the light of the passage quoted earlier about dogs being used to lick clean the bowls that people ate from, we need hardly be surprised at the prevalence of this disease.

The people of Iceland continued to live under the threat of most of the diseases mentioned above as long as their living conditions remained rooted in the traditional combination of poor housing, lack of hygiene and sanitation, poverty and cold. As the twentieth century progressed, with better medical provision allied to increased awareness of hygiene and sanitation, the quality of life improved steadily. Diseases such as diphtheria, which in the nineteenth century had reached epidemic proportions capable of wiping out whole families, were brought under control through widespread vaccination campaigns. The scourge of diphtheria is described eloquently in an article from 1895 in the journal *Eimreiðin* in which the unknown author reports on a new medicine introduced to combat the disease:

> That the disease is highly contagious is common knowledge. It comes with a fever. The child's throat soon starts to form white-grey spots, especially on the tongue. This film or growth soon spreads all over the throat, and often into the nose and down into the larynx if the disease is malignant. The lymph glands in the throat become inflamed and the neck becomes extremely swollen. At this point the child will die soon. Sometimes the disease starts in the gland and is then accompanied by a grating hoarseness with shortness of breath and a peculiar cough. The child then often dies within a short period from lack of breath. The growth that forms in the throat is covered with germs that spread rapidly and multiply. In this case a poison forms that spreads through the body in the blood, bringing either immediate death or death after a period of remission in which the disease appears to be over.

Typhoid was another endemic disease. Periodic epidemics ravaged whole communities, coming down particularly hard on families who lost their breadwinners, either permanently or for long periods. Those who survived were often left severely weakened and unable to provide for their families.

As the evidence presented in this chapter shows clearly, for most people living conditions in Iceland, both in urban and rural areas, remained extremely harsh until well on into the twentieth century. Despite the gradual improvements, poor housing and unsanitary conditions continued to foster a range of diseases that decimated families and whole communities. The situation was exacerbated by poor diet, which was limited in terms of both quantity and nutrition, and also by lack of clothing. In a well-known study Sveinbjörn Rafnsson has shown that the diet of eighteenth-century Iceland consisted mainly of fish and dairy products. Bread entered the picture as a regular item in the nineteenth century, along with coffee, which became an indispensable part of people's everyday lives.[14] Most clothes were made of wool. Woollen clothes are of course warm but of limited effectiveness in the damp and rainy climate of Iceland. Shoes were made of sheepskin. Sewn at home by hand, they offered only minimal protection against the elements. The lack of clothing during their childhoods is a recurrent theme of many of the autobiographers.

The hardships described in this chapter had a huge influence on people's ability to cope with the demands of day-to-day living. There is no reason to doubt the picture presented in the autobiographies of a hardworking people toiling desperately under almost impossible conditions. These conditions go a long way to explaining why much of the material in the advice literature was of limited value and had little effect: the general public was simply too poor to be able to act on their own initiative to improve their quality of life. There were, of course, exceptions, and the successes achieved by some sections of the population acted as a spearhead for the gradual change of society. This process of modernization, however, did not reach the majority of Icelanders until well into the twentieth century.

4

Icelandic Connections: The Lure of the New World

Background to the migration and the broader European context

The folk migrations of the nineteenth century touched the lives of hundreds of millions of people across Europe. The flood of emigrants to America radically altered the mental perspectives of both those who made the long journey west and those who stayed at home. The novelty of the situation, however, should not be overstated, since in many parts of Europe there were also large-scale movements within national boundaries, not least in Scandinavia.[1] This internal migration took a variety of forms – people moved from one part of a country to another in search of permanent future homes for themselves and their families, or seasonally according to labour demand. In the nineteenth century, for example, many Icelandic men moved regularly from the country areas to fishing camps on the coast at certain times of the year, and those who lived in the urban centres on the coast travelled to the country in summer to take part in the farm work at times of heaviest demand. These seasonal migrations from one place to another within the country had been a familiar feature of life in Iceland for centuries. Farmers went off for the duration of the fishing season, leaving their wives and children behind to tend to the farm, and came home at the end of the season stocked with sea produce that formed an important part of the family's food supply. In addition, unlanded people in bonded service tended to move home frequently, taking advantage of their right under law to change residence once a year. Even youngsters often had to leave their childhood homes and take up positions of service in other households. For nineteenth-century Icelanders, moving from place to place was a recognized part of their national culture.

The migration of people and families in nineteenth-century Iceland in search of new homes tended to be restricted to relatively small areas – the commune or neighbouring districts. However, in any commune there was always a number of resident families whose origins lay further afield. Thus Icelanders, like people in many other parts of Europe, were well familiar with the concept of moving home; such movement was a part of the pattern of their lives. But this kind of internal relocation was of a quite different order from migration to a new continent (or linguistic area) – though internal migration and the dislocation that went with it might perhaps be seen as providing an excellent preparation, both physical and emotional, for the emigrations to the New World. They were thus perhaps not such a massive leap into the unknown as might at first appear.

The Icelanders were the last of the Scandinavians to start emigrating to the New World. The main emigrations from Norway took place in the 1830s and '40s, from Sweden in the 1840s and '50s, from Denmark in the 1850s and '60s, and from Finland in the 1860s and '70s. In Iceland the exodus did not get under way to any appreciable extent until the 1870s, though there had been some small-scale movement in the previous decade. By and large the Icelanders stayed put throughout the first decades of the second half of the nineteenth century, in spite of difficult conditions at home such as sheep scab, deteriorating climatic conditions and poor fish catches. This failure to follow in the footsteps of their Scandinavian cousins was probably, more than anything else, down to simple lack of opportunity: until around 1870 shipping to and from Iceland remained very infrequent and irregular. Once this situation changed the Icelanders did not need to be asked twice and the trickle of emigrants became a flood, proportionally far greater than had been seen in any of the other Nordic countries. As the final decade of the century approached, 27 out of every thousand Icelanders were leaving for America each year.

We have a fair amount of information on shipping connections between Iceland and the outside world. Initially, most of the emigrants began their journey on livestock vessels going to Scotland, plying the trade in sheep exports to Britain. Later, after 1874, the shipping companies that arranged passages from Scotland to America started sending special ships to Iceland to pick up passengers. As the turn of the century approached the fare dropped considerably, from around 200 kr. to a little over 100 kr. Newborn infants travelled free and children from one up to eleven went half price. In the last years of the century there was competition for emigrants and the Canadian government invested considerable sums in subsidizing would-be immigrants.

The *Vesturfaraskrá* (Register of Emigrants to America) compiled by the historian Júníus Kristinsson is a fundamental source for anyone interested in the sociology and demographics of the Icelandic emigration – who the emigrants were and what classes of society they came from.[2] The Register contains the names of a large proportion of those who set

*Icelandic society changed dramatically after around 1870 with the emigrations
to North America. Around the same time Iceland started exporting livestock
to Britain (sheep and horses). This trade meant that, for the first time, the
ordinary people of Iceland had access to money; prior to this, all trade had
been in the form of barter. For most of the country's history the Iceland
trade had been a Danish royal monopoly, with the king granting licences to
favoured Danish subjects. Imported goods were exchanged for goods produced
by Icelandic farmers – wool, fish and sometimes meat. It was the Danish
merchants who decided prices and rates of exchange, and the country was
partitioned up between these merchants, with each holding sole trading rights
within his area. Icelanders were forbidden to trade with anyone other than
the designated monopoly holder for their area. The trade in live animals with
Britain created entirely new conditions on the internal market and provided
the means by which ordinary Icelanders were able to raise the funds for a
passage to the New World. Many used this opportunity and moved away
to settle in Canada and the USA.*

out on the long journey west. As Sveinbjörn Rafnsson notes in his
introduction, 14,268 individuals are listed as having left Iceland for
the New World in the years 1870–1914.[3] As Sveinbjörn also notes, this
figure is probably an underestimate: on top of those that appear in the
Register, there were conceivably quite a lot more – possibly thousands
– about whom we have no reliable records. In addition to their names,
the Register also lists the emigrants' last known place of residence in
Iceland, age, social status (and/or marital or family status), port of
departure and the ship they travelled on. Wherever possible, additional
information is given, such as sex, year of departure, and also where in
Iceland they came from originally. For instance, it emerges that twelve

harbours were involved, with the highest numbers setting out from Akureyri in the north and Seyðisfjörður and Vopnafjörður in the east.

While immensely valuable, the information from *Vesturfaraskrá* does not tell us everything we might wish to know. Work remains to be done on comparing the entries with information from North America, most notably Canadian immigration records that have recently become available. Another valuable source is the *Almanak Ólafs S. Thorgeirssonar* (Ólafur S. Thorgeirsson's Almanac), which annually over the years 1895–1954 published death notices of people of Icelandic origin living in North America. The historian Vigfús Geirdal has collated these records against the *Vesturfaraskrá* and come to the conclusion that, out of a sample of approximately 7,500 people born in Iceland, some 25 per cent do not appear in the Register.

In contrast to the other Scandinavian countries, most of whose emigrants headed for the USA, the vast majority of Icelanders settled in Canada. The commonest route started by livestock freighter to Britain or, after 1877, by the mail ships of the United Danish Steamship Company. Most of these ships stopped in Glasgow, from where the emigrants travelled by train to Liverpool to pick up ships bound for Quebec in Canada. From Quebec the routes diverged: the most popular final destinations were Winnipeg or the 'New Iceland' colony on the shores of Lake Winnipeg, but others headed further afield, including to settlements in the USA.

Aspirations and incentives

Historians in Europe and America have spent much time and effort trying to build up an idea of the reasons behind the emigrations – what it was, chiefly, that induced people to up roots and move away to a new continent and totally unfamiliar surroundings. From the sources presented here and others like them, it seems clear that the emigrations were motivated by a variety of factors. The most important of these need to be identified and taken for consideration.

First, it needs to be remembered that the Icelanders were not as isolated as has often been maintained. Geographically, of course, they had precious little direct contact with the world outside, but despite this news of international events reached Iceland fairly readily and many Icelanders took a keen interest in it. Writings preserved from nineteenth-century farmers and farm workers give copious evidence that the general public in Iceland, even in remote areas seemingly far from the centres of Western culture, was remarkably knowledgeable on what was going on in contemporary Europe and ideas that were circulating there. A farm labourer, schoolteacher, smallholder and seasonal fisherman from the remote north-west, Magnús Hj. Magnússon (b. 1873), for instance, notes in his diary news items from all around the world and often adopts a clear stance on the events and issues involved. In 1904 he describes the Russo-Japanese war thus:

> In this month there was a massive spilling of blood between the Japanese and Russians and I turn to this in brief. There were incessant battles, the fighting sometimes going on without let for days on end. The slaughter was terrible: all dips and hollows full of blood and corpses and the multitude of the dead piled up over those who were left standing to fight. The Japanese had the better of it. – Had our ancient sagas described such battles no one would have believed it, since they are supposed to be largely 'lies' and 'exaggeration'. But I think it is hardly possible to describe a battle so graphically that it is not even more terrible in fact, since few can describe the mental anguish of those who take part in the fighting.[4]

Quite naturally, Magnús sees this war in the light of the things he knew best – the Icelandic sagas – and uses the reports as evidence against those who chose to cast doubt on the veracity of his country's literary heritage, as will be discussed later. Here he had found proof that the things he read in the sagas could really happen. As his final comment indicates, Magnús was endowed with a powerful insight and imagination. He does not mention where he got his information but it is not unlikely that it would have been from a newspaper report.

Here we have a telling example of how international events could become part of the lives and imaginations of ordinary people in Iceland. We find a similar example in the autobiography of Tryggvi Emilsson (b. 1902), *Fátækt fólk* (Poor People), this time concerning an event from the second decade of the twentieth century. Once again we see how a major news story from abroad could find its way into the cottages of rural Iceland and the effect it could have on household life:

> One evening I went over to Gloppa and Steingrímur lent me a newspaper from Reykjavík. I tucked it away so it would not get wet and took it home to Gil. My father sat down with the paper and read it out loud and we discussed all the material in it, advertisements as much as anything else, but what affected us most was a report of the revolution in Russia, which had led to the overthrow of the czar and all his family being sentenced to death and this sentence being carried out. This was all the work of the Bolsheviks (hard-liners) and the people at Gil were

absolutely devastated to hear about it and went about in a daze for quite some time afterwards. My father considered it the greatest crime in world history and was quite convinced that the Bolsheviks would get their due deserts; the czar had been of divine origin and had stood next only to the Lord that would never be overthrown and was the king of heaven himself and had it in his omnipotence to wreak grim vengeance on the Reds, in addition to which they would never be able to govern for long, being a black-sheep proletarian riffraff. Guðný went even further and openly challenged the one from the nether regions to show his stuff and obliterate anyone that had had a part in it.

The examples quoted are from the early years of the twentieth century. But the situation in preceding times had not been dissimilar: news reached Iceland fairly readily and people had a surprisingly good knowledge of what was going on in the world outside and formed similar sorts of ideas about it as others in the West. In an interesting article on communications between Iceland and the rest of Europe in the journal *Saga* in 1995, Anna Agnarsdóttir pointed to a number of factors that helped Icelanders to keep relatively abreast with what was happening outside the country in the second half of the eighteenth century and the first part of the nineteenth. She mentions, for example, students who spent long periods of study in various European countries and wrote letters home or brought new ideas back with them on their return, and adventurers who journeyed to places as far afield as China, St Petersburg, France, Greenland and Turkey and wrote books relating their experiences. She also notes the frequent references to foreign events in Icelandic annals: as she says, 'Icelanders in bygone centuries were hungry for news.'

Anna's article also describes the curious attitude of earlier twentieth-century Icelandic scholars who, when editing the annals for 1400–1800 for publication, omitted all material that related to events outside Iceland – as if, as the national archivist Hannes Þorsteinsson expressed it in his introduction to one of the volumes, 'all this foreign stuff has been entirely left out of the edition, being totally without relevance to Iceland'.[5] This unfortunate practice has only served to reinforce the popular conception of Iceland as an insular and isolated society. Anna notes that many of the compilers of the annals followed world events closely and recorded those that struck them as most important. She also mentions the part played by the stream of foreign travellers who started visiting Iceland, especially in the nineteenth century, many of whom got to know the inhabitants well and so gave them an opportunity to acquire a new outlook on the world.

One lovely example quoted by Anna provides powerful testimony to Icelanders' interest in foreign news. It concerns a letter written in 1814 to Grímur Jónsson by Guðrún Skúladóttir, a woman well into her eighties at the time of writing. This Guðrún was the daughter of 'Governor Skúli', Skúli Magnússon, the eighteenth-century royal official who instituted a number of economic and industrial reforms aimed at dragging Iceland out of its medieval squalor and the founder of modern Reykjavík. 'It is a great shame and a pity if life has been cheated of Napoleon. It was to his valour and glory that he managed to keep his head amid such a calamitous change. If you write back to me, tell me whether he is still alive and how he is, and how well liked Louis XVIII is in France.' Whether Guðrún got any news back from France we do not know, but what is clear is that ordinary people in Iceland had some knowledge of foreign countries and the different circumstances of people in them.

Second, we need to bear in mind that the second half of the eighteenth century and the whole of the nineteenth was a time of major political changes in Europe, changes that affected every home in the continent and in fact further afield. The great emigration from Europe to America was to some extent the outcome of political developments both in Europe and the USA, the main feature of which can be characterized as an increased freedom for ordinary people. This wave of freedom touched the lives of people throughout the continent, including Iceland. It is fair to assume, therefore, that once the opportunity for movement to America opened up around 1870 the Icelanders greeted it with open arms. Up to that time, as mentioned earlier, sailings to and from Iceland had been sporadic and Icelanders had had to let themselves be satisfied with unfulfilled daydreams.

Third, it is clear that a major factor in the enthusiasm for emigration to America among the ordinary people of Iceland was the conditions under which they lived at home. Prospects for the young and people of limited means were severely restricted in Iceland in the second half of the nineteenth century. As elsewhere in Europe, poverty and lack of opportunity at home created a fertile ground for people's readiness to seek their fortunes elsewhere.

The biography of Einar Ásmundsson from Nes in Þingeyjarsýsla in the northen part of Iceland, who acted as chief spokesman for the transportation company, gives a detailed account of the events leading up to the early plans for emigration to Brazil. It is quite clear from what both Einar and others had to say that people felt bowed down by conditions at home, that society seemed at death's door under the weight of hopelessness and penury. In 1863 a group of enthusiasts sent representatives to Brazil to look into conditions there and the next year they

reported back, describing what the place had to offer. Jakob Hálfdanarson of Grímsstaðir describes the reaction to the news from Brazil
when summing up the year 1864 in his diary:

> Among the most notable and happiest things the past year has
> brought us we may count the letter that arrived on 2 May from
> our countrymen who set out for Brazil last year. This letter
> brought us who have sat in silence between hope and fear the
> glad news that everything had turned out as satisfactorily as
> could best have been hoped. For this reason a decision has been
> made to leave this country in summer for Brazil. Many new
> people have joined the group, while little is now heard from
> those who wanted to destroy this enterprise with their worst
> scaremongering, carping and groundless prejudice, and some
> have now changed their opinion entirely.[6]

It is clear that economic conditions at home made the prospect of
such journeys particularly appealing to impoverished Icelandic farmers
and farm workers. As mentioned earlier, one of the main obstacles to such
ventures was the lack of shipping. Einar Ásmundarson failed to secure
a passage for the group of 150 people waiting and ready to set out for
Brazil in 1865, and for this he suffered the odium of many of his fellow
countrymen who opposed the emigration and accused him of treason
and lack of patriotism, as well as of members of the group of would-be
migrants, who felt they had been cheated. Regarding Einar's patriotism,
the author of the account, Arnór Sigurjónsson, has this to say: 'Neither
can it be denied that he had mixed feelings about what happened in
the years immediately following; in all his attitudes he was a citizen of
the world.'[7]

The same might perhaps be said of more people than Einar, that they
were citizens of the world in their peculiarly Icelandic way. Though
economic considerations may have played an important part in shaping
ordinary people's attitudes to emigration, there was perhaps also a
fourth incentive, a desire for change for its own sake, a wish to see the
world. As Iceland's traditional isolation weakened, many people simply
wanted to try something new, to have the opportunity to test themselves
against new conditions and to benefit from the freedoms America
appeared to offer. The desire for freedom was not something drawn
out of thin air: the news got round that in America land was to be had
for free, or at very little cost, that there was a big labour market and a
great demand for people who reckoned they had something to offer,
that there were no constraints on trade, that people could decide for
themselves if and when they wanted to start a family, that educational

opportunities were many times better those at home, and that there were even full political rights for all men. Those who were touched by this hope of freedom were for obvious reasons eager to drink deep from the well of plenty. For many, the move to America became a simple necessity. This comes across, for example, in letters written by Einar Ásmundsson of Nes to many of his friends. He had no difficulty justifying his keenness to leave to the 'friends of the fatherland':

> We are arguing about what a fatherland is, and we all agree that, in the broadest sense, it is the whole world. But what are the boundaries of our fatherland in the narrower sense? Do I leave it behind if I move home to Greenland or St Croix in the West Indies or the Nicobar Islands in the Bay of Bengal? I am not leaving the country if I go to these places, any more than if I went to Norway or Shetland and the like. But if Iceland is our *only* fatherland in the narrower sense, could you not also call Grímsey the fatherland of the people from Grímsey? . . . I know that, to the Romans, their fatherland was wherever they felt at home, and I know that it is common nowadays to call the country a person moves to permanently that person's 'new fatherland'. According to this fatherland ought to mean *the land where someone lives*, as no one can be reborn in the sense that Master Nicodemus used the word long ago. – This also fits better with my opinion, since I view the whole world as a fatherland where a man should have the right to roam as fancy takes him, wishing all of it well . . .[8]

Doubtless similar ideas moved in the breasts of many of Einar's compatriots interested in moving to new places and finding somewhere to settle. Only few of them, probably, could have articulated these ideas as well as Einar did in his letter to Pastor Sigurður Guðmundsson, dated 18 April 1861. Einar closed his justification thus: 'Seen in this light, it was my duty to be an Eastfjorder as best I could in days gone by, and a Northerner now, and soon maybe a Brazilian – but whatever happens, I must always remain a *cosmopolitan*.'

A fifth factor influencing the decisions of people considering the move to America was family ties and connections with people who were already there. Correspondence from emigrants had a deep effect on those who remained at home. Here they got reliable information about the kind of society awaiting them. Letters from people who had moved to the New World appeared regularly in the newspaper *Norðanfari*, published in Akureyri and generally sympathetic to the emigrations. It was also not uncommon for people to travel back and forth between countries, for emigrants to return home and give first-hand accounts of conditions in the new land. It hardly needs saying the effect such visits would have had on people back in Iceland.

Contemporary sources contain several accounts of how people in Iceland talked about the New World and the affect letters from America had on their imaginations. Erlendur Guðmundsson of Mörk in Laxárdalur recounts one such story in his autobiography called *Heima og heiman* (Home and Away):

> When the first letters arrived they were printed in *Norðanfari*, which was then the only paper in the north of Iceland, and most of the emigrants came from Þingeyjarsýsla and Eyjaf-jarðarsýsla. The arrival of *Norðanfari* was greeted with great excitement, and nothing in it seemed so appetizing as the letters. They told of wonderlands, boundless in size, that were mostly unoccupied and just waiting for people to come along and, without a by your leave, turn themselves into great landowners out of nothing. This was something quite unheard of to people in Iceland, and no wonder it excited their longing to move. It was said, and probably not far from the truth, that no printed matter at the time except people's Bibles was read as much as these first letters from the emigrants. People stood in breath-less anticipation listening to these incomparable adventures. Then other stories were spun out of these adventures, and they were also believed, however improbable, and the local wags used this mercilessly on simple people when they got a chance, and there were plenty of them. I set down here a few examples.
>
> There was a man called Hallgrímur Erlendsson who lived at Meðalheimar at Ásar in Húnavatnssýsla, who I have men-tioned earlier. The next farm was called Hurðabak. There there lived a married man called Guðmundur Jónsson. This was around 1875 or 1876. One time Hallgrímur and Guðmundur happened to meet and the conversation turned to the emigra-tions, and Guðmundur had been thinking about moving to America. Then Hallgrímur starts to tell him various things he ought to know but was unaware of concerning what farm pro-duction was like in this promised land, such as for example that raisins grew in the earth there just like grass in Iceland, and people there did raisin-making just like they do haymak-ing at home. Guðmundur perked up at this, presumably with some kind of picture in his mind that he would likely be as good as anyone at this harvesting, probably reckoning he would be on to a winner in America, being enormously big and strong and

healthy. Then Hallgrímur let on that you could get blizzards in America that piled up in little heaps, only this was not snow but icing sugar, so there was no danger of the lady of the house being unwilling to sweep her doorstep and save a bit and bring it in for household use, because there are lots of uses for icing sugar.

Hallgrímur told Guðmundur a few more things it was useful for him to know about the journey to America, including this: for the passage every man should take with him a good-sized skin bag which people were supposed to use to put their excrement in, and when the bag appeared to be reasonably full it should be emptied into a tub assigned to each head of a household and hung on a hook over the ship's side, and the stuff that build up in this way on the voyage was a priceless asset when it got to America as it would fetch a huge price for spreading on the fields, and so everyone tried to eat as much as they could on the journey, on this depended how much or little went into the bag. When Hallgrímur had got to the point in the story where he was talking about the tubs on the hooks, Guðmundur's mother, who had been listening is silence up till now, said: Well, they seem to have thought of most things.

This Guðmundur arrived at Sauðárkrókur together with some other emigrants. They had to wait a long time for the ship and were forced to disperse around the neighbouring countryside to keep themselves alive, but no one would take Guðmundur in, and when the ship eventually arrived some of them had run so low on provisions that they got nowhere. One of these was Guðmundur. He made no further attempt to get to America, and from that day on he acquired the nickname Raisin-Guðmundur.

For all that nineteenth-century Icelanders may have generally been fairly well informed on international affairs, it must have been easy to string along more gullible members of society with fantastic stories of strange lands, as in the example above. The vast majority, we must suppose, knew quite enough about the world outside for tall tales like those Erlendur relates not to have had any appreciable effect. But it is worth bearing in mind that Iceland at the time was fertile ground for stories of this kind, since people lived with fairly tightly restricted liberties and so were only too willing to let themselves dream of better times. Young people would have been particularly susceptible to the allure of emigration, because in Iceland marriage was more or less out of the question unless they had acquired a tolerable level of wealth and status.

Finally, there may have been certain people who felt obliged to leave Iceland for reasons of politics or religion: this was certainly the case through much else of Europe. While freedom of conscience and worship was perhaps not a major motive among Icelanders, once they got to Canada and the United States their lives as recent immigrants were strongly shaped by politics and religion. More broadly, however, it is probably fair to say that there was a political element in many if not most Icelanders' decisions to leave for America, especially where this political element touched on social issues and the concerns of the poor and destitute.

Little is to be gained trying to weigh up between the six factors mentioned: each played its part, and there were as many ideas and motivations as there were people that set out on the long journey west. What is most important to understand is that many of the reasons put forward at the time say more about the people that put them forward than about the emigrants themselves. Those who left were neither driven out as a result of social or economic oppression, nor giving up on their homeland through personal defects of nature or nurture. Neither was it necessarily a case of an energetic and ambitious people unwilling to stay and watch on as their country went to wrack and ruin under the Danish yoke, as was sometimes claimed by emigrants in justification of their actions, nor of weaklings and slackers lacking the backbone to face up to the difficulties that went hand in hand with life in a harsh and unforgiving landscape. These arguments that were used for and against the emigrations are the product first and foremost of personal attitudes to the New World. No single reason provides the answer; the reasons were many and varied and differed from person to person. And just like the reasons, the effects of the emigrations were hotly debated, on the society that was left behind, on the new country, and finally on the individuals themselves, both those that moved away and those that stayed behind.

External influences

Whatever reasons individuals may have had for leaving their homelands and moving to America, it is clear that for a time governments in many parts of Europe took a generally favourable view of emigration where this meant a solution to the perennial problem of what to do with the poorest sections of their societies. In their book *Transatlantic Connections* the Norwegian historians Hans Norman and Harald Runblom note that in many places the authorities actively encouraged the emigration of poor people, especially those that were felt to be a burden on society. This, they believe, was the case throughout Scandinavia, including Iceland. However, there is reason to doubt that, so far as Iceland is concerned, Norman and Runblom's claim can be taken entirely at face value; or, at least, it requires qualification.

As has been noted earlier, Icelandic newspapers and journals throughout the second half of the nineteenth century and on into the twentieth were full of articles arguing that it was the first duty of each individual to shoulder the responsibilities that lay on all inhabitants of a country that aspired to independence. This was a repeated refrain and largely unquestioned, and we can take it as given that those in positions of power and influence in Iceland believed it. For this reason alone it is extremely questionable that the authorities would have set out deliberately to rid the country of its poor. In addition, it is worth remembering that the groups that held power in Iceland, especially landowning farmers, had a considerable economic interest in ensuring that an ample source of cheap labour remained available for use in production. It cannot, of course, be denied that there was a certain section of the pauper population that was entirely unproductive and played no useful part in the various stages of production. And there are certainly recorded cases of particular *hreppstjórar* (communal directors) who were happy to pack off to America paupers and dependants who had shown themselves to have nothing to offer society and were regarded solely as a drain on local finances. But this hardly justifies us in thinking that this was the dominant attitude among those in power in Iceland at the time.

In support of their thesis, Norman and Runblom refer to an article by Gísli Ágúst Gunnlaugsson in the journal *Saga* in 1978 under the name 'Milliþinganefnd í fátækramálum' ('Interim Committee on Pauper Affairs'). In this article Gísli Ágúst cites the emigrations as one possible reason for the reduction in the number of paupers during the period. He even provides a couple of examples of local officials subsidizing the transportation of poor people to America. Gísli Ágúst himself, however, points to the likeliest explanation for the decrease in pauperism in the second half of the nineteenth century: 'It is also possible that the large-scale migration to America freed up land and farms at home in Iceland and so improved economic conditions for those who remained behind.' This is surely closer to the truth, and it seems extremely incautious to conclude from one or two cases that the authorities actively promoted the mass transportation of poor people from Iceland.

Gísli Ágúst mentions that, according to stories going round at the time, a considerable proportion of those who emigrated to America were paupers, though it is not easy to say where these stories came from – other, perhaps, than from the ranks of those who opposed the emigrations. One thing that is absolutely certain is that contemporary sources discussing these matters cannot necessarily be taken at face value and must always be viewed in the light of the contemporary attitudes and opinions. A commonly found comment from the time, for instance, is that it was the 'worse' section of Icelandic society that was allowing itself to be tempted into emigration. This was just a logical extension of the contemporary debate in which all efforts were directed towards a single goal – to demonstrate that Iceland was the home of a responsible nation that was eager to face up to the future as free-born individuals. Those who 'jumped ship', as it were, were in some way inferior.

The social origins of the emigrants have never been subjected to proper scrutiny. But if at some time in the future they are, it is highly likely that it will emerge that the majority did indeed come from the poorer sections of society. A quick glance at the *Vesturfaraskrá* is enough to reveal that a large proportion of the names that appear were agricultural labourers, seasonal fishermen with very small landholdings and others of the sort, rather than, say, landowning farmers. It is very probable also that paupers made up a significant part of the emigrants and that in many cases they were aided by relatives and benefactors in raising the funds needed for the journey – it was no less of a relief to these people to see their dependants out of the way than it was to the local authorities, since people were obliged by law to support other members of their family. According to statute, which Gísli Ágúst refered to in his article, 'those who left the country were under obligation to provide a surety against their dependants becoming a burden on the local authorities in Iceland for at least three years from the time of their departure.' I am not aware that this statute was ever enforced but the spirit behind it is quite clear: a pauper's relatives were under an obligation of responsibility and this was an obligation that no one could evade.

According to Norman and Runblom, we have no information on how many people returned to Iceland after spending some time in Canada or the USA, or how they got on on their return. It can hardly be doubted, though, that such people would have had a considerable influence on those who were thinking of emigrating: the personal experience of friends and acquaintances could be all-important when it came to taking as momentous a decision as to abandon the land where one had grown up.

It appears, according to Norman and Runblom, that each of the Scandinavian countries acquired certain named individuals that became famous for having ventured out into the unknown and for their exploits in the New World. This was another group that would have influenced people's ideas on emigration. The Icelanders had had long experience of men of this kind – men like Jón Ólafsson 'Indíafari' (1593–1679), who joined the Danish navy and sailed to India, and Árni Magnússon of Geitastekkur (1726–1810), who travelled as far as Greenland, Russia, China and Turkey, both of whom wrote accounts of their travels on their return. Another Jón Ólafsson (1850–1916), literary editor, poet and later member of parliament, became a national celebrity by getting the US government to fund an expedition to Alaska with a view to assessing possible settlement sites for future Icelandic migrants.[9] The expedition went ahead and Jón found a region in Alaska called Kodiak that he felt was suitable. On his return he submitted a report of his findings to the US president Ulysses S. Grant and the idea became the subject of public debate. However, Jón's plans hit a snag since they assumed that the US government would be willing to fund the passage of Icelanders travelling out to the new settlement, and Congress balked at the outlay involved.

Jón Ólafsson went back to Iceland to promote his idea but his words fell on deaf ears: by this time large numbers of Icelanders were heading for the new Icelandic settlement around Winnipeg and the Canadian authorities were providing immigrants with free land, or as good as. There ensued a competition for Icelandic immigrants between the two governments of North America, the US and the Canadian, with each vying to attract new settlers, and Jón's idea fell by the wayside. In the event, it was the Canadian government that won out, simply by offering better terms, such as support for families once they had settled in New Iceland. Eventually Jón gave up.

Jón Ólafsson was not the only man to become a national figure in Iceland as a result of his travels in America; others included the later novelist Einar Hjörleifsson Kvaran and a number of church ministers. Almost certainly the most famous was Pastor Jón Bjarnason, who for many years acted as a kind of leader of the Icelandic community in America, later travelling regularly back and forth between the Old World and the New. All of these men had a great influence on how ordinary people in Iceland thought and talked about the settlements. Jón Ólafsson, for example, defended the emigrations with great vigour, as in the following title of a pamphlet published in 1888: *A word of sense about emigrants and emigration: Reply and address to editor Bjarni Jónsson occasioned by all the drivel, vilification and misinformation propagated in and by 'Ísafold'* [a journal]. *Benedikt Gröndal stripped, whipped and put in the pillory.*[10]

The critics of the emigration were in no mood to give up without a fight. The war of words between the two sides was personal and nasty, with the anti-emigrationists often resorting to highly colourful language in their portrayals of conditions in America and the character of those who fell for the propaganda of the emigration 'agents'. Their invective undoubtedly had the very opposite effect to the one intended on occasions: it simply served to direct greater attention on to the attractions of the New World. Here is not the place to follow the course of the debate that went on in the newspapers and journals, and little is gained by presenting a string of individual comments for and against in the great controversy. Instead, it is worth reiterating that the whole tenor of public debate on social issues in Iceland was united in a powerful opposition to any kind of going back. Men were urged to move forward in the name of the country and its people; the country had strong leaders and it was the duty of the common people of Iceland to follow their guidance across a whole range of issues from education to family affairs. Those who failed in this deserved only the severest censure. Yet despite this powerful undertone to the national debate, people continued to ignore the critics and leave the country in droves.

A single example of the anti-emigrationist lobby will suffice, in the person of Hannes Þorsteinsson (b. 1860), member of parliament, editor of *Þjóðólfur*, one of the two main national newspapers of the time, and later director of the national archives. Hannes talked about the emigrations in his highly outspoken autobiography, written in 1926–8, called *Endurminningar og hugleiðingar um hitt og þetta, er á dagana hefur drifið* (Memoirs and Thoughts about This and That which has Happened to Me). The following quotation provides a specimen of the approach and kind of argumentation used by those, including Hannes, who attempted to stem the tide of emigration. He saw his editorship as a platform from which to take an uncompromising stance on the issue and welcomed any opportunity to lay into his opponents:

> It was the inflammatory whispering campaign of the Americo-lunatic agents that whetted *Þjóðólfur*'s arrows and directed them against this farrago that newspapers in Iceland had up till now chosen largely to ignore, watching on year after year while unprincipled emigration sheep herders inveigled the people with various lying reports into leaving the land in droves to the Paradise Farm out west on the Canadian prairies. The most infamous of these 'agents' were Baldvin Baldvinsson, Sigurður Kristófersson and Sveinn Brynjólfsson, who were all travelling the land in the winter of 1892–1893, holding lectures here and there with the most ludicrous gilding of the wealth and happiness of our countrymen who had made the journey west, and presenting as proof printed statistics that showed every sign of being mere sensationalism, full of deceit and false claims, and handing them out in piles around the country, making people half crazed with the intoxication of emigration.

It is interesting to see how Hannes describes the people who promoted emigration. The language he uses to characterize the people and issues involved seems to bear the marks of the powerful winds of the independence movement that were sweeping through Iceland in the early years of the twentieth century. The style harks back to the ancient sagas, tightly worded and combative. Hannes goes on to discuss the role of *Þjóðólfur* in the dispute and how the paper became involved in it:

> So *Þjóðólfur* resolved to raise its hand against this scourge and give these gentlemen such a welcome when they came to the capital as they would scarcely forget and that would leave them with little to celebrate from their mission. Around the time that Baldvin and Sigurður arrived in Reykjavík, and while Sveinn was out east, I wrote an article in *Þjóðólfur* on 3 March (issue 10) under the heading 'A small sample of the agent proselytization', in which I described their methods according to what I had heard from reputable sources out in the country – an account that people found arresting. There was already quite a rumbling around town and groups had been formed to see that they did not get to parade their fanaticism and deceit in front of town-dwellers. And so it happened that when Baldvin and Sigurður were intending to deliver these customary lectures of theirs in the Goodtemplars House on the evening of Wednesday, 8 March, they were unable to make themselves heard for the furious whistling of 100 men which went on unabated for a whole hour, until the 'agents' finally scuttled away, and could count themselves fortunate that no one had laid hands on them, as some of the whistlers were only too eager to do. This singular and unusual occurrence is described accurately and impartially in issue 11 of *Þjóðólfur* (10 March) . . . Those who took part in this whistling were from various levels of society, assuredly not exclusively schoolboys and tradesmen, as Baldvin wished to maintain in a reply he sent to *Þjóðólfur* and which I published on 17 March (issue 12).

Here again it is the narrative style that attracts our notice – the humiliation of the agents, *Þjóðólfur*'s 'impartial' account of the events and Hannes's glee at having managed to whip up the masses against his enemies. Like many others, *Þjóðólfur* attempted to influence the course of events and the direction the debate was taking in Iceland, but it needs repeating that the results of this kind of intervention are far from clear. At least this text draws our attention to the activities of the agents and their personalities: what we appear to have is a group of highly skilled salesmen who under normal circumstances would have commanded the ear of their listeners. It would be very interesting to know more about their methods and results, but so far as I am aware the role of these men in Iceland has never been studied in any depth. Hannes's account gives a clear indication of how they operated, moving around the country and holding lectures and meetings to persuade people to try their luck in foreign lands. They were plainly forceful and determined men, willing to fight their corner hard.

Hannes goes on to describe how, around the same time, he published a poem in *Þjóðólfur* by one of the leading literary figures of the day, Benedikt Gröndal, another of the chief anti-emigrationists. The poem refers to the meeting and describes the whistling as 'freedom's call 'gainst foeman army'. Hannes adds that after their rout the agents turned vindictively against him and *Þjóðólfur* 'by bringing a case against me on account of some trifling comment I appended to Baldvin's riposte of 17 March, in which I talked about the Americo-lunatic "humbug" sermons they had delivered here in Iceland to gull people west across the seas to the barren plains of Canada, where everything "burns and freezes".' In the event, Hannes was acquitted, but he came to the conclusion 'that I was the most hated of all Icelandic-based editors among the newspapers and agent clique in America throughout my whole time as editor of *Þjóðólfur* as a result of my implacable opposition to the emigrations and the entire Americo-lunatic agent farrago. But then it rather faded into the background after the trouncing of these compeers, which knocked all the stuffing out of them, so that the tone became quite different from before, and the agents themselves, sent as fishers of men by the Canadian government, largely disappeared from the scene.' In other words, Hannes claimed the credit for bringing an end to emigration!

As noted earlier, the causes of the emigration were many, various and personal, and most of those who went probably reckoned they had little to lose. If there was anything at all in what those who were promoting emigration said, it was perhaps a risk well worth taking. Thus the debate in the press on general social issues, which in the overwhelming majority of cases focused on the position of the individual in society, had precious little significance: families and individuals moved away simply because the opportunity existed. So far as they were concerned, what the government wanted, or what the nationalist idealists would have them believe, was neither here nor there: the ordinary people went their own way, in spite of everything.

Erlendur Guðmundsson of Mörk, quoted earlier, was one of them. The extended extract from his autobiography below gives a strong idea of the kinds of motivations that lay behind people's decisions to emigrate. As he saw it, the most powerful factor was the promise of freedom and prosperity in the New World, a promise that had swept through Iceland like wildfire. People saw an opportunity to make a much better life for themselves and their offspring: to him, it was this that tipped the balance.

Although people here have claimed that the root cause of the emigration was a lack of faith in the country's future, there were other reasons too, such as discontent with the Danes, and it might also be said that every person had some personal reason for going, though common to all was the hope of improving conditions for themselves or their children. It was trumpeted everywhere that America was the land of freedom and progress. There ordinary farmers could vote on things that mattered to the land and its people and so count to some degree as stakeholders in the government of the country. There there were free schools for the children – the very opposite of back at home – and the further children went through school the greater their hopes of bettering themselves. Everyone educated within a few years – quite a difference from here in Iceland, where some farmers could barely write, let alone add up except to some extent in their heads. And then the women, wouldn't their freedom be a shock to the system? In America the men waited on the women hand and foot. They did only the finest jobs and of course lorded it over the men, did not have to touch a thing outside the house, did not need to milk sheep or cows. The men milked the cows, and there were not any sheep.

Neither were the prospects so unappealing for the young girls in service over there in America; more pay in a month than for the whole year in Iceland, and no need to be forever with their hands in cold water, but going around dressed better than the finest ministers' and merchants' wives, no need to feel embarrassed about what they were wearing on their feet, always in Danish shoes, nothing less would do. And there were theatres and dance halls – for there was lots of dancing in America – and no one making comments if some young man went out walking with a girl in the evenings. Was thought perfectly natural if the girls showed them the kindness of spending a little time together, and it was always the boys who paid. And on top of this, just think about those girls who were taking their first steps forward in life towards the estate of matrimony, how they would sail ahead in this women's paradise, in fancy dresses of every hue, multi-coloured like the feathers of the bird of paradise, dressed to the nines! They would come into the dance hall and swirl around the dance floor, calculated to sweep the young men gathered there off their feet. Not Icelandic ones of course – oh no, they would be such bumpkins, showing themselves up with their Icelandic – but some sort of English gentlemen, loaded in money. There would be plenty of them there. No problem.

How glorious they were, these daydreams that the girls in Iceland allowed themselves to dream, that kindled their yearning for foreign lands! For it was good for everyone to come to America, but for none so much as young girls with the blush of youth upon their cheeks.

Precious dream! Sweet is your rapture.

Precious dream! as a light in the wind.

Precious dream!

Such were the stories that were going round about America for a time, and many simple people believed them. Most people in Iceland had read Pastor Jónas's tale of Björn from Gerðum. I am convinced that when writing it Jónas was imagining some family supposed to be like real living people, and there was more than one Björn from Gerðum in Iceland at the time. What inspired young men most of all was this great hope of money to be earned for however little work they did, and then the desire for adventure that always exerts a powerful pull on the minds of young men.

No one need be surprised if it all ended in chaos. It hardly takes every fifth man in the household, that is to say in the country, to be moving away, if not this year then they might expect to be off the next if there was good news from relatives or neighbours, and everyone wanting to get letters and advice about whether it would be better to go or to stay. Many of those who went to America were restless the first years. They yearned for their family and friends and so many of the letters home were set rather to encourage than deter. And so many of those that stayed behind in pinched circumstances, they longed for any kind of change in their affairs in the hope that something would sort itself out.

One of the worst things about the emigrations was how they blocked the way to any progress for those who stayed behind. There was, as it were, little point embarking on anything of substance when men were already out in the yard with their bag strapped across their shoulders. Though it was those that longed to go but did not make it that cost the country dearest; they could talk about nothing but the hardships and oppression in Iceland and the bliss that was America. They were embodiments of defeatism, not just useless to themselves but demoralizing all they came into contact with, making them equally discontented and shiftless.

Such was how Erlendur Guðmundsson saw the emigrations. It is clear from his account that there was much that attracted people to the idea of North America as a future permanent home. The decision could depend on a variety of factors. Erlendur himself was averse to the emigrations and for the rest of his life he bitterly regretted leaving the land of his birth. In his autobiography he defended himself by saying that his wife had refused to waste her life in rural Iceland and it was this that made them decide to leave for Canada. The author's whole account bears the marks of the situation he found himself in and reflects how complex the process was as people weighed up the pros and cons of setting out for the New World.

5
Tactics for Emotional Survival: Education, Work and Entertainment

In the name of God

Education in eighteenth- and nineteenth-century Iceland came in two different but complementary forms. The formal education of children was generally provided by their parents and supervised by the Church; this included reading and, later, the rudiments of writing, and was religious in nature, leading up to confirmation at the age of fourteen. However, there was simultaneously an informal educational system, derived from and heavily influenced by everyday life. This informal education was unstructured and its benefits varied from person to person and according to circumstance. Although among devout families it too might have a strong religious content, it was primarily secular in nature. In essence, what we have are two different types of educational practice: one that was compulsory and rigid, and another that was fluid and fuelled by a desire for knowledge and entertainment and rooted in popular culture.

In a book called *Íslendingar* (Icelanders) published in 1933 the influential educationalist Guðmundur Finnbogason attempted to explain the circumstances that had led to this special system of popular education: 'The winter made outdoor work and communications difficult and forced people to spend time indoors and afforded them leisure. But how this enforced leisure was used depended on the character of the people and their level of culture from period to period.' In other words, according to Guðmundur, the long Icelandic winters forced people to find ways of filling their time and entertaining themselves. A traditional part of Icelandic social life was the *kvöldvaka* (lit. 'evening wake'), held on farms during the long winter evenings. And one important function of these gatherings in the nineteenth century was to provide a forum for the education of children.

Pétur Pétursson, historian and professor of theology at the University of Iceland, provides a good description of what went on at these winter-evening gatherings:

The winter-evening gathering was one of the central institutions of traditional rural society. This informal entertainment had great importance for the unity of the household and for the possibilities open to young people to develop as individuals and broaden their horizons. The household gathered together in the living room – Baðstofa – and did wool-working while one of the company read aloud to them – sagas, rímur, or whatever else was to hand. Hymns were sung, the children recited their lessons, and adults competed at composing verses. The boys in the foreground are playing with animal bones, which were widely used as toys in former times.

On those occasions the entire household gathered on winter evenings in the largest room (sometimes the only living room) of the farmhouse for various indoor activities, including the telling of stories, folk sagas and fairy tales. Ballads, the so-called *rímur*, were also recited on these occasions. Popularized versions of traditional narratives about old Nordic heroes and the sagas were often a part of the entertainment. Over the years they had been memorized and converted into popular ballads.[1]

The gatherings usually ended with a *húslestur*, 'a house-reading', that is, reading aloud from printed sermons by well-known preachers, followed by the singing of hymns. The whole activity was a welcome distraction for most people in rural Iceland, especially the children. Virtually every autobiographer and diarist confirms that it was in the environment of these winter-evening gatherings that they got their first real taste of culture and education.

In his autobiography Magnús Helgason (b. 1857), from the farm of Birtingarholt in the southern lowlands, describes his earliest steps in education. Initially, it was his father who taught him his alphabet. After that, his mother took over. 'She would sit at her spinning wheel and spin, with us on the bed or on the chest next to her with the book. While we were young and still learning to read she chose books she already knew well so her work would not be interrupted by her having to keep looking at the book.' Magnús was able to read confidently by the age of five. He was one of fourteen children and, once the older ones were literate, they took over the teaching from their parents – a delegation of important tasks to older children typical of life on Icelandic farms. Magnús also notes that no fixed time was appointed for these lessons, 'rather they took place in any free moments between jobs'.[2] Slowly but steadily children were exposed to writing and eventually to arithmetic, and this lay the foundation for their further education.

The most important part of children's early formal education consisted of memorizing prescribed religious texts. Soon after their eighth birthdays they started reading from the Bible and learning passages for recitation from the *Kverið*, an annotated version of Luther's *Minor Catechism* – by force if necessary. Most found the catechism difficult and dull. The pastor quizzed the children on their texts every year up to the time of confirmation. Among the many to express their distaste for the *Kverið* was Friðrik Bjarnason (b. 1880) in his autobiography: 'I was lazy when it came to learning the *Kverið* and I often got severely told off; I found some of the religious ideas hard to understand and disagreeable.' Critical of the value of this form of teaching, he added: 'I don't remember that learning the *Kverið* did anything much to make me behave better, and who knows how much it may actually have turned young people off reading books of other kinds?'

Not everyone agreed. Sigurður Árnason (b. 1877) recalled in his autobiography, *Með straumnum* (With the Steam), that 'I was probably one of the few who did not dislike the *Kverið*. I found it quite interesting and was quick to learn it off by heart. Long before confirmation I could recite the whole first section, word-perfect and in the right order.'

According to a law from 1790, every child was supposed to be able to read as a qualification for confirmation. No significant changes were introduced until 1879, when two new acts came into force requiring that children be able to read, write and do basic arithmetic before being confirmed. The act of 1790 also stipulated the ages at which children were to start the different parts of their education: the local pastor was to test children from the age of seven or eight, so it is safe to assume that in most households children started to learn to read at five or six.

The requirement for learning and memorizing the *Kverið* went back to the Pietist movement of the eighteenth century, according to whose tenets parents were charged with instilling piety and morality in their children and combating un-Christian thoughts and deeds in their daily lives. The means by which this was to be achieved was through the systematic inculcation of Christian doctrine, using harsh disciplinary measures if all else failed. Part of this indoctrination of Christian values required children not only to be able to recite their catechism but to understand it, and thus to be able to read.[3]

Children usually started their memorization of the *Kverið* relatively slowly, often doing only a few sections a year up to the age of ten, and building up steadily after that. Even though most of the autobiographers complain about having to learn their texts, it never occurred to them to simply refuse. In this, there were strong social pressures at play: to be officially received into the world of adults, and so have a chance of getting on in life, a child had to be confirmed, and parents were therefore very anxious to see that their children mastered their catechism. As part of their training, most children were expected to read or recite the *Kverið* at the winter-evening gatherings. If this failed, other measures were imposed. Jón Ólafsson (b. 1850) started learning his *Kverið* at the age of eight, but with little enthusiasm: 'My father then started hearing over what I had learned every morning before I got dressed, and if I had not learned what I was supposed to I was kept in bed until I had and not allowed to go out and play until it was done.'[4]

There were other factors that made it relatively easy for parents to motivate their children, most notably dread of the pastoral visits. Every farm was visited by a minister of the Church once or twice a year, principally to ensure domestic rectitude and to check on the children's educational progress. As Pétur Pétursson notes, the moral standard 'of each household was a part of pastoral care and the pastor was to use his influence and authority to improve the discipline and the well-being of the people'.[5] Just about every autobiography that describes the education of young people mentions these pastoral visits. The pastor usually enjoyed great respect and influence within the community and having to confront this representative of God in the flesh could be a daunting prospect. Björgvin Guðmundsson (b. 1891) describes his feelings before such a visit in his autobiography, *Minningar* (Memoirs): 'I remember especially the first time the Reverend Sigurður came to our home. Both Palli and I were agitated and on edge the day before, wondering how we would cope.' Parents were well aware that if their children failed to come up to the pastor's expectations this would reflect badly on their own reputation in the community. Similarly, children feared the displeasure of the pastor, since this jeopardized their desire to be treated as responsible adult members of the Christian community, a fear that drove them to put in the time and effort needed to learn and memorize their texts.[6]

The experience of Theodór Friðriksson (b. 1876), as described in his autobiography, *Ofan jarðar og neðan* (Underground and Above), provides a vivid example of the anxieties suffered by children in the face of the pastoral inspections, especially those that found reading and writing hard. His account tells in sad detail the tensions that went with mastering the *Kverið* and balancing the expectations placed on him by his parents and the Church.

Theodór was born in the west of Iceland and spent his childhood on Flatey, one of the islands in Breiðafjörður. His parents were poor and hardworking. His father was often away fishing and Theodór started to help out around the farm from an early age. He started to learn to read when he was nine – later than most children at the time – and it came to him very slowly: 'Lovísa from Neðribær set great store by teaching Sigurvin to read and write; he could not be seen to be inferior to his cousin Kristján at Nýibær. I, on the other hand, found it more fun to be with the sheep or go fishing than to read, so I could only read haltingly, while Sigurvin could read fluently. I was then told that I would turn out a heathen, like the man called Þorsteinn Grímsson who lived on Flatey at the time. Þorsteinn had had such problems learning to read and write that he had never reached confirmation.' Parents and society used the familiar tactic of invidious comparison with other children to pressure children into learning their catechism. In this case, it was formalized: at the confirmation ceremony the children were lined up before the whole parish in order of reading ability; the one who knew the text best was questioned first, and so on down the line. This was something the children were well aware of and there was competition to be first in line. Because of the public nature of the ceremony, held in full view of friends and neighbours, parents did all they could to encourage their children to perform well.

Theodór describes this Þorsteinn, who was apparently an extremely odd individual whose appearance and behaviour set him apart from everyone else: 'When I looked at Þorsteinn I realized it was a serious matter if I was going to end up a heathen like him. So I simply had to start getting down to it and learn to read like my friends in Flatey. But still it took a lot of self-discipline to do so.'

Soon after this a new pastor arrived in the parish and the word spread that he was a stickler on the matter of children's education. As the time of the pastor's visit approached, Theodór grew increasingly terrified:

> Still, I was very curious to actually see such a powerful man, to see how he would be dressed and how he carried himself. There was no doubt in my mind that the pastor would come down hard on me if I did not perform well. When I realized what was coming and that this test was unavoidable, I set down to learn the *Kverið* thoroughly. I now recited the passages from it like a man possessed. I rattled off chapter after chapter, my parents entreating me earnestly not to shirk my duty, so as not to let them down in front of the minister. I became more eager to do as well as my friends, and I realized that they were afraid of the minister too.

As luck would have it, the visit went well and the minister complimented Theodór on his performance. But it is clear that many children found the ordeal overwhelming, especially those who for some reason were slow learners. If they stumbled, they were immediately made to feel the weight of social disapproval. There was thus every incentive for children to put their full effort into learning their texts.

For some children, attending to their studies was simply a pragmatic choice, as providing a welcome break from other duties. Gunnar Ólafsson (b. 1864), one of eleven brothers and sisters, illustrates the point in his autobiography, *Endurminningar* (Memoirs). He mentions that at the start of each winter-evening gathering his parents gave the children the choice between working or studying. 'This was most often taken up. Or, more precisely, this was always taken up with pleasure and put life into the group since, even though studying could sometimes be boring, it was better than carding wool, winding yarn off the spindle, or knitting, which the boys found anything but entertaining.

No one was allowed to be inactive, and all this useful work was equally proper for boys and girls, according to my parents.'

For the most part, though, it is probably fair to say that children found learning to read and write a chore rather than a pleasure, and this only served to exacerbate the lack of emotional support that ran through their entire lives. There were perhaps compensations, since in some ways the pressure to learn might help to bring people together; it could provide opportunities for the sharing of duties and this at times produced a degree of emotional support. The effectiveness, though, was limited. Children, of course, associated mostly with other children, the elderly and servants, and the bonds formed were always fragile; children and the elderly were those most vulnerable to disease and death, and servants were liable to move away at any time, leaving those left behind in an emotional void. Children were expected to cope with the expectation that they contribute significantly to the work of the farm from an early age, as well as the social pressure that went along with learning their religious texts. This pressure was skilfully manipulated both by parents and the Church, and intensified year by year as confirmation grew closer.

Labour and literacy

For all its shortcomings, the formal education received by (almost) all children in Iceland had a profound influence on society and culture. We now need to consider its workings in a broader context. Loftur Guttormsson, who has written extensively on the history of education in Iceland, has argued that the increase in literacy in the eighteenth century was largely the product of ecclesiastical policy, implemented with the support of the state. There is no dispute that literacy rates did rise during the eighteenth and early nineteenth centuries. The question is where the credit for this lies – did the impetus come primarily from above, from the Church and state? Or were there other factors involved?

According to Loftur, the successes rested on the widescale dissemination of religious publications, backed up by persistent social pressure from parents and the local pastor, as described previously. He also points to the role of the reformers inspired by the principles of the Enlightenment at the end of the eighteenth century and the beginning of the nineteenth, as a result of whose efforts large quantities of secular literature became available, helping to underpin the foundations of universal literacy. Loftur maintains that these forces 'from above' had a deliberate agenda: according to him, 'they saw a clear benefit in the spread of literacy so that as many people as possible would be susceptible to the official rhetoric.'[7]

But, again, we need to ask, do these forces really serve to explain why children in nineteenth-century Iceland learned to read and write from a relatively early age? Historians of literacy throughout the world have had to face up to similar questions. Scholars in Scandinavia, for example, have frequently cited the concerted campaign instituted by the Church and state at the beginning of the eighteenth century as instrumental in explaining why the overwhelming majority of the public achieved literacy with little aid from formal schooling. The claim has been made that this advanced culture was the product of forces inherent in the formal structure of society, namely priests, parents and children, together with the social impact created by the interplay of these forces. The system looks both effective and functional: in both Iceland and most other Scandinavian countries at the time, children could be taken from their families and moved to another farm, at their parents' expense, if their parents neglected their educational obligations.

This argument can be accepted up to a point: under the formal system, parishes had a statutory duty to attend to the intellectual and spiritual development of their residents; the pastor had a supervisory role, parents and guardians had an instituted responsibility to educate their children, and the children could not become full members of secular or spiritual society without acquiring the required level of education. But this alone cannot explain the high level of literacy in Iceland. Nor can the environmental argument, that Iceland and the other Scandinavian countries were special because of the long dark winters and the opportunities they imposed for domestic activity. Throughout history rulers have issued laws and ordinances that have passed largely unheeded. Even though social pressures in Iceland and Scandinavia supported these policies, there was no guarantee that people would see them into practice unless they felt they had a good reason for doing so and circumstances made this possible. It still remains to be explained what exactly it was in Icelandic society at the time that made this particular campaign by Church and state so successful.

As I see it, the key to the dramatic rise in literacy in eighteenth- and nineteenth-century Iceland lies in the working practices on Icelandic farms, and in particular the fact that work did not preclude and even encouraged education. During the long winter evenings the household tasks divided into two types. First, the livestock needed to be fed and milked. This usually required between two and four hours a day. The rest of the time was spent working wool. Everyone was involved, men, women and children. Working wool hour upon hour can be a tedious business and it was essential that people remained as productive as possible. To entertain those involved, to keep them awake even, one of the family members usually read aloud. The autobiographies and diaries contain constant references to this interaction between work and education and many of the writers go into considerable detail about how it operated.

Gunnar Ólafsson, mentioned earlier, gives us a glimpse into this world from his childhood years. 'The teaching took place in the living room during the winter evenings, after the light had been lit and everyone had settled down. The grown-ups sat and worked along with the older children, if they were not learning. No one was allowed to sit idle and empty-handed if they had any capacity for work. In between, when children were not learning, they were given jobs to do, carding the wool, winding the yarn off the spindles, knitting or the like.' The grown-ups taught the children as they worked. They could hear the children read, correct them and give them directions when necessary, while still constantly occupied on their tasks. Moreover, these lessons became a form of entertainment for the adults too and therefore helped to ease the tedium and increase productivity. And productivity was all-important! Had it not been possible to combine it with the work, all attempts at improving children's education would have fallen by the wayside and children would not have had the opportunity to learn to read.

But this does not really explain the eagerness with which most children embraced the task of learning to read and write, an eagerness attested repeatedly in Icelandic autobiographies and diaries. They had, as I see it, another motive.

Literature, learning and emotional survival

The formal educational system, as we have seen, was founded on cooperation between the state, the Church and, most importantly, the individual household. This combination proved highly effective in delivering an education that centred largely on the intensive indoctrination of Lutheran orthodoxy. The whole process was supposed to inculcate discipline and obedience in society at large, producing virtuous and moral citizens. For all its apparent success, this arrangement would not have been as effective as it in fact proved if working practices in nineteenth-century Iceland had not allowed all households to combine work and education and so provide the general population with a solid foundation of functional literacy. But the nature of these religious texts and the means used to put them across only served to increase the social pressures on children who were in many cases already deprived of emotional support. So, even though the conditions under which they were presented help to some extent to explain *how* the vast majority of people achieved functional literacy, they do not explain *why*. We still have to face the question of why children showed such an intense interest in education in general and secular education in particular. It is worth asking how this interest came about, given the state of Icelandic society at the time.

We have seen the importance of the winter-evening gatherings in the formal education of children, in providing a forum where children could learn and practise their reading, writing, arithmetic and catechism. But there was another side to these gatherings that contributed to general education in a less formal way. As mentioned, it was common practice for one member of the household to read aloud to the others as they worked. In general, people were not particularly selective in what they read; they read whatever was to hand. Most families in the latter part of the nineteenth century owned a few books of secular literature or had access to some books and reading material, including the sagas, newspapers and magazines, poems and novels in translation. Lack of money of course meant that access to books was limited, but this was largely rectified in the last quarter of the nineteenth century by the establishment throughout the country of reading societies, open to the public and dedicated to the purchase of books to be loaned out among members.

An important element in the informal education children received at the winter-evening gatherings was the opportunity it provided for an emotional outlet in their lives – an introduction to new ideas and modes of experience that offered hope and relief in a forbidding world. It is useful to consider what literature it was that children encountered during these sessions and the best place to start is the Bible. The Bible was one of the most popular and frequently read texts at the gatherings and, to many children, was often appreciated simply for its tales of thrilling adventure. Many of the autobiographers mention that its moral and religious content was largely lost on them. Sigfús Blöndal (b. 1874) who later became one of the leading intellectual figures in Iceland, a translator of ancient Greek and compiler of the first large-scale dictionary of Icelandic, learned to read from the New Testament but discovered the Old Testament when recovering from measles: 'As soon as I got the Old Testament, it did not take me long to discover what a treasure it was. The fighting and bloodshed and all the stories from the historical books were like candy to a boy raised on the Icelandic sagas . . . The religious significance of the Bible – or religion in general – did not become clear to me until much later.'[8]

This informal, essentially secular, education probably played a far larger part in children's mental development than all their religious instruction. It also had a profound effect on how they viewed the world. After mastering the hymns and religious poems that all children were supposed to learn between the ages of four and five, they went on to learning secular poems. The mental and literary training children got from learning the religious verse proved invaluable when they came to be introduced to secular poetry, even if in many instances they did not actually understand what it meant. Many autobiographers mention this part of their education specifically. Elías Halldórsson (b. 1877) describes in his autobiography, *Heiðinginn* (The Heathen), how it would begin: 'During my upbringing it was the first step in a child's verbal training, once they had started to talk, to teach them religious poems and hymns. They were expected to recite them back in the evening when they went to bed, and on numerous other occasions, for instance if they needed to pluck up courage when they had to be away from home shepherding or running errands.'

Most children could recite an astonishing number of verses. A central part of the winter-evening entertainment was the art of creating and reciting *rímur*. *Rímur* are narrative poems composed in complex rhyming quatrains, 'in which the best examples can be real gems of poetry', in the words of Iceland's most celebrated literary critic, Sigurður Nordal.[9] There was often a strong competitive element in the recitation and performance of these verses. They were half read and half sung, a challenging task requiring people (mostly men) with strong voices. Good performers were in demand and considered welcome guests or additions to the household wherever they went. Clearly, the continuous learning and practice of this poetry, with its fixed and complex rules in which one syllable out of place destroys the entire metrical structure, served to inhibit morphological change in the language and helped to keep alive its rich traditional poetic vocabulary. As well as *rímur*, other forms of poetry were recited, discussed and cultivated – from verses going back to the Saga Age to contemporary nineteenth-century poets influenced by the romantic and realist movements of the time. Much of the poetry had nationalist overtones, either through being a living reminder of the glory of Iceland in ancient times or composed against the background of the struggle for political independence.

Poetry was held in high esteem – and remains so to this day; more poetry is published and read in Iceland today than in most other Western countries. Its importance and popularity is illustrated by the game, played with great enthusiasm by children and grown-ups alike, of *að kveðast á* ('capping verses'): one person recited a verse, at the end of which the next player had to recite another beginning with the last letter of the one before, and so on. The game could go on for hours. To compete successfully, participants needed to have as large a fund of verses as possible stored away in their memories. Eventually, most children managed to learn staggering numbers of poems. The fun involved helped to engender a love of poetry that shines out again and again from the autobiographies and diaries. Authors often mention the excitement and anticipation felt on a farm when a new book of poems appeared, perhaps borrowed from neighbours. Reading aloud was a fixed feature of almost all households on winter evenings. After that, the children would take the book and memorize it from cover to cover. In many instances someone would copy the poems out, providing the children with writing practice and entertainment for future evenings.[10]

Guðmundur Finnbogason, quoted earlier, attempts to explain this centrality of poetry to Icelandic culture. Although Guðmundur's explanation takes a rather romantic and heroic view of the Icelandic mentality, it contains the popular perceptions of the inherent strength of the Icelandic culture which strongly influenced children from an early age:

> A nation's deepest character and thoughts are often revealed in its popular assumptions. Icelanders have always felt that the art of poetry was more than just entertainment: it was more of a necessity, a place of mental health and healing and a source of energy, a defence against the danger of losing one's mind in the face of adversity and isolation. It was the only sport that was always there, ready wherever and whenever, available because it burned in the deepest recesses of the mind and spirit and provided lasting warmth for the soul.[11]

The informal educational system and the literature on which it was based were of immense importance to the emotional development and outlook of children in their peasant society. But there was another twist to children's experience, a darker one. As pointed out earlier, children often had great trouble coping with reality. They were burdened with heavy workloads and onerous duties, often spending large parts of their working days alone, far from their farms and isolated from the rest of their families. Moreover, they lived in a world where they had to come to terms with the frequent and sudden loss of friends and relatives. To be able to face up to the hardships of their lives they turned to literature, and above all the Icelandic sagas, for relief and moral support. However irrelevant ancient stories and poems might seem to a struggling peasant society, viewed from the perspective of a child growing up in rural Iceland in the nineteenth century this love of the written word was hardly coincidental: it provided an escape from the harsh realities of life and a flight into a world of the imagination. It is this interaction between work, death and education that best explains the almost universal, and unprecedented, literacy of nineteenth-century Icelandic peasant society. Without this interaction and the social and working conditions under which people lived their lives, all laws and initiatives from above would have been in vain. Education almost automatically became inextricably linked with working life, an integral part of the shared family effort to survive. The whole process worked like a tapestry of a peasant survival mentality.

It has sometimes been maintained that childhood as a life stage is a relatively modern invention. In Icelandic rural society the lives of children and adults merged into one; infant mortality was high and children were hardly given consideration before it was felt they were likely to survive their first years. As soon as they were able they were put to work and steadily picked up a greater and greater knowledge of the tasks on which farm life depended. However, this picture requires qualification. Children's lives on Icelandic farms were marked off from those of their parents in significant ways, and during their growing up they were given systematic instruction to prepare them for the problems they might later face in everyday life.

6

Death and Daily Life

Infant mortality

Our knowledge of infant mortality in eighteenth-century Iceland is hampered by lack of evidence and it is not until towards the middle of the nineteenth century that we start to get reliable information. The first discussion of the high incidence of child death in Iceland to offer any figures occurs in an essay by Bishop Hannes Finnsson (b. 1739) entitled 'Um barna dauða á Íslandi' (On Child Death in Iceland), published in *Rit þess Íslenzka Lærdóms-Lista Félags* (Writings of the Icelandic Society for Learning and the Arts) in 1784. Hannes calculates, for instance, that around 30 per cent of infants die in Iceland each year, while this figure falls to only two per cent among those who have reached the age of fifteen. He goes on to conclude: 'Man's nature changes most at around the age of 15. The natural life force is then at its peak, and it is then that the master of the household may first take the view that he has more than just a man in potential. At this point the choicest part remains, when the imperfect shoots have dropped off which fail to attain the time of fruition.' Hannes's ideas on natural selection are remarkably in line with new ideas on human development that were current in Europe at this time, providing an indication that Iceland's isolation was not as great as is often supposed.

Though information for the eighteenth century is limited, various sources allow us indirect insights into conditions. Most important of these is the detailed survey of Iceland produced by two Icelanders, the naturalist Eggert Ólafsson and the doctor Bjarni Pálsson, who travelled through all parts of the country in the years 1752–7 at the behest of the king and the Royal Danish Scientific Society and produced a wide-ranging account of its geology, vegetation, land resources and people. The work was published in Denmark in 1772 and translated in one form or another into German, French and English over the course of the next decade. As an example of how Eggert and Bjarni approached their material we can quote from the passage where they describe infant conditions in Iceland, and particularly in the Westfjord peninsula, in the middle years of the eighteenth century:

> It is not, however, that there is any want of human fertility, for it is not unusual for a couple to have 10–15 children, but the misfortune is that of this group rarely more than a third survive. We still lack completely reliable records of these children, how they are nursed, what kind of nourishment they receive and how much, and finally what diseases it is that bring about their deaths.

The authors spend several paragraphs listing various points that, from their conversations with people, they identify as contributing factors to the high level of infant mortality. They mention, for example, that breast-feeding is rare and that most children are reared on cow's milk. They note: 'There are cases of mothers who have lost all of their children that were given this type of milk, but if they have had one child on the breast because cow's milk was in short supply, then there has been no sign of sickness in that child and it has reached full age.' They also note that many people set great store by giving children undiluted cream straight from birth and in some places 'children are immediately weaned onto eating meat and fish by having their parents chewing it for them, as is known to be done in other countries'. According to Eggert and Bjarni, infants are made to 'consume this solid food within 3–4 months of birth, that is to say, long before they start to cut teeth, but to make it easier to get them to take it the chewed food is softened with milk, cream or butter'. They conclude: 'Everywhere in their ignorance people take great pains to get children to eat as much food as possible of every kind. People see it as a mark of good health that they eat well and preferably to excess. People assume that they will then grow quicker and become stronger.'[1]

The authors go on to describe the consequences of these practices: that they very often resulted in the death of the children. Eighteenth-century Icelanders were in fact to a large extent powerless in the face of infant mortality. The incidence remained high throughout the country, with slight regional variation, and people's ideas on infant nutrition seem to have been broadly similar in all parts of the country.

Children born into nineteenth-century Iceland had a shockingly low expectation of reaching their first birthday. During the early part of the century the mortality rate for infants in their first year stood at around 35 per cent. This figure fell markedly in the latter part of the century, to 20 per cent in the years 1881–90, 12 per cent in 1891–1900, and 11 per cent in the first decade of the twentieth century.[2] Davíð

Scheving Thorsteinsson, district medical officer for the county of Snæfells- og Hnappadalssýsla, described some of the general reasons for the high incidence of infant mortality in his annual report to the surgeon general for 1898: 'Space in houses is so limited that there can only be a tiny fraction of the minimum reckoned necessary for each individual. On top of this there is no ventilation. When we add to this the *downright squalor* on all sides which *poisons* what little air there is, then it hardly comes as a surprise to hear of 23 infants out of 112 dying in their first year, even without there having been any epidemic.'[3] Earlier in the report infant mortality had been given as 20.4 per cent for the district in that year, and Davíð also provided figures for exactly when in their first year these children had died.

One reason often cited for the drop in infant mortality during the nineteenth century is that mothers took to breastfeeding their children in ever increasing measure as the century progressed. There is almost certainly some truth in this; but it should be said that, when one examines the unpublished reports of the district medical officers, one finds frequent and repeated complaints about how difficult it is to get women in rural areas to breastfeed their children, and these complaints continue well on into the second decade of the twentieth century.

In his report for 1907, Guðmundur Scheving Bjarnason, the district medical officer for Strandasýsla in the north-west, writes as follows:

> *The treatment of infants* in this area, as in most other parts of the country, *leaves a huge amount to be desired*. Certainly, more care is generally shown about keeping babies clean here than hitherto, and they are also more suitably clothed nowadays, but there is still a long way to go. The problem really arises when we come to the nutrition of children. *With only a very few exceptions, all babies around here are brought up on the bottle*. The midwives have told me that it has become more or less impossible to get mothers to have their children on the breast. The mothers feel themselves unduly tied to the child and so unable to attend to the most essential jobs around the farm. The acute shortage of working women has a large part in this and means that farmers' wives have hardly a moment to spare from their most pressing domestic duties, and this is a great shame. Since, as things stand, children are generally nourished not on breast milk but on cows' milk mixed with water, and not always properly prepared, it is hardly surprising that *many of them are constantly afflicted by digestive complaints*, which are indeed *the commonest cause of death among children here*, followed by – at a considerable remove – *colds* and other chest diseases.[4]

To take another example from a different part of the country, Jón Blöndal, district medical officer for the Borgarfjörður region in the west, notes the following in his annual report for 1900: 'The treatment of infants seems to be improving somewhat here, albeit slowly. But breastfeeding is still far less universal than it ought to be and so digestive disorders remain very common. As things now stand, most mothers seem to want to raise their children on the breast but often do not know how to go about weaning them to it, and midwives are not insistent enough that children need to be taught how to suck. Only very few of them carry breast pumps, which ought to be an essential part of their equipment.'[5]

It was generally felt that at the root of the problem lay a lack of understanding among midwives and birth-helpers of the importance of breastfeeding and the limited time available to mothers to tend to their children. Another district medical officer, Sigurður Sigurðsson, from the Dalasýsla region, also in the west, goes into even greater detail on the rearing of infants in his report to the surgeon-general for 1907:

> Only very few infants are taken entirely on the breast. In 1905 I obtained a document on this matter from a midwife, in which it was stated that of 72 children born in the period November 1904 to November 1905, 9 were entirely breastfed, 31 on breast and bottle, 28 on the bottle alone, with 4 cases unknown. One may safely say that the ratio is the same or very similar still. Children who are on the bottle are given cow's milk and water; the vast majority boil both beforehand, but there are times when this safety measure is not followed, and so it is a wonder that fatalities are not more frequent. Many people fail to take as much care of the bottle and teat as they should; some reckon it a waste of time, others just turn a deaf ear to admonitions. In many places I have seen bottle teats carved out of wood with a hole drilled through; these are seen as convenient in that they last a long time. But they are rarely boiled in water, maybe washed from time to time . . . Many lay great store by getting children to eat as much as possible of various grown-up foods, often before the children are 1/2 year old. Digestive diseases in young children are common here and often contribute to their deaths if there is some other disease to complicate matters.[6]

Judging from descriptions like these, it is easy to see why the chances of survival among young infants were as low as the figures bear witness. What makes the account above particularly interesting is that it dates from the first decade of the twentieth century. The situation was in all probability much better in the urban areas, where cow's milk was not so easy for poor people to get hold of, compelling mothers to breastfeed their children. This comes out in the official reports of many district medical officers. The subject of infant mortality was taken up by surgeon-general Guðmundur Hannesson in his published public health report for the years 1911–20: according to this, breastfeeding was now more or less the rule among nursing mothers in Reykjavík, while still an exception in most other parts of the country.[7]

Grief contained

Death was very much a part of people's daily lives, a constant presence from which no one was immune. The sources present us with countless examples of how people's lives were shattered by the loss of loved ones and family members, as if their whole basis for existence had been pulled away from under them. This section will look at how people reacted to such events and how they attempted to deal with them.

The scourge of diphtheria is described in the passage from the progressive journal *Eimreiðin* quoted in chapter Three. This objective record can be 'personalized' by an account given by Elín Samúelsdóttir, the widow of Halldór Jónsson of Miðdalsgróf in Strandasýsla, in a letter to her brother-in-law Níels Jónsson of Gjögur. (This is the same Halldór and Níels as are mentioned in the Introduction, and we will meet them again later in this book.) The letter, written two years after Halldór's death, makes harrowing reading, describing the anguish of those living in a house struck down by disease and having to face up to the loss of their children.

Elín's letter is all the more striking for having been written in the middle of the events it describes, while most of her children were still desperately ill with diphtheria and one had already died. We can feel Elín's emotions with a special immediacy. She starts as follows:

> I am sending you a few lines. I can only write briefly, I feel so wretched, there is so much pain in me. But again it has pleased God to inflict a deep wound on me. I have lost my darling, fair-haired, my little angel, my youngest flower. Oh! my dear friend, there is no way I can describe the sense of loss. Nor any need, either. You can perhaps imagine for yourself how heavily this loss has fallen upon me.[8]

Elín, evidently, is in a state of great turmoil. In all probability she was writing directly after the burial of her child. She says at the beginning that she is only going to write a short letter, but in the event it turned out to be long and detailed. At the end she says, 'The letter has become longer than I thought when I started. Forgive me if it has become too long.'

After the introduction comes an account of the children's sicknesses that gives us a vivid insight into how life was for people when disease struck a community, leaving entire households crippled and unable to function:

> I had become a little tired, before the sorrow struck my heart, almost to death. The children had had whooping cough all summer. And then came this deadly enemy, diphtheria, before they could recover. It started with my sweetest little child, the one least able to complain or describe how he was ailing. It also started in him in a way that was very hard to recognize. The evening he fell ill he was so terribly cold and restive. Then he woke up in the night with vomiting. Slept badly that night. It was on Thursday evening, a little after 10, that this coldness came over him. But he seemed full of life during the day and had such an enormous appetite I thought it was just some everyday bug. He had fits of vomiting, off and on through Friday and Saturday, and was very hot. He more or less slept the whole time except when he was being sick and tossing about. Finally some green water came up out of him. By now his stomach was so empty that on Sunday morning I sent for Magnús the doctor; thought it better to get him to examine him, even if there was nothing to worry about. It torments me, more than I can say, that I did not send for the doctor immediately. Oh, but how little did I know! Magnús gave him and Þurý an injection. She was ill by then, took sick on Saturday. With her it started in the head and throat. The infestation in the throat spread out of all bounds on Sunday. But the diphtheria did not become so set in, it wasn't that that killed him. He was terribly ill, my dearest darling boy. He got worse on Monday. So I sent up for the doctor again but Magnús wouldn't come. He didn't seem to be suffering so much, but he was very ill, both his throat swollen and his whole body convulsed. He lay there the whole time half unconscious, didn't pay attention to anything that was going on around him, got upset when people talked to him, but always stayed just as sweet and cheerful towards his mother. He put his little limp arm around her neck with childish tenderness. It was something he always used to do, the little angel of mine; he was so given to tenderness, and obedience, toward his mother . . .

Elín goes on to talk about her lost son and the love and solicitude he had shown to his 'little bit careworn mother'. After this comes more about the other children's sicknesses: 'On the Tuesday before Sami died Nonni came down sick. Júla and I took him up the valley to Magnús the doctor. I had to go too because I was suffering from such a bad toothache, for so long, I had three teeth pulled out, but that was just a moment's respite. My darling child died on Thursday evening at 10 o'clock. He had lain ill for a week. Died at the same hour as this misery begins. It was 22 October. Was four years old on the 13th of the same month. And how happy and full of life he had been on his birthday!' Later in the letter she describes his final moments: 'My dear little child spoke to me the very moment he died. I asked him whether he wanted a drink of water and he said, 'Yes, mummy', but he couldn't get it down, sat up in bed, spread out his loving arms to me, and died that moment in my arms. Up to the very last he showed me only love. Now may God receive his soul, white and untouched by stain from this world. Your friend and mine Halldór has now received his flower, his angel, to his breast. They are happier than us.' Elín is presumably saying that father and son have been reunited in death. She continues with her account of the illnesses:

Nonni was in bed a week or more, was fairly ill. Þurý picked up quickly. Alli fell sick on the Monday after my little child died. We took him to the doctor, he wasn't very ill yet, just a headache and a rather high temperature, but by the time we got up there a white patch had appeared, not much bigger than a spot. Alli was very ill. On the Tuesday he had a fever and was delirious in between, but fairly cheerful. On the Monday he had had an appetite and it looked as if he would recover fast. But on the Thursday he was worse. On the Friday he was terribly ill, extremely hot and delirious at times, and his throat carried on swelling up inside and out. So I sent for Magnús, or asked for him. He didn't want to come, reckoned there was no point, though in my mind I thought I was going to lose him too for certain. The Wednesday before that Þurý had a relapse. Her whole body swelled up. She too had a bit of a temperature that went with this inflammation that made her all disfigured. She was in bed for two days, then got up, Friday, Saturday and Sunday morning, and by this time Alli was a little better. But then Þurý was back in bed, terribly ill, intensely high temperature, all covered in red blotches and couldn't open her eyes for the pain. She was rambling in her speech and I sent to Magnús to speak to him. He said to send for him if she didn't start to get better after a day or so, but by that time there was some sign

of improvement. So both of them are now in bed, Þurý and
Alli, but both on the way to recovery.

I have been ill myself, just about all autumn, though more
in my mind than my body. I do not have much experience, too
dispirited, and all these problems get so hard to bear. Feelings
so terribly on edge. But my friend! don't you feel as if the heart's
wounds are bleeding one into another, I do not think they
will ever heal. God knows how long I will get to keep those of
my blessed children that remain, or how long *I will get to be
with them.*

Elín and Halldór's children had been at death's door the whole time
since their brother died and were still ill when she wrote the first part
of her letter. She goes into the history of her children's health in some
detail, including the following: 'Eggi has not been ill yet, that is to say
this autumn. He went down badly with the cough in summer, the
whooping was so bad in him he could hardly catch his breath. He had
blood running from his nose and his eyes started getting a bit blood-
shot. If he has a bad turn, and Alli too, then there's a danger it will get
into the lungs, after diphtheria, if it gets cold or some other minor problem arises.' By this point in the story Elín is at her wits' end, exhausted
in both body and soul: 'I cannot write any more. My nerves are weak and
I am shaking. I must rest. I shall write some more if I find the strength.
May God be with me.'

The second part of the letter appears to have been written a few days
later as Elín now seems to have her thoughts much more under control
and she appears to have got some rest – though it is clear that the sorrow
still runs deep in her. Possibly it is simply that writing the first part had
given Elín a degree of emotional release. When she sits down to finish
off her letter, she turns to her own state of health, describing how she had
been quite ill for some time before the events she has already related.

Elín's whole life hung in the balance and she has deep anxieties about
how things will turn out: 'I have had to spend quite a lot on medicine
and the doctor. All these sicknesses this autumn have taken an enormous
amount out of me. Things like keeping the house clean and tidy get you
nowhere when sickness takes you over. God alone knows whether this
is over now.' She goes on:

But my friend! Toil and grind and cost (while there is anything
left) are one thing. But it is so much more painful losing a dear
growing flower of youth. It is more painful than I can describe.
I try to put my trust in God, put everything in his power, that
he knows what is for our best. I am full of tears, and 'The

Lord will take these tears of mine, So I *believe and solace find'*
. . . I can tell you nothing about how things stand on the farm,
or anything about that kind of thing. My thoughts are so all over
the place that I can almost hardly think at all, just let myself sink
down into my grief.

In time, Elín's response was doubtless like that of others of her age
who went through similar experiences. She would have attempted to
distance herself from the events and bear her grief in silence. It was
essential that she maintain a grip on herself and keep going, so as to
fulfil her duties towards those of her children that survived. It is only
at the end of the letter that she touches on these matters, when she
describes her anxieties about their financial situation. Sickness involved
considerable expense and the household was rudderless while everything was in a state of confusion.

There is no doubting the depth of Elín's grief, a grief shared by
many others at the deaths of their children and relatives. But the sources
also show that people were acutely aware of the need to master their
emotions as quickly as they could, that they had to take the attitude that
life goes on. As a result, most were never able to work through these
disasters emotionally and find an adequate outlet for them. It is perhaps
worth bearing in mind that this fateful episode in Elín's life occurred
in the middle years of the second decade of the twentieth century. It is
quite possible that by this time responses to loss and sorrow had started
to change, to the extent that people were now able to allow themselves
a greater emotionality than had been possible in previous times.

Death through the eyes of a child

In the last section we saw death and sorrow principally from the point
of view of a grieving mother – how she managed to establish control
over herself and get on with her life. Death was also a highly visible part
of the daily experience of children from a young age. Children were frequently witnesses to the deaths of friends and relations, people they had
even shared a bed with. It is interesting to look at how they went about
coming to terms with the grief they encountered year after year and
how it shaped their characters and ways of thinking.

The fund of autobiographical writing that has come down to us
from ordinary people of the nineteenth and early twentieth centuries
provides us with an insight into the kind of experience many children
had to go through. Over and over again we find it mentioned that people had to face up to adversity of whatever kind with equanimity and
stoicism and simply dismiss it from their minds. As an example we can

take the story of Sigurður Jón Guðmundsson (b. 1895) which he told in his autobiography called *Til sjós og lands* (On Sea and Land). Sigurður's mother died in childbirth when he was nine years old: 'Everything people could think of was done to cheer me up, but it all proved powerless. I was withdrawn and kept myself to myself and bore my grief in silence. My sister Súsanna was quite a bit younger than me and so did not understand so well what had happened. So I had to put on a brave face for her sake, because she looked up to her big brother.' The funeral proved very difficult for Sigurður Jón, so much so that his emotions completely got on top of him: 'a string snapped in my heart and the tears burst forth with such vehemence that it seemed for all the world as if the earth I stood on had all of a sudden turned into a raging waterfall.' Repeated attempts were made to calm him, but all to no avail: the grief was so overpowering. Eventually the tears stopped: 'Then I became taciturn and serious again. I had grown older by several years, but not a word could be got out of me, as if I had been struck dumb. My sister Súsanna cried a lot, but often she needed only to look me straight in my serious face to stop howling. When she saw that I was not crying, then she didn't want to cry either.'

What followed was hard for Sigurður and other children who found themselves in his position. They were either fostered with friends or relatives or simply farmed out to people with whom they had no connections, where the care and attention they received might be patchy at best.[9] Children came to understand at a very young age that life went on and people had only very limited time to attend to their grief. Hence the bitter irony of Álfgrímur in Halldór Laxness's novel *Brekkukotsannáll*: 'It was a wise man who said that, next to losing their mother, there are few things more beneficial for young children than to lose their father'.[10] Children were forced to grow up before their time and stand on their own two feet. There was no alternative.

Halldór Jónsson of Miðdalsgröf, the husband of Elín Samúelsdóttir, left a detailed account of the loss of his mother in his unpublished autobiography. What strikes the reader is the degree of fortitude and self-restraint. Having described how deeply he was affected by the news of her death, Halldór goes on to say that Níels, his brother, cried, but is keen to stress that he himself refused to let his emotions be seen: 'The way I see myself, I think I probably lack sensitive feelings, or so it seems at times.'[11] As we find in many autobiographies, people felt constrained not to dwell on personal catastrophes; as breadwinners, it was their duty to carry on regardless, since often the whole well-being of the family depended on them. People simply had to steel themselves and put their grief to one side; daily life took undisputed precedence. Under these conditions, literature became a kind of saviour to many children, somewhere with a defined form where they could seek spiritual shelter and guidance while the adults were occupied with keeping the family afloat. This, in part, explains the almost universal literacy of eighteenth- and nineteenth-century Icelandic rural society.

Emotional outlets

We often encounter in the accounts of people who grew up in the nineteenth century an apparent indifference to the slings and arrows of the times. A death in the family was accepted with stoicism, events of whatever kind were treated philosophically. Out of necessity, all emotional life was held in check. Children swiftly came to understand that they had to contain their emotions if they were not to risk losing all grip on life.

One might be tempted to conclude that people had difficulties coming to terms with their emotions under such circumstances. But there seem to have been accepted ways of formalizing, and thus tackling, personal feelings. Most notably, rather than suppressing them, people turned to verse in search of an outlet and release. Vast quantities of poetry have been preserved in manuscripts from the period, of various kinds and varying quality, testament to the extraordinary national trait of Icelanders of feeling a constant need to be composing and reciting verses about their loves and sorrows and everything in between. This need had its roots in the deepest recesses of the souls of Icelanders of the eighteenth and nineteenth centuries, people who had no other way of expressing their emotions.

Halldór Jónsson of Miðdalsgróf himself put together fifteen volumes of poetry, gleaned from sources both printed and unprinted. Some of these books are close to 500 pages. The collections are witness not only to Halldór's interest but to that of many of those around him. As described in his diaries, he got letters from people giving him new material or asking if they could have his collections on loan. This activity was pursued with such vigour and appetite that it must have arisen from some inner compulsion. The sheer scope of this grass-roots writing and collecting is attested by the extraordinary volume of elegies, laments and love poems preserved in the archives of the Manuscript Department of the National Library of Iceland.

This poetry conforms closely to the world-view of eighteenth- and nineteenth-century Iceland described earlier in this book. The form had to be tight and succinct, in line with people's general modes of expression and the ancient literary heritage – the *rímur*, the verses preserved in the sagas and other documents. This was poetry that spanned the whole range of human experience and people turned to it under circumstances of every kind. It provided people with an outlet for emotions that they would otherwise have felt compelled to leave unexpressed. This inter-connection of emotional life and literary form had a profound influence on people's outlook on life. People of all ages and at all levels of society found themselves drawn to literature and poetry, enabling many of them to express their innermost thoughts and ideas in verse with remark-able facility. The methods by which this facility was engendered were many and varied: 'Our father or someone else often liked to test which of us brothers could learn it quickest when a verse was recited', wrote Halldór Jónsson in his autobiography. 'I often managed to learn it even when I had only heard it once.'[12]

From the other end of society, the author and naturalist Benedikt Gröndal (b. 1826) provides an entertaining description of this compul-sion to make verses in a letter to Dean Árni Helgason from 1851: 'The storm within me and my soul have at times "conned" me into putting together poems. Just as reason and the necessities of life drive men to speak, so elevated and worthy emotions drive them to write poems. And just as language in general is the fruit of reason, so poetry is the fruit of the emotions, or, perhaps, a still higher reason. Poems are words that are inextricably bound with the heavenly music of song.'[13]

In her autobiography *Gamlar glæður* (Gleams from the Past), Guð-björg Jónsdóttir (b. 1871) describes several times how people turned to poetry in search of solace and strength to face the vicissitudes of life: 'The old folk chose the poems and verses that they mumbled off in accordance with the circumstances they found themselves in and how they thought about it. The old woman who had lost her grown-up only daughter, who was supposed to support her in her old age, was wont to repeat this verse:

> I sit alone so far from sunny skies,
> Ceaseless the cold, dry weather makes me sway.
> The weeping washes now no more my eyes,
> What point in tears when you have gone away.

Here in this poem the old woman found her emotions crystallized. It chimed with her experience and helped her to live with her grief. 'The elderly widower,' adds Guðbjörg, 'who had lost his wife after many years together, sang poems of regret under his breath when she had left this world, even though he had not always treated her with great respect or made a lot of her while she was alive.' Elsewhere Guðbjörg says: 'The poems and verses crept forth into the mind, sometimes as the answer to a hidden question, sometimes as a groan from the depths of a wounded soul, but always as a source of peace of mind, if only temporarily.'

People's thirst for reading material and knowledge set rural society in Iceland apart. Elsewhere in contemporary Europe the general citizenry was largely illiterate and had only limited opportunities to acquire education of any kind. It was not until these societies entered the modern age, with things like universal schooling, improved communications and even military service, that the ordinary people as a whole achieved the level of culture that the peasantry of agrarian Iceland had attained long since under considerably more primitive conditions.

Although much less is known about how young children of the eighteenth century thought about death, we have a certain amount of evidence to indicate that attitudes were similar to those we find recorded in the following century. One example may suffice. In his autobiography the Rev. Jón Steingrímsson 'Fire-Clerk' (b. 1728) describes how, as a child, he lost his father, then aged 36:

> There were now four of us his children left alive, with one in its mother's womb . . . He stayed up long into the night, reciting many verses from hymns. At this I fell asleep in a bed that was outside my parents' room. A boy called Ásmundur Einarsson, who worked in the cowshed, lay up against me. He woke me with these words: 'Wake up, Jón, your father is dead . . .' I woke up and saw and heard my mother sitting weeping over the body and my brothers opposite in bed. I got up, taking care not to show my feelings in any way, and I went outside to an isolated place and wept till I was weary. But then I found a new strength, pitiful as I was, so that from then on it seemed to me as if nothing had happened.

We can thus suppose that the 'the culture of emotions' developed over a long period of the country's history and took on a variety of outward forms under different conditions.

7

Childhood, Youth and the Formation of the Individual

In search of the past

Childhood has been an area of rich and varied historical research in recent years, particularly as regards the cultural, emotional and educational conditions of children. Much of the work of European and American social historians on the eighteenth and nineteenth centuries and on into the twentieth has centred on certain features and modes of explanation.

Traditionally, historians have formulated their arguments in terms of modernization theory: a social modernization is seen as having triggered an industrialization of the means of production, an expansion in trade, urban development, increased popular participation in politics, a growth in the flow of information between individual sectors of society, a progressive institutionalization of society, and so on. This development is in turn supposed to have encouraged education, in particular greater literacy, thereby improving the position of children.

The increasing power of the state is supposed to have led to an improvement in conditions for children by expanding educational possibilities. The aim here was to tighten the regulation of society – to encourage punctuality, to promote a greater awareness of property rights and the importance of control over the emotions. People needed to learn how to behave 'rationally' within the new environment of the cities following the mass migration from rural to urban areas. In the country, most people had lived in small villages where everyone knew everyone else and the rules of social behaviour were familiar and established and had developed from man to man over the centuries.

The social status of children was greatly affected by new, progressive ideas emanating from the middle classes, in particular a growing concern for the weak and underprivileged. Within the new urban societies the middle classes came to exert increasing influence over popular thinking. As well as striving to define and consolidate their own position, their representatives sought to impress their customs and mores on other sections of society. One of their key principles was the need to protect the interests of those less able to protect themselves, above all children. Within this environment a number of charitable and social organizations came into existence dedicated to supporting the weak and downtrodden.

Many historians have espoused the view that the increased education of children and young people was largely the result of a process initiated jointly by the influences of the Church and temporal powers. Both saw it in their interests to build up this area of society, and worked together to this end. This development went hand in hand with the growing status of the Protestant churches and the reform of Catholic doctrine in the early modern period (1500–1750), and the general attitudes of both denominations in the years that followed.

Gutenberg's printing press is seen as a highly significant step in the expansion of education, by making reading material available to the general public in a cheap and practicable manner. The opportunity that opened up for the mass production of books was an essential precedent for the initiatives that came later in the education of young people.

Arguments of the kind outlined above are often termed 'institutional'; that is, they look to the formal structure of society for explanations to the changing attitudes towards childhood and education. The institutionalization of society is seen as the crucial factor in initiating a process that continues to this day.

In recent years, however, an ever-increasing number of historians have started looking in other directions and two points in particular have captured their attention:

First, many historians have started approaching subjects where children are concerned from the perspective of the families that had to care for these children while they were going through their schooling. Older research tended to take for granted that parents automatically accepted the opinion of those who saw education as a good thing. This view has recently come under question. What has become increasingly clear is that the interests of families very often ran counter to the expectations that society made of its citizens and to middle-class conceptions of the proper arrangement of family affairs. Working-class families in European societies had their own agendas that, for them, often outweighed any vague hopes and ambitions for their children's futures. Thus, as soon as historians started to look away from conventional institutional reasoning – from the structure of the institutions that nurtured children – and towards their families and their everyday lives, a new perspective opened up. This change of emphasis provided a new dimension to people's ideas about how society operated.

Second, an even more recent trend has seen a further shift of perspective. The focus has been directed increasingly towards the individuals themselves and the ways in which they viewed their own lives. Historians have sought answers to problems such as what kinds of opportunities young people had open to them to shape their own destinies. With this emphasis on the individual, the spotlight has moved away from institutional reasoning and onto the daily struggles of ordinary people.

Where do we look for the children in history?

The life course of an individual may be broken down into a number of stages. Historians employ an analytical model called 'life-course analysis' to draw attention to particular areas and stages in the life course and define the boundaries between them. On the basis of these boundaries, important changes – transitions – are registered in people's lives, points at which there is often a clear 'taking stock' before the individual embarks on a new stage. An individual's life is thus broken down into discrete steps, their characteristics defined, and an attempt made to consider how the person tackles the issues that arise at each stage in their life.

The life course of children in Iceland, in the period we are interested in, can be split broadly into two: on the one hand, from birth up to the age of confirmation, and on the other from confirmation up to marriage. The first stage can again be broken down into smaller units: from birth up to the time when the child was given their first work tasks to do at home, around the age of five to seven, followed by the period during which they were expected to master literacy and Christian instruction, as well as the various duties that formed essential elements of rural society, from seven up to fourteen.

The vast majority of the autobiographers provide detailed accounts of their childhood, often in extraordinary depth. Many recount whole conversations and give long descriptions of the events, people and situations they encountered, all very much as though they had happened only yesterday. The authors are often keen to pass judgement on the things that had occurred in their lives based on their personal experience of them. 'Poor parents struggling to make ends meet did not always receive much sympathy,' says Kristján Sigurðsson (b. 1883) in his autobiography called *Þegar veðrið slotar* (When the Weather Goes Down), 'even when they had to see their children sent off into service the moment they were capable of helping around the home or minding sheep . . . You could never tell how they would be cared for. Parents were rarely asked whether they missed their children.' Kristján relates how his brothers and sisters were sent out into the world, one after another, around the age of ten, before going on to relate his own experience: 'Up to the very last moment I looked back over my shoulder in the hope of seeing my mother. She was still standing on the low hill by the farm. I was twelve years old and the fifth of her children that she had sent out into the unknown.'

The autobiographies are full of references to the value and importance of childhood, and people's ideas on the upbringing and status of children and young people are a frequent topic of discussion. Many of the writers look back on their childhood years with warmth and nostalgia, and in fact part of the reason behind the writing of these memories was to commemorate and celebrate people, parents and others, who had treated them well at this sensitive time in their lives. Others have unhappier tales to tell. But the vast majority weigh up and pass judgement on their childhoods in one way or another. The poet Matthías Jochumsson (b. 1835) describes in his well-known autobiography, *Sögukaflar af sjálfum mér* (Short Tales of Myself), how he was fostered out at the age of ten, and how difficult he had found it to adjust to the situation:

> Yet I have nothing to say that might show or suggest that I was treated any worse than was common among young people of my age without friends or relatives, who had to work for their food and shelter. It is quite another matter whether such treatment would be considered entirely right and proper nowadays. Neither can I think of much positive to be said for my progress over these years, since, emotionally, the first chapter of this period stunted my growth and development in various ways. But this was as much the fault of my youth, my peculiar character and timorous nature, as the influences from outside. Overall, as a result of this lack of somewhere permanent in my life, I was, so to speak, very late to develop. But however these vicissitudes that I met with are looked upon, I stood there at this time, a child of ten, at the first turning point of my life.

It is in fact striking how many of the autobiographers speak of finding themselves at a distinct turning point in their lives around this kind of age. From the age of five or six children had been given tasks to do that they were supposed to carry out conscientiously and often on their own initiative. They were expected to mind the sheep, alone, day and night, frequently a long way from the family home. Under such conditions the ability of children to maintain calm and self-control came under considerable strain, children who had been brought up on the wealth of stories about ghosts and elves told at the winter-evening gatherings. Matthías describes the torments he suffered thus:

> It did not make things any better when we got to hear the elf and ghost tales, and that was very young. It was an old woman called Solveig who told them, when our mother did not know, because she had forbidden her to fill us up with ghost stories. It was not long before I was seeing phantoms, especially at night and in the twilight, sometimes even out in the open. My mother has instilled in us that children had nothing to fear from this kind of thing so long as they remembered to say their prayers . . . The worst of it was how little profit I seemed to get from saying my prayers, since there was no let up in the visions while it was dark, even if I recited three times over all verses of the Bible that I knew.

Many other autobiographers express similar sentiments. Elías Halldórsson (b. 1877) discusses the significance of the world of popular religion and folk beliefs for the psychological health of children in his autobiography called *Heiðinginn* (The Heathen), and the motivations that supported this culture: 'But there were two sides. One was to instil in children a faith in God and trust in divine protection. The other was that, through the reciting of prayers, children were surreptitiously implanted with ideas about evil spirits, ghosts and demons set on doing them harm. To keep the children quiet and good, everything was done to terrorize them with bogeymen, witches, imps, the dark, etc. Then, as they got older, they got to hear stories of elves and hidden people, ghosts and monsters.'

To the considerable strain that children already found themselves under at this time in their lives can be added the constant proximity of death, as discussed in chapter Six. Children frequently had to watch as their closest relatives – brothers and sisters, parents, grandparents – disappeared from their lives, often long before their time. The loss often stayed with them for the rest of their lives. Many saw three or four of their own brothers and sisters buried.

In his autobiography, *Séð og lifað* (Seen and Lived), Indriði Einarsson (b. 1851) gives a poignant account of the loss of this brothers and sisters; out of a total of fifteen, only six reached the age of eighteen, and of these one brother died of typhoid fever. The rest were taken by diphtheria, which cast a terrible shadow over the whole family: 'All this loss preyed terribly on the minds of our parents and held us kids in fear. When we heard news of an outbreak of diphtheria, we would look at each other and ask silently, Which of us is going to die now?

An unusual aspect of Icelandic popular culture was the way it managed to combine work, education and entertainment. This picture, taken in 1920, shows how the heritage of the winter-evening gatherings remained a force in society even under the new conditions of the twentieth century. Housing and living conditions have clearly changed from the traditional farmhouse living room, but the activities are the familiar ones of the old society: the boy to the left is reading while the woman spins wool and the other boy knits.

Usually it was just a matter of time. For a period during my childhood years it seemed almost inconceivable that I would get past the age of diphtheria and reach the age of fourteen.' Accounts of this kind are given in an almost matter-of-fact way, without much fuss about the situation. Children grew up to take each day as it came, with its suffering. 'I was my parents' first child', says Jón Kr. Lárusson (b. 1878) in his autobiography *Ævisaga Breiðfirðings* (A Biography of a Person from Breiðafjörður), and adds: 'They had three altogether. Two died young and my mother died of the last, when I was in my fourth year. My father then gave up the farm and became a farm labourer.' So life continued; the rhythm of work and the seasons went on, whatever people's health and chances of survival.

Loss was an abiding condition of rural society, something that children had to contend with at regular intervals. In compensation, children started to learn to read and write around the same time as they were given their first jobs to do around the farm. Most children derived great pleasure and satisfaction from this part of their education. Mastering the skill of literacy, as I see it, made it possible for them to maintain a grip on their lives. It is striking how quickly most of them managed to learn to read, often with only limited guidance.[1] What is more, they were given pretty much free rein over what they were allowed to read – and in many cases simply read whatever was to hand.

Around the age of ten things changed. Now education became the burden and work the saving grace. Children started to work side by side with their parents or guardians, taking on much the same kinds of tasks as them and being treated accordingly. Around the same time began the preparation for confirmation, with its tedious rote learning from Luther's *Minor Catechism* (see chapter Six). This transition is apparent in many of the autobiographies, though perhaps not so markedly that it is possible to speak directly of this being a turning point in children's lives. The big change in the lives of all children in Iceland came a few years later following confirmation.

Adolescence to adulthood

The authors of the autobiographies normally end their accounts of childhood with their confirmation. For most, the future held one of three possible courses. Some stayed on, at least for the time being, in the parental household and continued to perform much the same tasks as before. Many children were sent out as servants to families they did not know, where they were expected to behave as adults, but with only very limited rights. A select few were able to go to school and continue their education. These were the sons of officials and more affluent farmers, and their way lay to the Latin School in Reykjavík, with some going on eventually to the University of Copenhagen. Throughout the eighteenth, nineteenth and on into the early part of the twentieth century this group was very small and the route they took was hardly an option for people from the poorer classes.

Some children had to leave home considerably earlier because their families were too poor to maintain them, or because their home had been broken up due to the death of one of their parents. Private paupers – *ómagar*, as such children were termed – did not always receive much care and attention and were frequently subjected to abuse and humiliation. Hafsteinn Sigurbjarnarson (b. 1895) had to stand on his own feet from an early age as described in his autobiography *Ævisaga*

Confirmation at the age of fourteen marked an important turning point in children's lives. At this point they were, as it was expressed, received formally into the Christian flock. At the same time they became fully legitimate members of the workforce. Most now had to make their own living. Very few children had any opportunity for formal schooling, only those from wealthier families or the occasional poor child who found some patron to sponsor its education.

(Biography), though in this case he, as it were, accompanied his mother into poverty. As a family they had been forced to accept financial support from the local commune. When her husband then died, his mother of course lost everything, but got to keep the children through the grace and mercy of the authorities. Hafsteinn's mother worked hard to pay off her debt and he describes what a turning point it was in their lives when she at last succeeded:

> When mother had listened to my story, she said, 'I am well aware that your upbringing has not been as I would have chosen. There is no way I can ever make it up to you. You are now over the worst stretch and I hope that the future will make up for what your childhood was lacking. The reason I asked Jóhannes to let you walk up here with me to the little hill by the farm was that you told me once that you were sometimes teased for us having had to receive support from the commune. Now you are my witness, both in sight and hearing, that the debt has been paid, and I am from this point on as free as if I had never

received a penny. You can henceforth direct anyone to the commune records if they are putting you down for being a private pauper.'

This incident engraved itself on Hafsteinn's mind, and is the more touching for his remembering it so clearly.

The accounts that have come down to us of people's adolescences can sometimes be fairly detailed, though rarely to anything like the degree of their childhood memories. The events from this period of their lives, when they stood alone but in no position to take much control over their destinies, tend to be viewed personally. Many of the writers spend considerable time trying to assess their own roles and their position within the environment in which they found themselves. Throughout both their childhoods and youths the writers tend to place themselves centre stage, and many actually employ the expression 'formative years' to describe this time, referring to their own personal experiences.

A characteristic feature of how writers present the next stages of their lives – for example the years after marriage – is their tendency, so to speak, to withdraw their own personalities from the narrative and let their actions speak for themselves. Little is said about the personal and emotional aspects of their lives. Family life tends to be dealt with something along the lines that, on some particular day, the author entered into holy matrimony and that their spouse was the greatest piece of good fortune that ever came their way. Those who go furthest in their presentation of marriage and emotional existence are men like Þorbjörn Björnsson (b. 1886) in his autobiography *Skyggnzt um af heimahlaði* (A View from Home). An eligible young girl of the district had caught Þorbjörn's eye but he reckoned he stood little chance – there were too many others competing for her attention. Þorbjörn describes how he finally managed to speak to her. 'After having been provided with excellent refreshments, Sigríður, the girl of the house, and I fell into conversation and we talked long into the night, and these discussions ended with promises to be together along the path of life still to come.' The match was agreed and everything arranged. Then the writer adds:

> I dwell on this a little because I do not think it out of order
> if I and others who record the incidents of their life histories
> speak out fairly plainly about the most momentous agree-
> ments they have made in their lives, and that is how I see the
> marriage contract. Also, it is rather fun to bring this all back
> to mind, from the first hours together with one's wife up to the
> present moment.

The author approaches the matter in hand just as he would any other job to be done. He needed to increase his landholding, build up his sheep and cows, and find himself a wife – all tasks that he took for granted and that were grounded on 'contracts' and 'agreements' between himself and the world about him!

This personal reticence on the part of the autobiographers makes it difficult to form any clear mental image of the emotional and intimate aspects of married life. The same is true of courtship. However, it is sometimes possible to get indirect hints by reading between the lines. Thus Hafsteinn Sigurbjarnarson describes the sickness of the wife of the farmer where he and his mother were staying shortly after the death of his father:

> One day Guðmann's wife and I were the only ones indoors. She started to wash a large sore that she had on one of her breasts. I had seen her wash this sore before and she made no attempt to stop me seeing when she treated it. It had become big and ugly and I reckon you could have hidden half a cup in the hole that had formed in her breast. The smell from the sore was unbearable when she was treating it. When I was in bed that evening, I asked my mother, 'What's the matter with Helga's breast?' She did not know what I was talking about and got me to describe it. I told her what I had seen and she hardly knew whether or not to believe me. The next day mother pressed Helga about what was wrong with her breast. She did not want to make anything of it. Still, in the end Helga showed mother the abscess, and it horrified her. In the end, mother spoke to Guðmann in private and asked him again and again whether he knew about the state of his wife's breast. It came out that he had no idea about it, had not even noticed the stench that was coming from it.

Eventually Helga was moved away to Reykjavík for treatment, where she died soon afterwards. The story provides eloquent testimony of the state of personal relations and emotional life that existed between many couples in the old society.

The autobiographers, most of whom were men, generally have little more to say about their children than their spouses. They are regarded as part of what the authors view as their 'achievements', something they have 'done' with their lives. This 'public' aspect of their lives in fact constitutes the principal subject matter of the later periods of the autobiographies, once the writers have married and settled down; their life's work is chronicled step by step, along with its victories and defeats.

Many of the writers name this section their 'productive years', with the interest centring largely on how they succeeded in getting on in the world, enlarging their farm and cultivating their land. Classic topics for discussion include anything relating to progress, in both the public and private arenas; the author relates his part in helping his country to move forward and in the ongoing struggle for national independence, a struggle in which each man must strive to do his best to improve conditions within the country.

This structure does not, of course, apply to all the autobiographies. In some the author keeps himself in the background throughout, with the emphasis rather on general living conditions, working practices and historical events. In other cases the 'productive years' are given much more personal treatment. But the broad pattern outlined above is hardly surprising: childhood and adolescence are times when every individual goes through great changes that stay with him for the rest of his life, and so it is perfectly natural that most space should be spent on describing the formative processes that take place in these years. It is at this stage of their lives that, for most people, the foundation for the future is laid. This is the structure we find repeated again and again in the various types of personal sources preserved in Iceland from the last three centuries and that bear witness to the unusual level of popular culture that existed in the country.

8

A True Passion: Writing as Personal Expression

In this chapter I will focus on the brothers Halldór and Níels Jónsson, with whom I started this book and whom we have met again since. Halldór and Níels grew up in the remote north-west of Iceland in the second half of the nineteenth century and to some extent can stand as representatives of rural society as it was at the time. The chapter describes the men and the environment they lived in, their stages along the road to manhood and, above all, the way they chose to spend their free hours, on learning and cultural activity – how they acquired their education, and their contribution to society through their tireless copying up of old manuscripts and other material that caught their attention. In the following chapter I discuss the lessons that may be drawn from these activities if we try to look at cultural history from the point of view of the individual.

The rediscovered people of Iceland

The setting is Strandasýsla, a region of cramped inlets and narrow valleys along the rugged north-east coast of the Westfjord peninsula. At the farm of Tindur in the parish and commune of Kirkjuból, nine brothers were born, sons of the farmer Jón Jónsson and his wife Halldóra Halldórsdóttir. Five of the boys died young. The other four, Níels, Halldór, Ísleifur and Magnús, grew up at Tindur and attained manhood.

From the short unpublished autobiography that Halldór wrote in 1906 covering the first twenty years of his life, it is clear that his was a happy childhood which he looked back to with fondness: 'Life in my parents' home was good and Christian, so far as I best remember, and as children we were constantly exhorted to adopt good habits and have the word of God at our fingertips.'[1] It seems that there was a strict order and discipline to all domestic life; for instance, everyone rose at 6 a.m. and was in bed by 10 p.m. Halldór also notes that the house was kept considerably cleaner and tidier than was general practice at the time, though not so well as later, at the time he was writing his autobiography:

> The living room and the whole farm was swept out daily, though the living room loft was washed only twice or so a year. By that time a thick layer of filth would have built up there, and snow was often brought in to dampen it, then most of the dung was shovelled out and the place then washed. Tables, shelves and bed frames were washed much oftener and the bedding aired. In my parents' later years on the farm this changed considerably, after the new living room was built in 1883, much brighter and more spacious than the one before. Then the loft was washed every Saturday evening, and the whole living room from top to bottom in spring.

The food was excellent, in Halldór's opinion, and every care was taken to ensure that it was clean and wholesome. The boys were not given coffee 'before we were six or older, and then just coloured milk to start off with'. Later the coffee drinking began in earnest and there was no stinting in its consumption. 'The dogs were permitted to remain untroubled up in the living room loft except at night, and at mealtimes they would go round from man to man, getting themselves scraps of food. No one then understood the danger of infection that goes with this, as in the recent outbreak of hydatids.' Halldór mentions that he himself was a rather fussy eater, but the brothers generally had enough to eat, except sometimes in spring when supplies began to run low. 'But we always got everything we needed when there was food to be had, and we never showed any sign of stunted growth and poor development even if good food was short for a while.' Halldór describes the bowl he had handed down to him:

> The first eating utensil I had, as I remember, was an old *askur* [a small wooden bowl with a handle and a hinged lid] that my grandmother gave me, now black and shabby with age, with a large domed lid, the carved roses half worn off, and the bowl itself cracked. Either those who had eaten from it before me had wanted to make use of every scrap they were given, or they had never got enough, for all the rims were licked smooth on the inside, and there was a round hollow at the bottom.

Halldór's bowl eventually met its doom when it fell apart in his hands, full of meat soup.

Halldór describes the games the brothers played and the jobs they did during their younger years, and it is clear they were well content with their lot. Everyone in the family appears to have got on well. Their games and the winter-evening gatherings, and much else to do with people's daily lives, remained firmly fixed in Halldór's memory. For example, he mentions that they got a fair number of visitors at the farm and always tried to be welcoming and hospitable. But he also notes that strangers were a rarity. Halldór himself was shy and self-effacing and found it difficult to put himself forward with people he did not know and contribute to the conversation.

On relations between Halldór's parents the autobiography has this to say:

> My parents' marriage was good and loving, and it was notice-able how thoughtful and attentive my father was towards his wife and children, and the household in general, whether he was at home or away. One saw less of this with my mother, that was just the way she was, but there is no doubt she loved him dearly. But her mind was not as strong as it might have been and this sometimes made life less happy than it might otherwise have been, together with other discomforts.

The brothers were set to work from an early age, though, as Halldór saw it, without ever being exploited. He especially enjoyed watching over the sheep so long as the brothers were able to do it together. But when the minister at Fell borrowed him to do some shepherding on his own he suffered horribly and, in general, did not feel comfortable anywhere outside the bosom of his family. Even his confirmation classes proved a trial to him because of his shyness, though the parish records note that all the brothers performed well at their confirmations.

The urge for self-expression

In 2002 Davíð Ólafsson and I contributed an article to a collection of studies on popular literacy in early modern northern Europe called *Writing Peasants*.[2] The article, entitled 'Barefoot Historians', dealt with the group of uneducated Icelanders in the eighteenth and nineteenth century who, with great energy and zeal, wrote up material from previous centuries for the use of their friends and relatives. These people came to constitute what can almost be seen as a kind of informal 'institute of culture' and their importance for the continuity and development of popular culture in Iceland is impossible to overestimate. Their work is described further in chapter Eleven.

It should be borne in mind that nearly all printed material at this time was religious in content; very little secular material was published formally in Icelandic until well into the nineteenth century. There were, however, 'unofficial' channels of distribution – an 'underground press', one might almost call it – in which these barefoot historians played a central part. In this sense they were the glue that held Icelandic popular culture together, giving children, youngsters, and in fact people of all ages the chance to immerse themselves in the world of the sagas and traditional poetry, as described earlier in this book – and so be better placed to face up to the hardships and struggles of everyday life.

The reason it is possible to follow the lives of Halldór and Níels Jónsson in such detail is that both left behind them enormous amounts of written material in the form of diaries, letters and other sources. The brothers provide one example, out of many, of how the barefoot historians went about their business. Halldór started his diary in 1888, a seventeen-year-old farmer's son from a poor community in the remote north of Iceland. For two years prior to this he had already been recording various bits of information relevant to the management of the farm. He kept his diary up to the day of his death in 1912. Elsewhere, and alongside this, he wrote various pieces describing his ideas and speculations, as well as practical material about himself and the running of the farm. Five large volumes of this type have been preserved. Also from his hand we have fifteen collections of poetry containing copies of poems taken from both printed and manuscript sources. Finally, we have copies of the local newspaper *Gestur* (The Guest), which he edited and wrote out entirely by hand, as well as, along with his brothers, writing the vast majority of the articles. The paper came out for two years in 1907–8, fourteen issues in the first year, 23 in the second, and acted as a kind of small-sized version of the conventional newspapers published nationally. It was distributed around about ten farms, with each paying a small sum to read it.

To my knowledge, one of Halldór's descendants also preserves copies of the local paper *Dalbúinn* (The Dalesman) that the brothers Halldór and Níels wrote while they were still living with their parents in 1891–3. Initially they edited the paper together; then, after the first year, Halldór took over the work on his own. The paper was not distributed widely, according to what Halldór says in his autobiography. Another descendant has recently been discovered as having a book that contained the brothers' drawings of people, animals and other objects that Níels later used as inspiration in his love letters. In total these sources amount to a massive corpus, particularly in view of the fact that the writing was done under difficult conditions in old turf farms, often

The picture shows some of the manuscript material produced by the two brothers Halldór and Níels Jónsson. Halldór and Níels came from a poor farming family in the northwest of Iceland in the second half of the nineteenth century and their lives and writings form one of the main sources for this book. We can only be amazed at the sheer quantity of writing they produced in their lives, especially in view of the straitened circumstances under which they lived. The brothers were far from unique in this respect; large numbers of Icelandic peasants, with little formal education, spent many of their hours collecting and copying up written material to enrich their own lives and those of people around them.

in extreme cold and with no light, by a man who had to labour with his hands every day of the year. It should also be said that all of Halldór's literary activities are characterized by great precision and accuracy, as well as being in an elegant and aesthetically pleasing hand.

Níels started to keep a diary in 1893 at the age of 23 and the entries extend over 40 years, up to 1934.[3] The same may be said of Níels's diary as of Halldór's: it appears to be a labour of love, carried out with great care and attention to detail. Níels's book is large in size and broad in extent, providing a detailed account of his day-to-day toils and those of the people around him. Both these men's writings constitute contemporary sources of the first order, not least in being from the hands of ordinary young men of the peasant working class.

From the effects of Níels and his relatives we have just under a hundred letters, which can be divided into two groups. On the one hand there are the letters, described in the Introduction, that Níels wrote to his later wife in the years between 1890 and 1895 and covering the period of their betrothal. These letters are highly unusual in several respects: they are beautifully produced and some are ornately decorated with drawings in Níels's hand. Their contents are no less colourful; they are not only love letters in which Níels opens up his deepest feelings and desires, but also letters of encouragement and exhortation, holding up a revealing mirror to contemporary society. They express the future visions of both parties and can be seen as representative of the thoughts, hopes and aspirations of young people in general as the nineteenth century drew to its close.

Secondly, there is Níels's correspondence with his brothers and other friends and relatives. Of the letters from his brothers found among Níels's effects the most were from Halldór (45), followed by Ísleifur (21), with only seven from Magnús. There is also the heart-rending letter Níels received in 1914 from Halldór's widow, Elín Samúelsdóttir, containing the news of the death from diphtheria of her youngest son, quoted extensively in chapter Six. In addition, we know that the brothers undertook writing and copying work for people from the surrounding farms but little of this material has found its way into the manuscript collections. This vast quantity of writing, in its modest way, bears testimony to the brothers' importance to their local community, and to Icelandic popular culture in general.

The brothers and their families

The farm of Tindur in the Miðdalur valley in the commune of Kirkj-bólshreppur was considered an excellent holding for sheep rearing, with enough land to support the family tolerably well. On top of this, the father and sons worked at sea during the fishing season from the fishing stations on Steinsgrímsfjörður, and sometimes travelled all the way west to Ísafjörður for the same purpose.

Just as elsewhere within the farming community, working patterns in rural Strandasýsla were very much bound up with the seasons. In general, one task followed on from another, with seldom much free time in between. Very often in difficult times the jobs piled up, and people had to work night and day so that years of toil would not go to waste. For this reason there was close cooperation between the farms of the district on jobs both great and small. People lent each other their labour and materials and banded together in groups to handle particular jobs and projects. This created a basis for a kind of specialization within the district: men and women became known for their skill in certain tasks and were called upon in case of need. In addition, whole households took on work for parties from outside.

Work on Strandir consisted chiefly of the customary tasks of the Icelandic rural economy, but with clear signs of a change that we find

*Though rural society in Iceland was fairly simple and homogeneous, the
various tasks associated with agriculture called for a certain division of labour
among people. Good haymakers were in great demand over the summer season
and were paid well for their services; everything depended on getting the hay
dried and stored away as quickly and efficiently as possible. The haymakers
in the picture are holding their scythes and appear to have taken a break to
sharpen them. They are sitting under a house wall built of earth and stones,
the typical method of construction of most houses in the Icelandic countryside
until the twentieth century.*

in various other rural societies in Europe at the time, a move towards
what is known as 'proto-industry'. This term is used to describe a stage
of production where traditional agriculture remains the staple occupation but space has developed for a degree of specialization. This often
had major consequences for the productivity of regions where such an
arrangement was possible. Sources for this kind of practice are known
from Iceland. The writer Þórbergur Þórðarson, for instance, mentions
households in Reykjavík where they did net making, the work being
organized in one of two ways: 'Either people bought all the materials
in the shops and chandleries, made the nets, and sold them on to dealers, or the dealers themselves provided the materials and paid a fixed
rate for the net making. The dealers then sold the nets in their shops
to fishermen from outside.'[4]

We have further witness of this early form of domestic industrialization in an article called 'Fyrir 40 árum' (Forty Years Ago) by Þorkell
Bjarnason, published in 1892 in the journal of the Icelandic Literary

Society. He describes a poor farmer of his acquaintance who saw his family through the winter by taking on wool work for people from outside:

> He was an impoverished man with several children, and he provided what he needed for himself and his large family over the winter by taking wool on credit from traders in autumn and producing knitted goods, paying for the wool with the knit-wear and buying food with what was left over. He worked in this way for himself and his large family year after year, without either him, his wife, or the children ever falling idle.

Here we have a clear example of one form of proto-industry. In fact, a fair amount of this kind of activity went on, entirely outside the self-sufficiency farming of the country districts as it is typically portrayed by Icelandic historians. This kind of nascent specialization is significant for the conditions under which Halldór and Níels led their lives, particularly when we try to assess the possibilities open to them to take control of their own working lives and establish themselves socially and economically. The society in which they grew up was considerably more complex than historians have generally allowed for when discussing rural economies of a similar type, and the interplay of its different elements in all probability served as an incentive for people seeking to improve their conditions.

The local community was equally close-knit in other areas of life, with constant coming and going between the farms of people seeking each other's company. Organized gatherings and formal socializing were, however, notably rare. The church was the midpoint of such social activity as there was in the parish; other entertainment was sporadic and occasional. Beyond this there were a number of societies and associations operating in the district and their meetings were generally well attended, especially by men.

This is the environment in which the brothers grew up. In 1893 their father quit farming and he and all his sons became *lausamenn* (wage-earning free labourers resident on other people's farms) in the surrounding districts. Halldór for the most part remained in the area where he had grown up, as did his brothers Ísleifur and Magnús. Halldór supported himself by teaching and building work, mainly house construction and drystone walls, together with writing and anything else that happened to come his way. From this he managed to earn a decent living and it is revealing to trace his life course and career in general during his time as a farm labourer. This is possible as he recorded all his financial affairs in conscientious detail, including making estimates of the value of everything he owned, down to the underwear and the other clothes he stood up in while conducting the valuation!

Early in the new century Halldór married a young woman, Elín Samúelsdóttir, from the farm of Miðdalsgröf in the same district. At the time Halldór was 31 years old and Elín eighteen. Together they had five children. Halldór died in 1912, in the prime of life, drowned while fishing just off the shore of his native area.

After he set up as an independent farmer Halldór carried out various official functions for the local agricultural, trading and reading society. Even during his years as a farm labourer he was renowned for his skill in wall-building and as a writer and he carried on doing work of this kind as a sideline for people of the district as his family started to grow. Halldór enjoyed considerable respect within the local community and was entrusted with important jobs on other people's behalf. He seems to have been a self-possessed man, careful and deliberate, but exceptionally progressive in his outlook. To give an insight into Halldór's character it is worth quoting from the letter he wrote to his brother Níels on the occasion of his wedding:

In summer, on 20 September, Elín and I were joined in wedlock by the Rev. Arnór and we held a little party. We did not invite many as I had always taken the view that, if I should ever happen to marry, I intended not to be such a fool as to squander what little I had on things for a reception, since usually one gets nothing in return but ingratitude, or worse. There were 12 people present (the folk from Geststaðir and Tindur, brother Mangi [Magnús], etc.). Witnesses were brother Mangi and Grímur from Geststaðir. I would have wished you could have been there at that hour, with all best wishes. But I knew there was no point asking you to come as you would not be able to get away from home at this time.

What we have here, clearly, is a man who knows what he wants and has no hesitation about taking charge of his elder brother's interests! So far as we can see, Halldór's days at Miðdalsgröf were happy and profitable. The family was tolerably comfortable, even though Halldór did not always have the chance to give his various schemes for improvement the kind of energy and undivided attention he would have chosen. To get a taste of family life at Miðdalsgröf it is worth quoting Halldór's own description. He had been having trouble sleeping because the main room was still hot after the Christmas baking earlier that day. He sat up in bed, looked around him and set down a description of what met his eye under the title 'Evening, 1906':

In the living room there is a bed under each sloping wall. I am in the bed under the south side. It is a free-standing bed [i.e. not built into the timberwork of the house]. Above me my little son Alfreð, in his fifth year, is sleeping soundly. He went to sleep with a wooden horse in his hand, which he was saddling up, as he put it. In the slope of the ceiling there is a window on each side. In my window hangs a large watch in a silver case, with a gilt chain, and a gold ring on the same nail. On the peg above the bed opposite hangs a little lamp, the oil chamber of green glass, with a round lampshade behind, burning with a dim light. In the bed opposite me sleep my younger boys, Eggert and Jón, three years and one year, one at each end. At the centre of the gable end there is a table, unpolished and fairly insubstantial. On it stand a washing bowl, a matchbox and a soap tray. Up above it is a cupboard in the panelling with three compartments. In it there are all kinds of papers, *Alþingistíðindi* for 1905 [the official gazette of the Icelandic parliament], *Ísafold* 1884–86 [a newspaper], 'The greatest cause for joy', an Easter sermon by the Rev. Jón Helgason. A clothes brush and various items. Above the cupboard hangs a little clock and a round barometer. It is foul weather outside, too, windows frosted and snowed up. Right by me hangs an oil lamp, waiting clean and polished for Christmas. On one side of the cupboard hangs a sewing basket with various things in it; on the outside is a silver-coloured picture of a falcon on a blue background, the symbol of Iceland. On the other side of the cupboard are two shelves. On the lower shelf there are some scraps of paper belonging to Alfreð; on the other, books and newspapers.

Halldór goes on to list the varied selection of books housed on these shelves. Then he continues:

High up in the roof above me in a rack are a carving knife, two spoons, a knife, scissors and wool combs. In the roof on the other side there is a rack with a broom and a file. From the rafter hang four hats, two of them mine, one for each of my sons. While I have been writing these lines, sleep has crept up on me unawares and I must give in to him and end this now.

Such was the sight that met the eyes of a young family man as he looked about him in the living room at Miðdalsgröf in the early years of the twentieth century.

When their parents gave up the farm Níels started travelling, often working at the fishing camps at Ísafjörður and Gjögur. For the first years he was frequently on the move but eventually he settled down at Gjögur. In 1896 he married Guðrún, the daughter of Bjarni Sæmundsson, the farmer at Gjögur, as described in the Introduction. Níels was 25 at the time, Guðrún 23. Together they had one daughter. Land at Gjögur was limited but the place was an important fishing centre, and so Níels spent much of his time at sea, but also kept some livestock, which he and his wife tended together.

Like his brother Halldór, Níels enjoyed considerable respect in the area where he lived, despite the harrowing events described in the Introduction. He was much sought after for repair work, building and carpentry of all kinds, and for his copying of poems and stories. One of his most noteworthy enterprises was his work on the construction of an ice-house at Gjögur, in which he was involved first in 1905 and then again in 1912, running both places in partnership with others. Ice was necessary for preserving the fish catch and Níels's part in these projects enhanced his reputation greatly. However, for much of his life Níels lived in poverty and this cast its shadow over his whole life. His undoubted abilities never found the kind of outlet they perhaps merited. By nature he was a far more sensitive man than Halldór, and the other brothers customarily turned to him for advice on personal matters.

The story of these brothers is interesting in many ways. In their childhoods and early manhood they worked side by side on the family farm, but later their paths diverged and their fates turned out rather differently. Both spent times as farm labourers, but in different fields. Such men enjoyed an uncertain social status, but their individual lives and the sources that tell of them provide good indications of how such people might achieve some kind of position within nineteenth-century rural society. It is also interesting to consider these men as examples of young Icelanders as their country entered the twentieth century, in particular in the tension between their outlooks and attitudes and the realities they lived under. Both were men with ambitious ideas about life and human existence, ideas they were never really able to see through to fruition due to the hardships and toil of their everyday lives.

9
The Shaping of Modern Man

In the early years of the nineteenth century there was a man
who lived in Þingeyjarsýsla [north-east Iceland] by the name of
Jón Kolbeinsson. Jón was a peculiar man, cared little about
work and was constantly with his nose in a book, at all times,
opportune or not. About him is told this story: One day during
the haymaking Jón's wife was outside all day up to her neck in
work while Jón spent most of the time indoors. In the evening
his wife laid into him for idleness and irresponsibility. To which
Jón replied: 'I haven't been wasting the day either, because I've
got a fair bit forward in German.'

This little anecdote comes from a book by the writer Gunnar M. Mag-
núss, *Saga alþýðufræðlunnar á Íslandi* (A History of Popular Education
in Iceland), published in 1939. The picture presented here supposedly
exemplifies the foibles of a well-known type of Icelandic eccentric, men
who chose to follow different paths from their fellow farmers and
immerse themselves in books and study. Gunnar passes the following
comment: 'This is a true and simple account of a man taken by a passion
for study and learning, a passion he had never been able to satisfy in his
younger years. It is not alone. Lots of men struggled against the odds
to achieve a level of learning through self-study and their efforts were
often viewed with disapproval.' Whatever we choose to make of Gunnar's interpretation, there is no disputing his assertion that the example
does not stand alone.

Conflicting interests

If we look into the legal and regulatory changes to the education system
in the nineteenth century and early years of the twentieth, there is
plenty of evidence of genuine progress. This period saw the laying

down of the foundations for the future shape of education in Iceland. Of particular significance was the passing of the Education Act of 1907, which introduced general compulsory schooling for all children in the country. This legislative framework has been under constant revision ever since, which continues to this day. The picture usually presented of the development of the education system in Iceland is one of a series of little victories, of discrete steps forward taken by the country on its road towards a modern society.

Until now the history of education in Iceland has generally been discussed in terms of economic factors. Scholars have shown how developments in education went hand in hand with the great economic upturn that was seen as having reshaped society as a whole during this period. Developments in one area automatically led to changes in the other. However, if one looks deeper into the public debate that went on in the newspapers and journals at the time, what emerges is a marked divergence of opinion between two groups, those who advocated a wholesale expansion of the education system, and those who favoured slower and more cautious reform. The latter took the view that the existing system had served its purpose well and was likely to continue to do so, and included especially the more affluent farmers and conservative elements among the powerful elite. The other group was made up chiefly of the educated classes of Iceland and many from the working class. Between these two groups there was a sharp difference of views about the future shape of society.

The position of the working class in this debate merits particular attention. Both sides to the debate repeatedly comment on the level of interest shown by ordinary working people in progressive reforms to public affairs. Working-class Icelanders were eager for education and were often ready to make considerable sacrifices to get it. Many conservative commentators in fact saw in this evidence in support of their belief that working people were not to be trusted to take charge of their own affairs. A commonly heard refrain was that the eagerness of working people to go chasing after education was simply a pretext for slacking; when it came to work itself, those who had acquired a certain amount of education were felt to be prone to being workshy and unreliable.

There was thus a partly negative tone to the debate, as regards both education itself and the working classes, particularly unattached free labourers (lausamenn). Mixed in with this debate was a widely held perception that increased general education would exacerbate the problems of agriculture and encourage further migration from country to town. Initially, most people took the view that schools represented nothing but a threat to the agricultural way of life and would make it more difficult

For most of the eighteenth and nineteenth centuries Icelandic society existed within tight constraints and allowed little room for flexibility. The age of matrimony was high, around 30 for both men and women, and people did not marry until they could show they could support themselves. There was only one way for people to build up the funds they needed to set up on their own, and that was by entering positions of service on other people's farms. Their pay chiefly took the form of livestock. This situation was the lot of just about everyone, for a time at least, except for a few tramps and itinerant workers. Very often these were people who suffered from some kind of mental or, in some cases, drink problem. They moved around between farms and districts, settling here or there for a few days and entertaining the people with their stories and antics, which at times could be highly bizarre. Tramps were famous people in Iceland, on a par with poets and political leaders. The pictures show 'Love' Brandur, one of the best-known drifters, said to have had various 'faces of love' in his repertoire, whatever that may mean, and 'Rat' Petersen, who specialized in catching the rats that abounded in Icelandic urban areas.

to resist this trend. Later, in the first decades of the twentieth century, the tone changed somewhat. Calls were heard for schools up to a certain level to be set up in rural areas, and eventually, towards the end of the 1920s and at the start of the '30s, a programme of secondary schools was introduced to cater for the needs of the farming community, many with boarding facilities. As a generalization, however, it is fair to say that the moves to reform the education and schools system in Iceland were characterized above all by caution and conservatism.

Enthusiasm and discouragement

Some of the comments aired during the public debate indicate that popular attitudes to education and schooling were not necessarily as progressive as has often been claimed. The Education Act of 1907 attempted to steer a middle course between those who wanted a large-scale and comprehensive expansion of the education system and those who wanted to maintain the older system based on peripatetic teaching. Under this system each commune appointed teachers who travelled round the district from farm to farm, staying at each for an appointed time and teaching the children the rudiments of reading, writing and arithmetic. The debate on the pros and cons of this system went on for over 80 years and a satisfactory solution was only reached after a century of squabbling over the same main idea: whether schools were likely to help or hinder the economic position of rural areas.

In this book I have attempted to assess the effects that the legal framework and the various social impediments in Iceland had on the opportunities open to ordinary working men like Halldór and Níels Jónsson. The brothers regarded it as their mission in life, in fact their most pressing mission in life, to create for themselves a freedom of action. Over and over again in their writings we find a deep awareness of the contingent nature of personal freedom. All their thoughts and actions point to such an understanding of the concept of freedom. But how did it come about?

Halldór and Níels accepted and made their own, quite literally, the exhortations of the poets and the educated elite that it was the duty of all Icelanders to look forward, to strive towards bringing their country into new age. They appear to have been utterly untouched by the reservations of the conservative forces at work in nineteenth-century Iceland. This is remarkable on its own, since these men were coming to adulthood at precisely the time when the opponents of formal education were at their most vocal. The resonance of the poems of the Romantics seem to have drowned out all dissenting voices. This manifested itself in various ways.

A keen desire to face up to the task of the times, seen for instance in their faith in progress, appears repeatedly in the brothers' writings. Their work ethic and ways of approaching the problems of daily life are strong indications of how ordinary people thought about their world. Judging from what Halldór says in his autobiography, a predisposition in this direction showed itself early in the brothers' lives. He tells, for instance, about an idea they had to move the water source at Tindur closer to the farm to make life easier for those who had to fetch supplies. The source often got snowed over in high winter and 'It sometimes

happened we could only find it after a lot of digging and searching . . .
We brothers found this tedious and uncongenial work as we grew bigger and it became part of our job to bring in the water.'[1] They suggested
changes, 'but when we put it to the older people they would have nothing of it, thinking it would cause the stream to fail during the winter
freeze or disappear underground, and then we would lose the source entirely.' The brothers saw no logic in these objections to their 'water source
improvement idea', as Halldór put it, and one day when their father went
off for a visit to another farm they took matters into their own hands. But
when their father arrived back before expected and found them in the
middle of the work he ordered them to fill in the channel they had cut:

> So time went by, but we were not happy to leave things as they
> stood, as we were convinced that this would be a real improvement, even if it was going to be hard to get it accepted. We put
> our heads together and talked the problem over in secret, and
> eventually came to the conclusion that we might use some night
> in spring to finish off the work while everyone was asleep. I was
> put to stay awake until the people sleeping, because I found it
> easy to stay awake at night, and then wake the others. This went
> fine, and we all got dressed very quietly and set to work. We
> uncovered everything that had been dug before, completed the
> channel and let the water in. We were well satisfied. The water
> supplies were now 2/3 closer to the farm than before. We were
> pleased to get praise for the work from most people, or at least
> silence from others. To tell the truth, we expected to get told
> off. In the autumn we lined the pool with stones and put in a
> spout you could put a bucket under – previously you had had
> to scoop the water up – and built a roof over it. It made quite a
> difference; now you never needed to shovel snow away from
> the stream, or go digging after it, and the stream did not fail in
> the hardest part of winter. The water supply has been there
> ever since.

Halldór does not say how old the brothers were when this took
place, but it seems to have been during their teenage years. The incident
demonstrates the difference between the old time and the new. The
brothers were full of a hunger to take on new ideas and projects, and
this spirit characterized everything they did throughout their lives.
They had drunk in this way of thinking with their mother's milk, so to
speak, since they started reading newspapers and journals while still very
young, and there encountered the works of the poets and the arguments of the educated urging progress.

The wide-ranging cultural and educational aspirations of Halldór, Níels and their fellows proves beyond all question the extent of the popular desire for progress. The extraordinarily keen literary and cultural life in the communes of Strandasýsla is particularly notable in light of how little there was in the way of other social activity there at the time. Things remained largely unchanged through the first decade of the twentieth century. All such activity was of course hampered by lack of facilities. It was not until 1897 that the school house at Heydalsá was taken into use, built by one of the local farmers on his own account and with his own money and later sold to the commune on generous terms.

Throughout their formative years Halldór and Níels constantly sought out the company of other people with similar interests to their own. They borrowed material for copying and lent others their own copies. They were regular members of the local reading society, borrowing books from there and from others in the neighbourhood, or buying those they felt to be of special interest. Their book collection suggests that Halldór and Níels were voracious readers of just about anything they could lay their hands on. To a certain extent the varied reading material they managed to acquire laid the basis for Halldór and Níels's entire outlook on the world and their life's work. Libraries were their schools. It was there that they went in search of answers to the call of the poets and the advocates of independence, for the working people of Iceland to find ways to improve the conditions of the land and its people. There is no mistaking the optimistic spirit that inspired these informal cultural activities and aspirations; wherever one looks in the early parts of their lives one is faced with a keen and abiding desire for knowledge and learning. Halldór and Níels were part of the group of nineteenth-century Icelanders who felt they could foresee a time when they might, despite all the impediments, improve conditions for themselves and their country and look to the future with optimism.

The spirit of progress

We may well ask ourselves how it was that these brothers, Halldór and Níels Jónsson, never lost their faith in this idea of progress. What was it that actually drove them forward? Is it really conceivable that the words of the poets were so potent that they not only ignited a spark in men like Halldór and Níels but were able to keep it burning though all the shocks and disappointments that life held for people at this time? This question is particularly apposite in the light of the external conditions under which the brothers and many of their contemporaries lived. It is easy to think of countless occasions during their lives when the rallying call of the poets and the arguments of the educated elite for a better society might have faded and eventually died out in the everyday struggle to stay alive. The lack of schooling on its own should have been enough to kill off all their enthusiasm. It is as though something special must have been present that enabled this motivation to survive and continue to resonate through the brothers' formative years. We need to cast the net wide if we are to come to any satisfactory answer to what lay behind this unquenchable interest in learning and education.

Earlier in this book I suggested that the desire for education among children can partly be put down to the various hardships they had to put up with in their daily lives. These hardships led them into reading as a kind of refuge from the anxieties and tribulations of everyday life – in the harsh and often unforgiving world of nineteenth-century Iceland, where leisure was brief and rare, the imaginary world of literature provided a place into which children could escape. A world like that of the ancient sagas not only provided children with respite from the vicissitudes of their actual existence, but, equally importantly, the values and world-views of the saga characters became for them a guiding light on their path from cradle to grave. Children learned to face up to life with the fortitude that characterized many of the heroes of the sagas. What made this world so credible was precisely the fact that the events described in the sagas were set in the very same environment as people knew from their own experience. The literature filled a gap in people's emotional lives and so provided not only an outlet for their emotions but a pattern for guiding their decisions and reactions to events.

Halldór and Níels's attitudes become more comprehensible in the light of what was said in chapter Six about death and its influence on people's thinking. There we noted the self-restraint and self-control that people felt forced to adopt in the face of personal grief. This element of self-discipline comes out in many ways in the brothers' actions and behaviour, as in the following account from Halldór's autobiography, where he talks about his partiality for coffee and alcohol:

The year before I moved to Fell I stopped drinking coffee at home but could not bring myself to refuse it in places where I was a stranger. But at Fell I made a decision to give it up entirely, wherever I was; there they made coffee out of all kinds of rubbish, such as rye coffee and the like. I was incredibly fond of *brennivín* [Icelandic schnapps] before the time I was confirmed, it almost brought tears of longing to my eyes if it was there but I could not have any. One evening I had a couple of tots and got fairly tipsy, and I felt so extraordinarily easy wandering around with the sheep that evening, it felt amazingly good. When I was confirmed I took it upon myself to stop drinking, and I have kept to this up until now, spring 1905. Coffee I did not touch for 13 years.

The diaries give an insight into the lives of the brothers in their formative years (between the ages of fourteen and 30) as they were preparing to launch themselves into life. When we try to account for their enormous interest in reading and their ambitious writing projects, the most obvious place to start looking is in the troubles they went through in their childhood years with the loss of their mother and brothers. We can imagine that their responses to these events laid the foundations for their great interest in learning and culture, as with many other young people of the time. When we first meet the brothers in their diaries, half grown up, this affinity for literature takes on a rather different significance. By then they would have had far more diverse connections with different elements of society than we suppose they had as children, and thus far greater possibilities for emotional outlets through their reading of cultural and political material. There thus seem to be two types of motivation for this interest in literature and education: on the one hand, directed towards national issues, and on the other literary and aesthetic.

Anticipatory grief and a better future

We can suppose that the reading material the brothers had access to had a profound influence on their emotional lives, helping to shape their characters during their formative years and creating a foundation upon which they were later able to build. But as they reached maturity there was a change in how they used their literacy. This comes out when we examine their emotional reactions to love and grief.

From a reading of Halldór's diaries it becomes clear that the very fact of keeping the diary – recording and ordering his life, so to speak – provided him with a form of outlet for his emotions. The diary also allows us an insight into other areas of his life and thinking, for example when he discusses the interrelatedness of people, animals and nature. How Halldór talks about these things gives us a better idea of how he thought about death and how it impinged on his consciousness. The way in which nineteenth-century men like Halldór understood life was inextricably bound up with the interplay of these three main elements of rural society. When accidents, misfortunes or disease struck, mankind had no choice but to yield to the vagaries of nature. The animals, many of them linked to man by bonds of fealty, were killed in autumn. Nature both gave and took without any observable pattern or rule. Men like Halldór were clearly keenly aware of this cycle of life and death, and that there was little they could do about it. They had encountered it in their childhoods and adapted their thoughts and ways of living to this reality. They were intimately familiar with deep sorrow at the loss of friends and relatives, as we see graphically in the reactions of Halldór's wife Elín to the death of her son, described in chapter Six. But, out of necessity, people contained their grief as much as they could. Anything else was impossible. The round of work, linked strictly to the seasons, demanded that people got on with things without fuss or bother if the lives of those who remained were not to suffer irrevocable damage.

As we saw in chapter Six, a man like Halldór had to be constantly prepared to come to terms with the deaths of those who were nearest and dearest to him. The method he adopted was to direct his thoughts not to the particular instance of death but to the whole idea of death. There was really no other option, since death and the grief that accompanied it were such tangible and ever-present parts of his daily experience. Halldór's method was thus to be constantly prepared for grief. Grief theories, especially those that focus on *anticipatory grief*, maintain that individuals who have considerable time to prepare for loss base their strategy for dealing with death on *hope*, in particular, the hope that the dying person will recover. In Halldór's case – the case of someone for whom grief was a constant presence – we can perhaps conjecture that this hope, which is usually directed towards an individual, might also be directed outwards and more widely. Anticipatory grief was, as it were, projected onto society as a whole, and its outlet – through the hope of recovery – becomes a faith in *progress*, a hope for the improvement of society as a means for making life more tolerable. For Halldór, and perhaps for many other Icelanders, reaching forward to a better future became a tactic for channelling and conquering grief. This idea of progress became a part of the brothers' identity and an inescapable prerequisite of their search for a better life. One clear reason why this route lay open was that the way had already been prepared by the exhortations of the poets and men of letters: the way out of life's problems lay in hope for a brighter future, and the key to this was education. Education, by providing a foundation for making a better future a reality, made it possible for the brothers to face up to grief in the way that they did.

This leads us to theorize over the mental resources available to nineteenth-century Icelanders. The emotions engendered by both love and grief were circumscribed within definite limits. These limits came about as a result of particular external circumstances in people's lives. From this we may conjecture that nineteenth-century Icelandic society lacked any strong tradition of inward and introspective expression like that which characterizes love. As a result of the siege mentality that built up in response to the ever-present imminence of grief, people simply did not know how to channel their emotions inwards. Emotions were therefore directed outwards, manifesting themselves in works and actions designed to move the country forwards.

The restrictions on emotional expression meant that people sought clearly defined outlets for both their love and grief. Broadly speaking, grief was channelled in one of two ways. On the one hand there was religion, with its teaching that God received all true Christians, young and old, and that those that died were happy to be now in a better place. On the other, grief was channelled into literature and learning through which people looked for ways to come to terms with the uncertainties of human existence. For men like Halldór and Níels, this connection with learning and education fed into the desire for progress. This desire manifested itself extremely powerfully in their behaviour and outlook and, as noted earlier, ran through much of society at the time. As a result, for the most part people bore their grief in silence. To give an example, when Halldór himself died his death came as a terrible blow to his family, and in fact to the whole community. And yet, according to the sources, the entire family's reactions were along the same lines –total silence about Halldór and his death. His children, who were all young at the time, heard copious testimonials to him and his qualities from people from outside the family who had known him. But the memory of Halldór's death was so painful to those who had been closest to him that his name was never mentioned. This is very much in the same spirit as Halldór's own reactions to the sorrows that poured down on him at regular intervals, as described in his diary.

Optimism, doubts and limitations

We can perhaps adduce strong evidence in favour of the theory presented above regarding personal expression and the shaping of the individual in eighteenth-, nineteenth- and early twentieth-century Iceland from the way that these people looked at the future. They *were going to* move forward, come what may. This strength of purpose on their part reveals itself most clearly in how they conceived their aims in life.

None of the brothers was prepared to let things remain as they were – 'stasis', as Níels called it. Despite as good as no outside support their faith in the future remained undimmed. We see this, for example, in the descriptions they give of themselves at the time when they were just about to emerge into independent adulthood. But it was not only external circumstances that limited their options in life; there were also personal factors that needed to be overcome. Within the brothers' personalities there was a tension between boldness and enterprise on the one hand, and shyness and insecurity on the other. This manifested

itself in various ways – though, when it came to it, it was generally the
insecurity that came out on top. For instance, in the chapter of his autobiography where he speaks about learning and education, Halldór is
highly self-deprecating about his achievements in this area:

> Though I put in a chapter here under this heading, it will be
> neither long nor rich in content, for I have little to say on the
> subject. It is possible that I could have been a fit receptacle for
> general education like most people, but my main fault is and
> has long been a timidity and lack of self-confidence. I *wanted*
> to learn in my childhood years, but I found the way hard, or
> thought it would be so, because of poverty, regretted leaving
> my father and brothers while there was a chance. So, when I
> started to educate myself, I felt I was too old to be setting out
> on study, and did not keep at it as diligently as I should. And
> so nothing ever came of it.

Here we find Halldór laying himself bare and trying to come to terms
with his own personality, how he has turned out and taken shape as a
person. He blames himself and his lack of determination for his failure
to achieve the fulfilment that formal education might have given him.
We can surmise that in reality the more significant factors were his
poverty and a general lack of support. Education was a major matter
that required the backing or economic security that most ordinary
farmers lacked. The passage casts a new light on the connection between
the formal educational policy in the country and the real lives of people
like Halldór and Níels. Such people had precious little chance of acquiring a formal education. Yet despite this obvious deficiency in the system,
the brothers at Tindur continued to allow themselves to dream.

This optimism had its dark, almost tragic, side. The rallying call of
the poets and other progressively minded people faded into insignifi-
cance in the face of the country's poverty and lack of facilities. Guidance
towards the desired goal was as good as non-existent. The schools were
simply not there. The Education Act of 1880 fell well short of meeting
needs and there were precious few opportunities for young men like
Halldór and Níels, let alone women, to realize their educational ambitions. For the vast majority of working-class people confirmation
marked the end of formal education. The constant discussions on education and progressive reform were, when all was said and done, little
more than empty words. The wealthier parts of society – better-off
farmers, government officials and merchants – balked at the cost that
went with increased education and schooling. The conservatism of the
authorities, evident for instance in their extreme caution in matters of

One of the consequences of life in the twentieth century was that all Icelanders came to be cast in the same mould: everybody went to school, read similar books and newspapers, listened to the same radio station (the only one in the country). As a result, society became ever more standardized and homogeneous. But long after the middle of the century echoes of the old times could still be felt in Reykjavík wherever eccentrics and tramps young and old gathered together. Many of these people did some kind of work for the city authorities or had links with people or companies that held a protecting hand over them. When they disappeared from the scene, something valuable was lost with them. In former times these people had fulfilled a valuable role in Icelandic society, representing a life where people could come and go as they pleased and acting as some kind of model for those who yearned for the freedom of the open road but were inextricably bound into a system that offered little flexibility.

public expenditure, served to hobble those who tried to do something to change the conditions of their daily lives. In these hidebound attitudes lies the tragic element within nineteenth-century society, something that cut far deeper than appears at first sight. Nearly all suggestions put forward for change to the structure of society were stifled, or tossed back and forth for years on end, without achieving anything. The debate on a national educational system is a clear case in point. Those who held the reins of power were only too ready to cavil at any new ideas that were suggested, and preferred to let them fade into oblivion.

The matters discussed here touch at the very heart of Icelandic popular culture and its conditions for growth and development. The presentation has of course focused on the lives of only a tiny number of individuals, viewed in as much detail as possible, in line with the general approach in this book. But there is every reason to believe that the brothers Halldór and Níels Jónsson were not alone. They maintained strong links with others who shared similar interests and tried to shape their lives under equal circumstances. It is thus the story of many nineteenth-century men and women who, in spite of external difficulties, forged for themselves effective ways of facing up to the problems that the world set before them with the help of their cultural background, rooted in the medieval period.

10

The Middle Ages and Beyond:
A Cultural Foundation

Culture and independence

For Iceland, the nineteenth century was the time of political awakening. As in many other parts of Europe, the growing middle class – specifically, middle-class men of a sufficient social standing – started to assert itself and demand greater political rights. The campaign for Icelandic independence was conducted mainly from the country's capital, Copenhagen, where a group of educated Icelanders coalesced around the figure of Jón Sigurðsson and began publishing writings urging their compatriots to throw off the colonial yoke. They justified their claims by arguing that Iceland had never formally submitted to the Danish Crown when the country had followed Norway into union with Denmark in the fourteenth century. From the outset, therefore, the country's medieval legal tradition and ancient literature formed a central part of the demand for independence.

It was against this background that the classical view of Icelandic cultural history took shape, a view that was of immense importance in moulding the Icelanders' sense of national identity and that was to play a major part in the political developments of the nineteenth and twentieth centuries. The independence movement built on the idea that the Icelandic people needed to break free of Danish hegemony in order to be able to grow and mature like healthy individuals. The country had undergone one hardship after another under foreign rule, while in its days of independence its history had been one of splendour and success. The independence campaigners deliberately fostered the myth of 'the saga nation', a myth that remains at the heart of Icelanders' image of themselves and their country. At the centre of this myth lies the concept of 'the Golden Age' of medieval Icelandic literature, an age manifested tangibly in the manuscripts preserved from the period.

Icelandic cultural history is rooted in this manuscript culture. Handed down from medieval times, the extraordinarily varied corpus

Large numbers of calves or lambs were needed to provide the vellum for a single manuscript. Book-making in the Middle Ages was therefore the prerogative of the rich. The processes for turning the skins into books were complicated, time-consuming and expensive. After the skin had been treated and prepared, the scribe took over and marked each page with a frame for the text. Pens were made of feathers and the ink was home-prepared from plants, chiefly bearberry (Arctostaphylos uva) and other naturally occurred colouring materials. The pages were sewn together and the covers put on, usually of wooden boards or leather. The manuscripts in the photograph are from the thirteenth and fourteenth centuries and come from the Árni Magnússon Institute for Icelandic Studies at the University of Iceland.

of manuscript material remained alive and current well into the twentieth century in the endless copies made by ordinary Icelandic peasants on impoverished Icelandic farms. Beyond all doubt, this literary and manuscript culture has completely overshadowed all other areas of culture in public regard – so much so that to modern commentators it often seems as if writing and the copying of ancient texts was the only kind of cultural activity practised in Iceland from medieval times down to the present age. Whatever the case, it is remarkable testimony to almost a thousand years of literary activity among the ordinary people of a poor and isolated land.

The cultural and literary history of Iceland is conventionally broken down into periods. The opening period, often called the Golden Age of Icelandic literature, covers the years from about 1100 to about 1400, but above all the thirteenth century, from which most of the main texts are thought to originate. At the core of this period lie the 'sagas of Icelanders', also known as the Icelandic family sagas. But this was a time of extraordinary literary activity that produced works of many different types. There are biographies of Norwegian kings and more strictly historiographic writings such as *Íslendingabók* (The Book of the Icelanders) and *Landnámabók* (The Book of Settlements). There are more fanciful sagas and romances recording ancient legends and courtly adventures. There are sagas dealing with contemporary events, and learned works in areas like grammar and astronomy. Finally there is the codification of poetry preserved from preliterate times. This poetry, ancient already at the time when it was written down, is of two types. Firstly there is skaldic verse – formal, occasional verse, usually by named poets – largely found embedded in the sagas. Much consists of praise poetry addressed to Scandinavian monarchs and used by the saga writers as historical source material. Second, there are the so-called Edda poems (the Poetic Edda), known to us almost entirely from a single late thirteenth-century manuscript, the *Codex Regius*. These are traditional poems either dealing with the Norse gods and mythology or reworking themes from the common Germanic heroic heritage.

The subsequent period, from the fifteenth century up to the end of the eighteenth, has been called 'the Dark Age' of Iceland. This darkness covers both the state of the country under foreign rule and the literature, which is sparser and generally considered inferior in value and quality to that of the earlier age, lacking any of its fire and originality. Much is of a fairly conventional religious nature. In the earlier period we have the impression of a literature created by or for chieftains; now the interests and attitudes seem to come more from the ordinary peasantry. Significant genres include verse, particularly *rímur* (see chapter Five), and historical material and annals. One interesting innovation of this period is the appearance of personal sources such as the first autobiographies and travel books.

Finally there is the modern age. Early in the nineteenth century the 'official' culture of the educated elite began to come under the influence of cultural currents from Europe, notably Romanticism. From this point the country starts to emerge from its isolation and move gradually towards the European mainstream. However, the conventional view of the nineteenth century as a nationalist-romantic period of revival and rebirth in Icelandic culture needs a degree of modification. This was also the time when the common people of Iceland started to make their voices heard in far greater numbers than before. To older forms such as *rímur*, which continued to be written and recited, we now find added new modes of expression. This emergence of popular culture in the late nineteenth and early twentieth centuries forms the background of the next chapter, in which I consider the importance of these peasant writers and their influence on the society in which they lived.

For the remainder of this chapter, though, I intend to look back to the material from the earlier two periods and examine its influence on the later development of Icelandic culture.[1]

The Golden Age

From its first introduction into Iceland, writing was used for both secular and religious purposes – though by medieval standards it is astonishing how much there is of the former and how little of the latter. Going back to the twelfth century, the anonymous author of *Fyrsta málfræðiritgerðin* (First Grammatical Treatise, ? 1175) lists the kinds of writing that already existed in Icelandic in his time: laws, genealogy, 'þýðingar helgar' (either religious material in translation or biblical exegesis) and historical lore. Towards the end of the century, then in a flood in the course of the thirteenth, there was an outburst of writing of all kinds, in particular the various types of semi-historical and semi-literary narratives known as sagas.

Probably the earliest type of saga to develop were the kings' sagas, biographies of the rulers of Scandinavia, particularly Norwegians of the Viking Age. As well as recounting the lives of great noblemen, the kings' sagas act as histories or pseudo-histories of the countries concerned. The genre reaches its climax in Snorri Sturluson's *Heimskringla* ('Orb of the World'), probably written in the 1230s, a series of sagas of the kings of Norway extending from the mythical and legendary prehistory up until the twelfth century. After about 1200 the Icelanders started to apply the techniques they had developed in the kings' sagas to various other types of narrative, most famously the sagas of Icelanders (family sagas), but also legendary sagas, chivalric sagas, lives of churchmen, sagas of contemporary events and others. Apart from some of the kings' sagas, just about all are anonymous.

The 'sagas of Icelanders' comprise about forty texts, the longest being of similar length to a modern medium-sized novel.[2] Most of the best appear to have been written during the thirteenth century but are clearly based on older material, both written and oral. They deal with Icelanders who lived in 'the Saga Age' – the generations after the settlements, up to around 1030 – and in particular their feuds and disputes. There is clearly some kind of factual basis behind the events recorded. Equally clearly, the sagas are not to be treated as purely historical records; the people and events are clothed in an epic grandeur whose roots lie in the common Germanic heroic heritage. There are certain similarities in construction to chronicles, but the sagas are tightly and consciously plotted so as to come to aesthetically satisfying conclusions.

While most of the events described take place in Iceland, Icelanders of the Saga Age travelled widely and there are many scenes set in other parts of the Viking world – Norway, the British Isles, Greenland and even farther afield. There are strong elements of popular superstition (ghosts, portents and so on) and in places we find themes and motifs that can be traced back to religious or mythological material, both Christian and pre-Christian. In general, though, the world of the sagas is firmly secular: the impression is very much of real people in real settings, heightened by powerful moral considerations such as the sense of honour, and social themes, such as the struggle for resources in a harsh environment. Another element in this realism is the central part played by the political and legal background of the Saga Age: a loose federation of competing local chieftaincies bound together by a single law. This political structure, called the *þjóðveldi* or, in English, the Icelandic Commonwealth, is discussed later in this chapter.

The sagas are noted particularly for their style, their narrative technique and their characters. Stylistically, the prose gives an impression of naive simplicity, using concrete vocabulary and short, compact sentences. This, however, is a very calculated simplicity, the mark of a high literary sophistication on the part of the authors. Events are always presented externally, with an appearance of detachment and objectivity, and are reported but never explained. The author 'pretends' to be impartial between the protagonists and the characters are allowed to reveal themselves only indirectly, through what they do or say. Exceptional in this respect are the verses with which many of the sagas are studded and which purport to come from the characters concerned; here we are sometimes allowed direct insights into personal feelings and attitudes.

Much of the appeal of the sagas lies in their characters; people are depicted with a heightened naturalism, giving a strong impression of reality, only more special and glorious. Characters are generally introduced formally and formulaically into the narrative. The introduction starts with a detailed genealogy, family connections being central to the interests of the saga writers. These genealogies also add to the impression of verisimilitude. Then follows a personal description that gives clues to the character and future fate of the person concerned. The following is Skarpheðinn Njálsson, the son of Njál, the central character of *Njál's saga*:

> Skarpheðinn was the eldest, a big and strong man and a good fighter. He swam like a seal and was swift of foot, quick to make up his mind and sure of himself; he spoke to the point and was quick to do so, though mostly he restrained himself. His hair was reddish-brown and curled and he had fine eyes; his face was pale and sharp-featured with a bent nose and a

broad row of upper teeth. His mouth was ugly, and yet he was every bit a warrior.[3]

The mental world of the sagas is characterized by a strong sense of fate. Death and destiny are pre-ordained, and the characters go to meet whatever life throws at them with equanimity and unflinching stoicism. This ethical outlook had an incalculable influence on Icelanders' attitudes to life over the succeeding centuries. Another recurrent preoccupation is the contrast between the proper behaviour of the calm, self-possessed and rounded man of moderation and the arrogance of the troublemaker. The former is plain-spoken and trustworthy, slow to take offence, and often drawn into conflict against his will; the latter is generally shifty, impulsive, violent, and indifferent to the consequences of his actions. The qualities that are valued highest are honour, intelligence and courage in the face of adversity, presented either through the actions of the characters or, at times, through their absence. A common theme is the conflict between public duty and personal inclination – between, say, honour and friendship: the epic dilemma in a particularly pure form. At their best – in works such as *Laxdæla saga*, *The Saga of Gísli* (*Gísla saga*), *The Saga of the Confederates* (*Bandamanna saga*) and, most famous of all, *Njál's saga* – the sagas are writings of extraordinary literary skill, full of incident and with a rich array of characters, giving a vivid insight into a world very different from other European societies of the time.

A second type of saga, though less highly regarded today, had an almost equal influence on Icelandic thought over the subsequent centuries, the so-called *fornaldarsögur* (legendary sagas, sagas of ancient times).[4] These purport to relate events from pre-Icelandic Viking Europe and are marked by a stronger sense of the supernatural and a greater emphasis on pure heroics. Another genre that enjoyed considerable popularity with ordinary Icelanders over the centuries – though less so with modern literary critics – were the *riddarasögur* (courtly or chivalric sagas). These, originally at least, were based largely on material from France and are firmly within the western European courtly tradition. They tell of knights in armour, jousts and tournaments – all things that were entirely foreign to the people of Iceland. There is often a sense of mystery to them and love forms one of the principal interests. The foreign models led to native imitations, and here these sagas, sometimes known as *lygisögur* ('lying sagas'), come close in their themes and attitudes to the legendary sagas. All these types of 'adventure saga' appear to have been treated as recreational reading whereas, to the ordinary people of Iceland, the sagas of Icelanders were their country's history. But in reality it is impossible to draw absolutely sharp lines between the different types of sagas; sagas of Icelanders merge into legendary sagas, courtly sagas incorporate elements from kings' sagas, and so on.

At the other end of the scale are writings that we can unhesitatingly call historical. Many are fairly early. Other than the laws, the first work we know of as having been written in Icelandic is *Íslendingabók* (The Book of Icelanders), by Ari fróði ('the Learned') Þorgílsson, in about 1130. This is a short, sober account of the history of Iceland from the settlements up to the time of writing, intended to establish a chronology for events in the country. It bears witness to a familiarity with foreign historiography, notably Bede, and in this sense can be placed within the 'learned' tradition of the twelfth century and seen as an attempt to establish links between Iceland and the broader world of European culture. In other respects it is remarkably modern in its historical approach: for example, Ari cites and discusses the reliability of his sources and admits ignorance of and differences of opinion on certain points.

Shortly after this, it seems, people started recording genealogical material. Genealogy was of crucial importance to Icelandic society; who people were related to determined whom they could marry, whom they had obligations of support and vengeance to, and what claims they had over landholdings. Over time these genealogies coalesced into the various versions of *Landnámabók* (The Book of Settlements) put together in the thirteenth and fourteenth centuries. The Book of Settlements records several hundred of the leading settlers, their origins, land claims and descendants, often with short passages of information about their lives and disputes.

Also among historical works we can perhaps place the sagas that treat events in Iceland after the Saga Age. At the centre of this group is a collection of 'contemporary sagas' known as *Sturlunga saga*, which describe the unrest and political manoeuvrings of the thirteenth century. Some of these sagas were probably written only very shortly after the events they describe; in cases the author may actually have been a participant in the events. Despite this unusual closeness between author and text, the contemporary sagas are written with the same narrative detachment as we find in authentic saga style.

It is clear from the sheer volume of work produced that literary culture, both oral and written, played a large part in the lives of early medieval Icelanders. This activity was only possible because the economy of Iceland, then as in later centuries based largely on sheep rearing, provided an almost unlimited supply of vellum for writing purposes. It needs to be borne in mind that Iceland was at the time a comparatively simple and homogeneous society, and that this is long before the age of print. What is important is that this literature was kept alive and in constant use long after it was first written down. Stories were altered and adapted and new characters added to suit changing tastes and conditions. They were read aloud and retold at gatherings for entertainment and copied repeatedly. The saga literature thus remained a living heritage that formed an intimate part of people's daily lives until well into the twentieth century.

The Icelandic Commonwealth

The question then arises, why was it that a small and isolated community put so much of its time and effort into composing works celebrating its immediate past? To attempt to answer this question, we need to look briefly at the society that produced the sagas, essentially the thirteenth century, and the society the writers were writing about, the Saga Age, and their image of it.

Around 930, towards the end of the settlement period, the chieftains of Iceland agreed a system of government and a body of law for the new country. This constitution lasted with only minor modification until 1262/4, when Iceland submitted to the authority of the king of Norway. The system of government was known as the *þjóðveldi*, customarily translated as the Icelandic Commonwealth, though perhaps 'Free State' would give a more accurate idea of the kind of social structure involved.[5] Uniquely in Europe at the time, there was no king – a fact reflected in the demands of the independence movement in the nineteenth century that never envisaged Iceland as anything other than a republic. Power lay in the hands of an oligarchy of chieftains, none of whom was supposed to have greater influence than any other. These chieftains were called *goðar* (sing. *goði*) or *goðorðsmenn*, and their position of authority was known as their *goðorð*.

Each free farmer had to ally himself to a *goði*, though he was free to choose which one. It is estimated that for most of the Commonwealth period there were perhaps around 5,000 free farmers in Iceland. Slavery seems to have died out early, but women, children, servants and workers were under the control of the heads of their household, whether chieftain or free farmer. There are of course no reliable figures for population in the early period, though the Book of Settlements provides an invaluable starting-point for making estimates. Different historians have suggested figures ranging between 20,000 and 35,000 for the end of the settlement period, rising to perhaps 60,000 in the thirteenth century.

The word *goði* presumably originally meant 'priest' or that the holder's power was conferred by the gods. We can assume that in pre-Christian times these men were both secular and religious leaders, for instance through their maintenance of temples and local shrines. In a sense, this dual role survived the conversion, since many chieftains took holy orders and continued to treat church benefices as their personal property; that is, there was far less separation between the secular and ecclesiastical authorities in Iceland than elsewhere in Catholic Europe – the chieftain and the priest were often one and the same man.

The constitution of the Commonwealth was specifically intended to distribute power and limit the ambitions of individual chieftains or families. The *goðar* of course came from the most powerful families in the country, though this was to some extent fluid, with new families coming to prominence able to buy themselves *goðorð* or obtain them in other ways. In return for their support, free farmers could expect their *goði* to protect them and their interests and to support them in matters of law and in disputes. Under the original constitution there seem to have been 36 *goðorð*. This later rose to 48. After the conversion the two bishops of Iceland were accorded the status of *goðar*.

Legislative and judicial power was exercised through various types of assemblies (*þing*). The spring assembly (*vorþing*) was a local assembly, incorporating a court presided over by the local *goðar*. The national or 'General Assembly' (*Alþingi*, Althing) was held in summer at Þingvellir, beside the largest lake in the country, about 30 km inland from Reykjavík. All the *goðar*, from all parts of Iceland, and a proportion of their client farmers (*þingmenn*) were expected to attend. The Alþingi acted as both the legislature, with laws decided by the *goðar* sitting in session with their advisors, and the highest court in the land. The laws of the Commonwealth were written down in the twelfth century and exist in copies of a lawbook called *Grágás* dating from the thirteenth. Up to this time the laws were memorized and recited regularly in the open air at the Law Rock (*Lögberg*) at the Alþingi by the only official of the Commonwealth, the lawspeaker (*lögsögumaður*), whose job it was to adjudicate in matters of legal dispute. The sagas make repeated references to the law and how it operated, and it is clear that it was a very powerful and active force within society – indeed, the only formal institution that held society together.

During the twelfth and particularly thirteenth centuries, the *goðorð*, and thus power, became increasingly concentrated in the hands of a few influential clans. These clans were able to manipulate the law and the courts to their own advantage, at first locally, eventually nationally, and the entire constitution came under increasing strain. The country began to break down into warring fiefdoms and the rights of individual free farmers became increasingly subordinated to the interests of their chieftains. For long periods of the thirteenth century the country descended into anarchy; this period, known as the Sturlung Age after one of the leading families of the time, is synonymous in Icelandic tradition with bloodshed and contempt for the law. Eventually, in 1262/4, in an attempt to restore stability, the Icelandic people invited the king of Norway to take over the country. From this point until 1944, the Icelanders remained subjects of the kings of Norway or Denmark, and merely a minor factor in the politics of continental Scandinavia.

There can be little doubt that the constitutional structure and history of the Icelandic Commonwealth were an important element in the conditions that gave rise to and made possible the creation of a literature like the sagas of Icelanders. One of the reasons for their composition – particularly relevant to conditions in the thirteenth century – seems to have been to provide examples of how disputes could be reconciled. Another was to promote the status of the leading families by recording incidents of significance to particular power interests to ensure their domination in society. Thus the sagas are usually highly localized; even if many range farther afield, they tend to concentrate on events in one particular part of the country, in accurate and circumstantial geographical detail. The power struggles of the thirteenth century thus acted as a motive for their production; the sagas had a function in the disputes between the competing clans at the time when they were written.[6]

However tempting it may be to view Iceland as a remote island far away in the North Atlantic whose people had little contact with the world outside, this would be a false assumption. From the earliest days up until the end of the Commonwealth, many Icelanders travelled abroad, spending time at the royal courts of northern Europe and at centres of culture and learning, bringing back with them a wide range of knowledge and experience. These journeys influenced both the literature produced in the country and the form of Icelandic society. As an obvious example, Christianity was accepted by largely peaceful agreement at the Alþingi in the year 1000, traditionally as a result of pressure from the king of Norway, but in all probability because this made it easier for Icelanders to conduct trade and commerce with the Christian countries of northern Europe.

Contacts with the world outside Iceland also provide another reason for the flowering of Icelandic literature. It was of course the Church that taught the Icelanders to write. But, more importantly here, Iceland seems to have long been regarded as a storehouse of culture and traditional lore in northern Europe. For example, Icelanders seem to have more or less monopolized the role of court poets to the kings of the North after about 1000. This trade in literature continued into the era of writing: Icelanders produced manuscripts for export and were commissioned to write biographies of kings and chieftains abroad. They thus fulfilled an important function at many of the northern courts and seem to have been rewarded by the institutions of power in these countries with considerable advancement and respect.

It is often claimed that many of the sagas were written by monks. Evidence for this is scanty, and in many ways it is an irrelevance. Unlike elsewhere in Europe, many of the chieftains of Iceland took holy orders, in part to control Church lands and benefices. It is quite clear that the sagas are the work of educated people and probably of people from chieftainly families, and that in many cases the sagas reflect their interests and outlook. This close link between the chieftainly class and the ecclesiastical authorities was undoubtedly another important factor in the development of the saga form.

While we of course cannot rely on the thirteenth-century sagas to provide an undistorted picture of tenth- and eleventh-century Icelandic society, there is no doubt that most of the sagas are based on real events, polished into coherent narrative over the course of two or three hundred years. Popular tradition has always been to take the sagas at face value, as reliable records of past events. This is, in fact, the way the sagas are still popularly regarded in Iceland; to Icelanders through the centuries, characters like Njáll and Egill Skallagrímsson have been very much real people. Academic views on this, and on the oral background to the sagas, have shifted back and forth. After years of emphasizing the literary and written elements of the sagas, there is currently a move back towards a modified form of oral theory. While it is quite easy to point to things in the sagas that are wrong, there are also striking cases of their evidence being confirmed by later research, for example in the case of the exploration of parts of the coast of North America. And if this is true of 'far away' events, it is likely to be all the more true of events at home in Iceland, where there were more people to preserve and pass on the knowledge.

What we seem to have is a development in which the 'semi-historical' attitudes of kings' sagas broadened, producing a spectrum of works ranging from the intentionally historic to almost pure fiction. The sagas of Icelanders lie somewhere in the middle, imaginative reconstructions of a past that still had immediate relevance to the people that wrote them.

The Reformation and the printing press

Iceland became Christian in the year 1000. The conversion seems to have gone through extraordinarily smoothly and peacefully for a country that had no central authority to enforce the change. Late in the thirteenth century Iceland was annexed within the Kingdom of Norway. The Norwegian royal court and entire administrative system were seriously weakened during the Black Death and in 1383 Iceland followed Norway into royal union with Denmark. In 1397 all three continental

Scandinavian countries, Denmark, Norway and Sweden, were joined into a single monarchy as the Kalmar Union, with Iceland as only a very minor player. When the Union broke up in 1523, Iceland reverted to Denmark. Iceland's association with the Danish Crown, begun in 1383, lasted until the establishment of the Republic of Iceland in 1944.

In the middle years of the sixteenth century, under pressure from the Danish Crown, Iceland abandoned Catholicism and went over to was what called 'the new rite', Lutheranism. The Reformation greatly increased the economic, religious and cultural power of the Danish king in Iceland. Within a few years the Crown had seized large amounts of Church property, making it by far the largest landowner in the country.

One crucial factor in the growth of Danish royal influence in Iceland was that the Church, now controlled by the king, had a monopoly on printing. Nearly all books printed in Iceland from the mid-sixteenth century until after the middle of the eighteenth were religious in content. However, at least books were being printed, and in Icelandic. Scholars have argued the importance of this from various points of view. For example, the Bible translation known as Guðbrandsbiblían, published in 1584 by Bishop Guðbrandur Þorláksson (b. 1541), is often cited as having been crucial to the survival and later development of the Icelandic language.

The first printing press had in fact been brought to Iceland, probably in 1530, by the last Catholic bishop, Jón Arason (executed 1550). After the Reformation this press was taken over by Bishop Guðbrandur. Guðbrandur embarked on a large-scale publishing programme intended to confirm the acceptance of the new Lutheran creed among clergy and laity alike. During his long episcopate from 1571 to 1627, Guðbrandur was responsible for the publication of more than a hundred titles, among them a new collection of hymns (*Ein ny psalma bok*, 1589) and a service hymn book or *graduale* (*Grallari*, 1594), both used widely as late as the nineteenth century both in church and at home at winter-evening gatherings. As well as promoting orthodoxy of faith, such publications were intended to replace what the new Church viewed as the ridiculous, violent, lewd and tasteless secular poetry that circulated among the general public. In this Bishop Guðbrandur's efforts met with only very limited success: traditional secular literature continued to be composed and copied for centuries to come without the aid of printing. Guðbrandur, though, was no fanatic: while the vast majority of his publications were religious in nature, he was also responsible for the first secular text printed in Iceland, in 1578, the lawbook *Jónsbók* that had superseded the laws of the Commonwealth (*Grágás*) on Iceland's loss of independence.[7] Over the preceding three centuries *Jónsbók* had been copied many times by hand and, interestingly, despite Guðbrandur's edition and two reprints in 1580 and 1620, continued to be copied by hand as late as the twentieth century.[8]

The introduction of printing did little to change Icelandic literary tastes and it is a gross exaggeration to claim, as some historians have, that it constituted a great turning point in Icelandic cultural history. Only 42 titles were published between 1534 and 1600, plus seven more in Icelandic or by Icelandic writers published abroad. It was not until the middle of the seventeenth century that any books appeared whose roots lay in the medieval manuscript tradition. However, by this time it was clear there was a large demand for such material. One of the first such works to appear in print was a version of *The Book of Settlements*, shortly before the end of the seventeenth century. However, it was still many years before the publication of sagas and secular literature was put on a regular footing. Of around 250 titles published in Iceland or abroad by Icelandic authors in the seventeenth century, only very few were secular in content. This heavy religious bias continued through most of the eighteenth century. However, around the middle of that century twelve of the shorter sagas were issued in two volumes, as well as two translated chapbooks containing material adapted from or similar to Daniel Defoe's *Robinson Crusoe*. The publication of sagas continued to be sporadic until quite late in the nineteenth century and the bulk of the Icelandic literary heritage remained unavailable in popular printed editions. Around 1890, seeing a potentially lucrative untapped market, the publisher and bookseller Sigurður Kristjánsson launched a series of sagas in affordable small-format editions. In many cases this was the first time these sagas had become generally available to a mass readership. The new editions proved enormously successful and some titles were issued with an initial print-run of 4,000. By the time Sigurður retired in 1929, the most popular had achieved sales of up to 10,000.

The same is true of much of the rest of the ancient manuscript heritage: many of these works did not become available in printed editions until the twentieth century. But by this time readers in Iceland had access to a wide range of secular material of other kinds. Starting in the late nineteenth century there was a concerted campaign, inspired by the principles of the Enlightenment and the nationalist movement, to improve conditions in the country and help it to move forward into the modern age. For this purpose, large amounts of practical and educational material of foreign origin were translated or adapted for publication in newspapers and journals, particularly in areas such as the natural sciences, the humanities, politics and economics.

Historians of Icelandic culture have tended to judge the post-Reformation period first and foremost on the basis of the printed material produced and have paid only scant heed to material published in other ways. In the opinion of most critics, the literature published in print after 1500 is of a far lesser stature and quality than the manuscript material passed down from the Golden Age. This is seen as reflecting the general degeneracy and degradation of the country under foreign domination. Recently, however, interest has started to be directed at the production and distribution of handwritten material through unofficial channels, quite separately from the ruling forces of society.[9] Icelandic scribal culture after the introduction of print manifests itself both in the reworking of the medieval literary heritage and in the production and circulation of original texts of poetry, history, law, natural history, geography and so on. This material had an enormous influence on how people after 1500 viewed and led their lives. We need to remember that this was not just a question of members of the rural peasantry copying up old material for their own and others' entertainment, but of their creating new material out of this material, and thereby also creating possibilities for making interesting links between their own times and the ancient past. New texts and new forms of poetry and prose reveal a literary culture far wider and more diverse than either the medieval canon or the surviving printed works might suggest.[10]

The vast majority of this post-medieval writing has never been published, either in scholarly or popular editions. On the other hand, the archives of Iceland are full to overflowing with unpublished manuscripts, created by ordinary working people, that constituted an integral part of Icelandic popular culture all the way down to the twentieth century.

The autobiographical impulse

One of the most notable features of the period after 1500 is a growing interest in factual and documentary material such as annals and personal sources. The details of this development lie beyond the scope of this book, but by way of illustration it is worth looking briefly at the remarkable growth of autobiographical writing, since this provided the foundation for the explosion of autobiographies in the late nineteenth and early twentieth centuries quoted extensively in this book.

The earliest writings of this type were travel books, usually the account of some adventurous voyage made by the author. In these accounts it is often difficult to distinguish between fact and fiction; at least, a lot of material in them strikes the reader as highly improbable. The first such travel books produced in Iceland date from the seventeenth century. Among the most remarkable is *Reisubók síra Ólafs Egilssonar* (The Travel Book of the Rev. Ólafur Egilsson). Ólafur (b. 1564) was kidnapped from Vestmannaeyjar (the Westman Islands) in the so-called Turkish Raid of 1627. On 16 July that year, out of the blue, a band of around 300 pirates from Algiers in North Africa landed on the islands off the south coast, indulged in three days of looting and pillaging, killed 36 and made off with 242 prisoners. About 200 of the islanders managed to hide and escape their clutches. The raiders were of course Moors rather than Turks, but Icelandic knowledge of the Islamic world was limited, and the Turks were at the time the most powerful Muslim power known to Western sources. The Rev. Ólafur was among those who were sold at the slave auction in Algiers but was eventually redeemed and returned to Iceland. His story recounts his captivity, the loss of all worldly comforts and pleasures, and his wanderings in unknown lands. Simultaneously it describes the author's struggle with himself and despair and how he managed to gain control over his life through the help and grace of God. The narrative is cast in the conventional form of a 'passion story' or the trials of a Christian saint, which tends to obscure the element of personal experience. But the material is both exciting and informative and was much to the taste of readers at the time.

Better known is *Reisubók Jóns Ólafssonar Indíafara* (The Travels of Jón Ólafsson, India-farer).[11] Jón was born in 1593 and served in the Danish royal navy. His book tells of his journeys through most of the world's oceans, reaching as far as the East Indies, and describes the many wonders he encountered on the way. His style is lively but rough and unpolished, the authentic voice of an Icelandic commoner. As Guðbrandur Jónsson, editor of the second edition of the *Travels* in 1946, notes in his introduction: 'One needs to treat Jón's exaggerations with some caution.' But he sees other qualities in the writing:

> The *Travels* show that Jón had a wonderfully percipient and enquiring mind and, equally strikingly, that he was endowed with a remarkable memory. The reader should never forget that Jón was fast approaching seventy when he wrote his *Travels*, and 35 years had then passed since the end of his travels. Despite this, he recalls most of the things he relates in such detail that errors or inconsistencies are rare, as is largely confirmed by comparison with other sources, such as the [Danish] account by Ove Gjeddes of his voyage to India in 1618.

Guðbrandur notes various sources to which Jón Ólafsson would have had access and shows that much of his account is based on sound geographical detail, despite the generally arbitrary and impressionistic nature of people's knowledge of distant lands at the time.

Other writers of autobiographical material from the same period include the Rev. Jón Steingrímsson (b. 1728) discussed below, the Rev. Þorsteinn Pétursson of Staðarbakki (b. 1710), Jón Þorkelsson

(Thorkillius) (b. 1697) and sheriff Bjarni Nikulásson (b. 1681). Of particular interest to modern readers is the 'Trials of the Rev. Jón Magnússon' (b. 1610), written at the height of the witch-hunts and detailing Jón's conviction that he was being persecuted by evil spirits, and a terrifying portrayal of schizophrenia. These and other such stories influenced the way the general public regarded the times they lived in. In the introduction to his 1947 edition of the autobiography of the Rev. Þorsteinn Pétursson, Haraldur Sigurðsson noted:

> The manuscript of the autobiography is enormous, 764 sheets, plus a few loose pages, of which there were probably more at one time. It is now preserved in the manuscript collection of Landsbókasafnið [the National Library of Iceland], JS. 207, 4to. I do not know where Jón Sigurðsson obtained the book: this is not recorded in the manuscript index and the manuscript itself gives no indication of who its owners were from the time the Rev. Þorsteinn died until it came into the hands of Jón Sigurðsson. The Rev. Þorsteinn's literary remains came to the National Library from various directions, suggesting that they became dispersed after his death.

The Jón Sigurðsson mentioned here is none other than the leader of the independence movement in the nineteenth century, a historian and archivist and owner of a large manuscript collection. The editor's account gives us an idea of how manuscripts were preserved and distributed, and how it is often a matter of pure chance as to what found its way into collections and what was lost. It also gives us an idea of just how big these kinds of eighteenth-century texts could be, in this case over 1,528 pages.

Guðbrandur Jónsson, editor of the *Travels of Jón Ólafsson, Indiafarer*, also provided an introduction to the published edition of the autobiography of the Rev. Jón Steingrímsson, 'Fire-Clerk'. Jón became nationally famous for having preached such a powerful sermon in his church at Kirkjubæjarklaustur, southern Iceland, that it halted a lava flow that was threatening to engulf it at the time of the terrible Skaftáreldar eruptions of 1783. Guðbrandur starts by maintaining that the so-called vice of curiosity is

> the foundation of all human progress in all areas. All sciences, whether practical or other, are the product of man's curiosity, and without it there would be no knowledge. Man would still be little more than a beast, and would probably be sitting naked or clad in just a few scraps of skin, without fire, in a damp, dim

cave, gnawing raw meat off the bones of wild animals that he had caught unaided with his bare hands, if divine providence had not breathed inspiration into his breast, the spark of the divine, which drives man constantly onward to greater and greater knowledge. To condemn curiosity is to condemn God.[12]

This grandiloquent apology for curiosity of course provides a justification for the human desire to try to make sense of life and man's position in it. 'One's fellow man is no less remarkable than other phenomena of nature,' Guðbrandur continues, 'and knowledge of man and his nature is an indispensable precondition for the existence of a healthy civil society and for our ability to see where human customs and circumstances are in need of amelioration. Meddling in the affairs of others with this end in mind is thus also conducive to progress.' Guðbrandur points out that the success of the autobiographical form is the result of people's desire to learn things at first hand. Another guiding motive is the desire for truth. All these, in Guðbrandur's opinion, are reasons to treat this type of writing as deserving of attention. In his account of the literary antecedents Guðbrandur notes that there are no autobiographies in old Icelandic literature, but adds: 'though it is worth mentioning that *The Saga of Bishop Laurentíus Kálfsson*, which is thought to have been written by the Einar Hafliðason of Breiðabólsstaður in Vesturhóp [northern Iceland], who was for many years the bishop's chaplain, bears unmistakable signs that Laurentíus himself played a part in its composition, directly or indirectly, since it contains much that evidently can only have come from him himself.' Guðbrandur is thus claiming for this fourteenth-century bishop's saga the honour of being the first attempt at autobiography in the language.

Guðbrandur describes various qualities of the autobiographical form in similar terms to those he used to justify the reading of such works, viz. curiosity: they can help us to gain a better understanding of society, not just of man himself, and thus act as a spur to progress. The autobiography of the Rev. Jón Steingrímsson definitely falls into this category. This work marks a clear turning point in the development of the genre, since it is considerably more open and unreserved than most other writings of the period. The author presents an apologia for various things he has done in his life, intertwining this with an account of things he has seen and lived through. Written in a succinct and energetic style, Jón's autobiography provides a vivid picture of the life, customs and thoughts of the people of his part of southern Iceland through good times and bad. Despite the prominence of external descriptions of people and places, Jón frequently turns the narrative inwards on himself, describing his inner struggles, especially in his relations with God.

The Rev. Jón starts with a justification for his writings addressed to his five daughters: 'My dearly beloved daughters, Sigríður, Jórunn, Guðný, Katrín and Helga, for you, for those whom you love and for your descendants who are now or may ever be, and for all charitably minded readers of the words and accounts hereafter written, I ask God's mercy in the name of Jesus Christ.' The introduction that follows reveals a particular attitude towards time, the view that the past has relevance and value for the well-being of people in the present and future. This is interesting in itself, but Jón also articulates the concerns of all who may follow his example in giving public expression to their thoughts about themselves and their times:

> When you, my dear children, read these pages, you will find from what I have previously told some of you that I have passed over much that is true, for I have seen fit only to mention that which has revealed God's most special mercy and protection over me from first till last. To this I have added true examples of virtues and vices in this world, showing how God is the one and only object of faith. I have more often written little rather than too much about this or that, but so openly and simply, without any affectation of style, that if fantastical and captious detractors, those who envy and hate me, who you can imagine who they are, see or hear this, they will pour out over me dead, no less than in life, and on you too, their vitriol and revilement, and so these pages are therefore never to come into their hands. I dedicate here not to one of you alone but to you all this the story of my life, for I know your loving harmony of spirit, which I ask may ever endure, and that your descendants be of like mind, and then can they too have this book for their information and entertainment, until it moulder into dust.

Jón's approach sounds a new note of personal examination and self-analysis in Icelandic writing. The outcome is one of the most powerful works of Icelandic literature of later times.

Seventeenth- and eighteenth-century travel stories in their various forms give us a good insight into how people of the time in Iceland viewed their lives. In a sense, we can see the travel stories as a sort of staging-post in the development of self-expression on the way to the full-blown autobiographies that followed. However, the connections should not be pushed too far: throughout this period Icelanders continued to write and copy other forms of literature, and these too continued to influence how ordinary people expressed themselves and judged their lives and their surroundings. Above all, we should never underestimate the continuing appeal of the ancient sagas.

The development of autobiography as a major literary form has parallels elsewhere in Europe. It is when we get to the nineteenth century that this development began to take its own special course in Iceland, especially in the part played by the working-class in such writing. In Iceland ordinary farmers and farmhands of limited formal education appropriated this new way of thinking and the opportunities it opened up and made them a central part of their own world of learning and experience. The result was an outburst of cultural activity, pursued in the rural areas of the country by dedicated peasant scholars who permitted themselves no respite from their labours of copying and learning. Their work vastly increased the opportunities open to ordinary people of the nineteenth and twentieth centuries to acquire knowledge and information of every kind. Their literary heritage, both ancient and modern, thus formed part of people's day-to-day spiritual sustenance long into the modern age.

11

The Barefoot Historians and the 'People's Press'

The Icelandic rural bookshelf

Conventional wisdom in Iceland has generally been that the legislative reform of the education system in the eighteenth and nineteenth centuries was one of the leading factors in propelling the country towards the modern age. While there is no question that these laws were a step forward, it can be argued that the advances they produced were both small and makeshift. This comes out clearly if we consider matters from the standpoint of the ordinary people these laws were supposed to benefit: as noted previously, for a large part of the population the provision of formal education remained at best sketchy, at worst non-existent. Very few young people had any opportunity to take their education beyond the age of fourteen until new laws on compulsory schooling were brought in during the 1930s.

If we look back for a moment, an interesting but apparently contradictory picture emerges. On the one hand, popular culture in Iceland managed to produce a surprising number of people who took a deep and lasting interest in education and learning. Moreover, many showed the capacity to apply their acquired knowledge in productive ways. Some even managed to use it to grapple with abstract arguments and theoretical concepts in an attempt to come to a better understanding of the conditions under which they lived their lives. On the other hand, we see an extremely primitive education system and a minimal infrastructure that, despite everything, succeeded in providing and sustaining a basic level of education in the country. The result was the almost universal literacy of the Icelandic population from the late eighteenth century onwards. This is all the more astonishing since the ownership of secular books was fairly rare, especially before the last quarter of the nineteenth century.

According to studies based on parish records and household inventories, in around 1800 over 97 per cent of Icelandic households had at least one book of a religious nature in them. Pétur Pétursson in *Church and Social Change* points out that ownership of such books was very high when compared with other countries; in Sweden, for instance, only approximately twenty per cent of households had books. In Iceland the parish priest was supposed to make sure that every home was supplied with Christian reading material; if poverty prevented this, poor relief could be used to buy it.[1]

Earlier in this book I have argued that it was in fact generally secular literature that determined whether children came to take an interest in reading. If this is true, the high literacy rate in Iceland would appear to be something of a puzzle, since until fairly late in the nineteenth century formal publication of secular reading material was negligible. Earlier in the century a number of progressively minded people, inspired by the principles of the Enlightenment, had published a certain amount of secular material, mostly of a practical nature, but this had been on a very limited scale. In the last quarter of the century things changed dramatically, with an active press producing ever-increasing amounts of secular literature. However, throughout the period the general public had other, unconventional, methods of ensuring access to reasonable supplies of reading. This activity, although absolutely crucial to the continuity of Icelandic popular culture, has often been overlooked, with most historians choosing to focus almost exclusively on the formal channels of education, publication and distribution of books.

To explain the avidity with which children from the Icelandic peasant class took to literature and reading, access to written secular material had to be considerably greater than the printed cultural legacy would suggest. Despite the significant expansion in publishing in the second half of the nineteenth century, printed material had only limited distribution and fell far short of meeting the demands of a hungry market. Print runs were small and few ordinary people had the money to buy these books; there were more pressing demands on their resources. Obviously, then, another explanation is necessary.

The manuscript tradition

The modern historian is faced with conflicting clues about the state of literary culture in nineteenth-century Icelandic peasant society. Over and over again, from all over the country, we are told of young people being categorically forbidden, under pain of dire punishment, from getting involved in writing, and there are countless satirical tales of obsessive bookworms becoming the laughing-stocks of their local communities. Set against this there are many attestations to a deep general love of literature among the common people. They read, wrote and retold stories and recited poetry, and – despite limited means, despite the lack of schools, printed material and everything else we normally see as necessary for the development of literate culture – put great efforts into disseminating knowledge of every kind.

The priceless collection of manuscripts preserved in Landsbókasafn Íslands (the National Library of Iceland) and local libraries around the country stand as indisputable testimony to the determination of many Icelanders to let neither worldly nor spiritual adversity hinder their pursuit of knowledge. This living manuscript culture, sometimes referred to as 'scribal culture', covered all areas of literary activity, both original writing and copying and reproduction. In spite of – or because of – the dearth of books in the country, it prospered over hundreds of years and persisted well on into the twentieth century. Unlike the medieval manuscript tradition discussed in chapter Ten, to which there are obvious parallels, the manuscript tradition of later centuries has hardly been researched, and not at all from the perspective of contemporary cultural history. The tendency among historians has been to view 'book culture' as distinct from society, an isolated phenomenon of the elite. To really understand the Icelandic literary tradition and its status, function and meaning in the lives of ordinary people, we need to turn this approach around and study the diverse strands of culture together and as a whole. Viewed this way, culture becomes a part of daily life, and vice versa.

The spread of writing skills among the general populace of Iceland has been the subject of some debate. Some historians have seen this as an autochthonous process, the impetus coming 'from below', and until the late nineteenth century largely separate from and ignored by official channels and institutions. Writing is seen as sprouting directly from the grassroots in response to a public need, most notably in the period between about 1830 and 1880. Such self-generated interest, especially among younger people, was often met with resistance from adults and the governing classes. According to this view of the events, this rapid surge of literary activity in the nineteenth century was markedly different from what had happened a hundred years earlier when the nation as a whole first achieved basic literacy, where the impetus was, at least to some extent, the result of the joint efforts of state, Church and home.

What do we really mean, though, when we speak of 'self-generated interest' in education and literary culture? The suggestion is that these areas of culture evolved largely unaffected by legislation and the formal institutions of society. No further explanation is deemed necessary. But this view raises certain questions: where exactly did this interest stem from? and what lay behind it? And, indeed, what precisely were the needs that writing skills were supposed to meet?

Recent research into the cultural world of the Icelandic working-class diarists has shown that manuscript material played a much more significant part in the Icelandic rural community than was hitherto thought. The historian Davíð Ólafsson, working on the nature and development of the diary tradition in Iceland in the eighteenth, nineteenth and the twentieth centuries, has come increasingly to the view that some of these diarists used their diaries in part to give themselves a fuller perspective over their other literary activities. Some of them were much more than simply writers of diaries; they were also collectors and collators of all kinds of written material from within the popular culture, and indeed were largely responsible for keeping it alive. These characters Davíð and I have named 'barefoot historians'.[2]

Lay scholars as 'literary institution'

To anyone who acquaints themselves with the collection of personal manuscripts in the National Library of Iceland it rapidly becomes obvious that many of the authors can be viewed as 'literary institutions' in their own right, on an equal footing to the publishers and printing houses, schools and writers of the 'official' literary world. When we speak of a 'literary institution', what we mean is any individual, group or formal institution that influences, in one way or another, the ways in which literature is produced, consumed, regarded or discussed by other members of society – in the modern world a role filled by publishers, critics, academics, establishments of education, the media, writers and authors, and, of course, the reading public. In nineteenth-century Iceland, it seems, many of these roles were also filled by lay scholars, dedicated amateurs who took it on themselves to cater for the needs and guide the tastes of other people from the same background as themselves.

The thirst for knowledge of these people, and the importance of their activities for the community at large, cannot be overestimated. Although the diarists and others were, without exception, working people, taking an active part in the daily routines of their family farms, every spare moment of their lives seems to have gone into intellectual activity – reading, writing, calculating and speculating about their surroundings. Such was the case with Halldór and Níels Jónsson, described earlier in this book. These lay scholars were very often keen collectors of books and manuscripts, possessing or handling far more than one would ever expect of poor rural farmers and labourers. They took time off work if necessary to write up material they had not seen before to ensure that it would not be lost to the community. It was often an expensive, arduous and time-consuming occupation, and the gains were neither obvious nor certain. One has to wonder why they took all this trouble.

These barefoot historians did not operate alone and in isolation. Together they constituted an informal grouping, exchanging material, organizing meetings and providing each other with mutual support. In fact, the network of lay scholars in the west of Iceland, the area we have been specially focusing on, was so tight that we are almost justified in speaking of a 'Westfjord Academy' that flourished up to the end of the nineteenth century and beyond. The collaboration among its members was so extensive and their productivity so great that we know they exercised considerable influence on the general population around them, functioning as a sort of quasi-institute of cultural affairs.

To give an idea of the methods and activities of these lay scholars, it is worth quoting from the diary of Magnús Hj. Magnússon (b. 1873), one of the best known of the Westfjord group. Magnús gained national recognition after his death as the model for one of the characters in Halldór Laxness's epic novel *Heimsljós* (The Light of the World), published in 1937–40. Magnús's diary provided Laxness with one of his main sources. The passage in question is for 28 February 1899 and Magnús is recording his activities for the day:

> Fair weather, clear skies and no wind. This month I copied out the *Rímur of Jesus Christ's Childhood*, or *María Rímur*, written in 1654 by the Rev. Guðmundur Erlendsson, pastor at the farm of Fell in Sléttuhlíð in the district of Hegranes. This poem is hard to get hold of. In this county [Ísafjörður] I know of only two copies, one of them in the possession of Sighvatur at the farm of Höfði, the other being the one I have copied. Originally also in the possession of Sighvatur, it now belongs to Sveinbjörn Kristjánsson, labourer from the village of Flateyri. Sveinbjörn is a little over thirty years old now. He was born with good mental and physical capacities but as a young man, living in Dýrafjörður, he got lost in a storm and spent the night in the open without shelter. He eventually made it on his knees to a farmhouse but suffered serious frostbite and had to have his right hand amputated at the elbow as well as the tips of the fingers of his left hand. Since then he has been one-handed but he is still extraordinarily skilful in many activities.[3]

Magnús mentions here some of the members of the same 'school' as he belonged to, in particular the 'super scholar', Sighvatur Grímsson of Höfði, originally from the Borgarfjörður region. Sighvatur's vast output was of central importance to the 'Westfjord Academy'. He was an extremely prolific copier of manuscripts and left a diary spanning over sixty years and a large amount of other material. His writings shed

The Icelandic horse is a remarkable animal, small but exceptionally hardy. It is the descendant of the horses introduced by the original settlers. For centuries it provided the main means of transport about the country, proving particularly effective in the mountainous terrain and harsh conditions of the Icelandic landscape. Maintaining communications between different parts of the country presented enormous problems. Often travellers and itinerant workers were employed as messengers, carrying things such as letters, books and manuscripts on loan between farms and districts. In the second half of the eighteenth century communications were put on a regular basis with the introduction of the so-called Landpóstur. This was a postal service that carried delivered letters between the quarters of the country three times a year using trains of horses to carry the boxes in which the mail was kept. The post carriers acquired a reputation for being daredevils and were famed for the dangers and adventures they encountered on their journeys across the mountains, rivers and wildernesses.

considerable light on the world-view of the nineteenth-century peasant class.[4] Also mentioned is Sveinbjörn Kristjánsson, an obscure farmhand whom Magnús held in high esteem. It is notable that Magnús appreciates the work of these men with a clear eye to the often difficult conditions under which it was performed. The text shows that one of Magnús's conscious aims was to save rare material from destruction, in this case a religious poem from the year 1654. Elsewhere Magnús compiled a list of all the lay scholars and copyists of whom he was aware, and came to the conclusion that at the time of writing there were something like 210 of them scattered around the country! These people formed the core of the informal network of the barefoot historians.

The records reveal that the picture found in the Westfjord region was repeated in Skagafjörður in the north-west. Here we again find a vigorous and unbroken succession of lay scholars and barefoot historians, extending from the late seventeenth century up until modern times. The activities and outlook of this Skagafjörður group have been the subject of detailed investigation by the literary historian Viðar Hreinsson and bear many of the same characteristics as the Westfjord group, and we can safely assume that some kind of connection was maintained between the two throughout the nineteenth century.

In the first half of the nineteenth century a remarkable group of popular scholars coalesced in Skagafjörður around the figure of sheriff Jón Espólín (b. 1769). Its members were mostly ministers of the church, public officials and farmers, all united by a shared interest in history and the compilation of annals. Another barefoot historian, Gísli Konráðsson, who lived most of his life on the island of Flatey off the west coast, acted as a sort of link between the 'Skagafjörður Academy' and the 'Westfjord Academy', being both a central member of the circle around Espólín and mentor and friend to Sighvatur Grímsson. This impressive coterie of scholars seems to have fuelled a powerful interest in writing among the young people of Skagafjörður. One significant result, according to Kristmundur Bjarnason, the most important modern historian to research the subject, was that Skagafjörður was almost universally literate well before the implementation of the Education Act of 1880. 'The youth of the region was held up as a proud example ... Manuscripts were handed on from one person to another, from farm to farm, for the purpose of copying, and young people showed great eagerness in being able to express themselves in this way.'[5]

The cultural importance of these 'informal institutes' like the groups around Jón Espólín, Gísli Konráðsson and Sighvatur Grímsson raises a number of questions. Precisely how much influence did they have on popular attitudes in the first half of the nineteenth century? And what about the 'Westfjord Academy' around Sighvatur Grímsson later in that century and surviving into the twentieth? The output and sheer energy of these men is undeniably remarkable and deserves our admiration. But, when all is said and done, how important were they? And what was their true role in and influence on the society in which they operated? Were they isolated groups of eccentrics who lived in a sealed off world of literature and learning, outsiders to society at large? Were they viewed in some way as a danger to children and young people, their values a threat to the work ethic that held peasant society together? Or were they regarded as examples for emulation? Are we justified in seeing in them a sign of increased specialization within rural society, men who were able to make a living out of a specialist skill, filling a public need for reading material, almanacs, bookkeeping and even letter-writing for both private and public purposes? And if so, did they possibly impede the spread of literacy, either as negative examples to be avoided or by removing the need for others to become literate?

Icelandic popular culture at the time was too complex and multi-stranded to allow for precise and unequivocal answers to these questions. But one thing is certain: the barefoot historians played a major role in the dissemination of written material in every commune of the country, and in many instances won the respect, gratitude and friendship of their communities for their efforts. This was often all they won. Many of these men sat and copied manuscripts day in and day out – not only on their own initiative but also on commission – material that was later handed on from person to person, home to home. And for many, both rich and poor, this material became the principal source of knowledge, information and entertainment in a country where print publishing was small-scale and limited in scope.

In rural Iceland, formal institutions of the kinds that modern historians tend to concentrate on were only one of the channels through which the popular desire for knowledge and education were served – and in most cases not even the main one. For the majority of people, especially children, there were compelling psychological factors that came into play. Reading and education provided a way of coping with the emotional stress that formed part of daily life and became an important tool in many people's tactics for mental and spiritual survival. Without the network of barefoot historians and the sort of 'People's Press' they established to provide the materials, there would have been no way of satisfying this popular hunger. The activities of these poor farmers, farmhands and lay scholars are probably largely responsible for the fact that the Icelandic peasantry in general took great pride in their own reading and writing abilities, many of them capable of producing texts that can stand the most exacting examination – diaries, autobiographies and letters, both personal and public. It was all part of the peasant mechanism for survival.

12

Urban Living: Industry, Labour and Living Conditions

Industrialization

The first four decades of the twentieth century in Iceland can be seen, in essence, as an extended period of transition in which the appearance of change outstripped the reality. Existing daily routines and fundamental attitudes altered surprisingly little, and this undoubtedly helped people to adjust to the changes that did occur. We should treat with some caution the remarks of contemporary commentators who, unsurprisingly, tended to notice particular indications of change and often exaggerated their significance. To them the transition often seemed dramatic and bewildering.

The socio-economic and demographic changes discussed earlier in this book led among other things to the steady growth of the urban settlements scattered around the coast. Reykjavík was the only town of any size. Around 1860 it numbered about 1,500 inhabitants, most of them officials, merchants, craftsmen and unskilled labourers. For most of the nineteenth century Reykjavík acted mainly as a service and administrative centre, with little or no industry until commercial fishing took off towards the end of the century. This expansion of fishing attracted an influx of new migrants. Between 1897 and 1908 Reykjavík grew at the unprecedented rate of 8.3 per cent a year. By way of comparison, the annual population growth for the country as a whole over these years was 0.8 per cent.[1]

In the final decades of the nineteenth century Reykjavík developed into the main centre for manufacturing, commerce, services, transportation, communications and administration. By 1890 its population had grown to almost 3,900, 5.5 per cent of the total population of the country. By 1910 this figure had risen to 11,600 (13.6%), by 1920 to 17,450 (18.5%), and by 1930 to 28,300 (25.8%). Over the country as a whole, the number of Icelanders living in urban areas (villages and towns of over 200 people) rose from 3 per cent in 1860 to 12 per cent in 1890, 44 per cent in 1920, and 57.3 per cent in 1930.[2] But for all its rapid proportional increase, in absolute terms Reykjavík remained tiny by any international standards. And Reykjavík was a very special case, far outstripping any other urban centre in the country. This again gives us cause to be sceptical about exaggerated claims of the degree of change in people's general outlook and behaviour patterns in the wake of increasing urbanization.

Nevertheless, in the area of working practices Iceland was beginning to emerge into the modern world, notably in the growth of urban occupations such as industry, trade, transport and services. In 1860 such occupations had accounted for 6.3 per cent of the national workforce; by 1930 this had risen to over a third. Accompanying these changes there were significant changes in family structure and living conditions. In particular, the rapid urbanization of the years 1880 to 1930 led to a large increase in the number of households. In both rural and urban areas households were growing smaller: extended families living under the same roof became less common and the age of marriage fell, as did the illegitimacy rate. The effects of these trends on living conditions were felt throughout the whole of Icelandic society.

According to one analysis, Icelandic society in the 1930s can be broken down into four social classes. Needless to say, any categorization of this type is open to challenge and at best gives only a limited view of the social differentiation within Icelandic society. According to this analysis, two-thirds of the working population are classed as lower or working class, taking in both skilled and unskilled workers. This group does not, however, include farmers, since the analysis is based largely on people's relationship to the means of production; farmers tended either to own their farms and/or to employ some workers, and for this reason are placed among the upper class (12.3 per cent in 1930) or petty bourgeoisie (9 per cent). While it is certainly justifiable to categorize some farmers as upper class, it should be remembered that the majority of farmers were very poor and one could equally argue for including them among the lower class. The remaining 11.4 per cent of Icelanders in 1930 are categorized as middle class.[3]

The make-up of the workforce changed dramatically with the industrialization of fishing in the late nineteenth century and the subsequent rise in manufacturing and other industries. Industrialization outside the fishing sector came fairly late and was initially limited to Reykjavík and the surrounding area. Between 1901 and 1940 about 24 to 29 per cent of the working population of Reykjavík was employed in industry,[s] and its share of the total industrial output rose from 34 per cent to 63 per cent.[4] This development can in large part be put down to changes in manufacturing methods, starting in the late nineteenth century and continuing on through the twentieth. Initially, manufacturing was almost entirely restricted to providing for local markets and was based on domestic production by artisans and skilled labourers serving their own local areas. Early in the twentieth century we see the beginnings of a change in production methods as a result of the growing market in Reykjavík. Later still, once the population of Reykjavík and its surroundings had reached a sufficient level, it became economically viable for manufacturing companies to start looking towards mechanization.

Mechanization remained fairly limited and small-scale until the 1930s, when the government initiated a major programme to promote domestic production to counter the effects of the Great Depression. Manufacturing was dominated by domestic consumer products and service-oriented industries, usually labour intensive and technologically primitive. The firms involved were generally one-off enterprises, set up and operated by small-scale owner-managers and employing no more than a handful of staff. Industrial manufacturing accounted for barely one per cent of exports, tiny when compared to fishing and processed agricultural goods such as wool, skins and butter.

Probably the most far-reaching innovation of the early twentieth century was the introduction of the motorized trawler. In economic terms, these trawlers increased the productivity of each fisherman many times over. This had two important consequences for the Icelandic labour market. First, the size of the catch increased massively. In the absence of significant mechanization, this required a large workforce on land to process the fish. The main product was salted cod. This was a highly labour-intensive process, relying largely on female labour. Saltfish had been Iceland's main export since the nineteenth century and continued to dominate exports up until the Second World War. The fall-off in demand during the Depression marked the end of an era. Second, the fishing boom added further impetus to the existing trend in settlement patterns, changing Iceland beyond recognition. The stream of people abandoning the country and moving to Reykjavík and other fishing centres reached unprecedented levels. The capital came to dwarf all other urban areas, as a centre for both fishing and industry and for the development of trade and services. This huge expansion of Reykjavík at the expense of all other parts of the country was to have enormous implications for Icelandic society in the later years of the century.

The changes of the early twentieth century had other consequences. Fishing became a uniquely specialized occupation, demanding new levels of training and expertise. As the size of boats increased, the means of production became more centralized, modifying and opening up the country's existing social structure. Even so, in 1915 trawlers accounted for only about a half of the total Icelandic catch; the rest came from smaller motorized vessels, owned and run by single individuals with small crews and scattered in ports all round the coast. In many cases these were family boats, manned by a father and his sons, and thus with social similarities to the farms from which these families had originally come. Ownership of the means of production thus remained widely distributed across society throughout the first half of the twentieth century.

The urban family and lifestyle changes

Increasing urbanization was accompanied by a change in the composition of households, as noted in chapter Two. This was true in all parts of the country, farming areas as well as towns and villages. For example, in both rural and urban parishes the number of servants per household fell dramatically.[5] This decline in the number of servants can be viewed as one of the most significant changes of the period; from accounting for over a third of the general population, servants, at least in their traditional form, almost disappeared from Icelandic society in the early part of the twentieth century. During the same period, the greater freedom of choice of occupation and accommodation led to a rise in the number of single tenants: people living alone. Rather than being forced to seek accommodation as domestic staff in the households of established families, young people in urban areas now had the option of seeking work outside the home in industry or the fisheries.

If an attempt is made to categorize the period between 1880 and 1930, it seems reasonable to identify two phases, as the historian Magnús S. Magnússon has done: an early transitional period from about 1880 to 1910, and the capitalist breakthrough between about 1910 and 1930. The migrants who settled as tenants in coastal towns and villages and took up work as labourers suddenly found themselves able to realize long-cherished dreams of independence. In 1930, for instance, migrant workers accounted for the majority of lodgers and tenants in Hafnarfjörður, a fair-sized fishing town near Reykjavík. This increase in the number of one-person households and single tenants had profound implications for the social, economic and political status of the family. Particularly in urban areas, the family gradually began to change into a different kind of unit from the extended household of traditional peasant society, that is, from a unit of production to a unit of consumption. However, it should be remembered that the socio-economic changes involved were not felt equally throughout the country and their significance varied between rural and urban areas and between different urban settings.

There are also limits to how far the changes of the late nineteenth and early twentieth centuries affected people's actual lives. The industrialization of the fishing industry and growth of manufacturing obviously had an impact on working patterns in Reykjavík, the only town of any size, and other coastal communities, but not to such an extent that one can justifiably speak of Iceland moving decisively from a traditional rural society to a modern, urban, industrial one. For most people, the business of daily life went on largely as before, with similar tasks performed in similar ways. For instance, as noted below, agriculture and horticulture remained an important part of life for many town dwellers. Perhaps more importantly, attitudes to work did not change fundamentally; migrating from country to town did not involve any major recasting of people's world-views or ways of living. People did not have to adapt to totally new rhythms of work and were able to draw on their previous work experience. The labour-intensive and un-mechanized nature of work in towns made it comparatively easy for rural Icelanders to adjust to the new working patterns. The changes involved were of a very different order from what peasants elsewhere in Europe had experienced when adjusting to the far higher levels of technology in nineteenth-century industrial factories.

For the vast majority of those involved, the fishing industry did not provide a steady job and a reliable source of income. The gap was filled in various ways. Many households in urban areas, of almost all classes, kept sheep, cows, and often horses for personal use. With the head of the household and older children employed elsewhere, the job of tending the livestock fell mainly on women and younger children. Better-off families hired others to perform these tasks, creating a source of employment for people with relatively unstable incomes. Indeed, it can be argued that well into the twentieth century the area of the country that saw the greatest growth in agriculture was in fact Reykjavík and its surroundings, particularly in order to serve the demands of the growing urban population, but a similar phenomenon can be observed in the smaller urban settlements around the coast. Many urban families relied for their survival on a combination of employment in the fisheries for the main breadwinner (generally the husband) and agricultural work of one kind or another in the surrounding areas for the other members of the family. Contemporary sources are full of descriptions of farm work of this kind, often seasonal, which appears to have brought people considerable satisfaction as well as providing a significant supplement to the family's income and food supplies. This period also saw a marked increase in people establishing vegetable gardens for domestic consumption. Local authorities and various societies encouraged this development by providing land for use as allotments. The most important crop was the potato, the introduction of which made a huge difference to the family's food stock and nutrition over the long winter months.

Female labour was an important part of the economy of families that moved to the growing urban areas in the twentieth century. Cleaning and drying fish demanded considerable manpower and this work was mostly done by women. They were often accompanied by their children, who were expected to contribute from an early age. The working day was long and the work dirty and messy, and generally only short-term. When the work ran out people were often obliged to move. Many headed for the country where there was work to be had on farms over the summer. The picture shows a line of women in protective overalls, hard at their monotonous tasks. They probably spent the whole day there cleaning fish, from six in the morning to past seven in the evening, as long as there were boats landing and catches that needed processing.

An article published in 1904 in the journal *Stefnir*, 'Vöxtur Akureyrar og afkoma bæjarmanna' (The Growth of Akureyri and the Inhabitants' Way of Living), gives us a vivid snapshot of urban life in Iceland around the turn of the century. The article describes the situation in Akureyri, the largest town in the north:

> Akureyri has grown quite big in recent years. The population has doubled in the last ten years and now stands at sixteen to eighteen hundred. Most of the people of the town live by commerce, crafts, agriculture and fishing, and I want to discuss each of these in turn. Agriculture and raising livestock is widely practised as a sideline but few have it as their main occupation. It is mostly those who work in commerce, crafts, fishing or as

day labourers who do some farming part-time. By raising livestock I mean that many families try to have one or two cows and a few sheep, and many also have horses ... Agriculture and livestock cannot therefore be considered more than a secondary or ancillary occupation for most townspeople, but they often provide a good source of work for day labourers since those who put up the money for them often do not do the actual work themselves, and this therefore provides a source of casual labour for others. Working the vegetable garden in summer, preparing the hay meadow in spring, haymaking in summer, and tending the livestock in winter – all these activities are mostly done by hired day labourers. Agriculture and livestock are thus fundamental to the labour supply for jobbing workers and many families rely on this for their ability to survive in town.

The urban poor of the early twentieth century not only had close relations with agriculture within the limits of their own towns, they also had more direct links with rural areas. At the end of the fishing season in spring many faced unemployment and were forced to seek work elsewhere. This of course was the time when work in the country was heaviest, for example in haymaking, and many men from towns travelled to rural areas and hired themselves out as labourers on farms. Often their families went with them. Alternatively, if their husbands had work in town over the summer, many women would go to the country on their own or taking some of their children with them. As noted in chapter Fifteen, children were also sent alone to work in the country, either for the summer months or in some cases for longer periods.

For many this seasonal migration was considered a welcome break from life in the coastal settlements. The movement between town and country forms a recurrent theme in many autobiographies. The tradition of sending children to the country to work in summer persisted long into the second part of the twentieth century. This was the case for myself, for example, though I was born in 1957 and brought up in the West End of Reykjavík by parents who would certainly be categorized as upper middle class. Every summer, from late May to the beginning of September, I worked on a farm which belonged to people who were totally unrelated to my family, from the age of six to fifteen. Earlier in the twentieth century, though, the system was more formalized and often essential to the family's economy.

Migration in one form or another was not new to the people of Iceland; it had formed a central part of most people's experience in rural society in earlier times. As servants or as young couples setting up home for the first time, the majority of people lived for longer or shorter periods away from the parish of their birth. As described in chapter One, male farm workers were often sent over the winter to work as fishermen at fishing stations along the coast. In this sense migration can be viewed as an important stage in the life of the typical nineteenth-century peasant and a part of the general culture, something that each generation was accustomed to inherit from the one before. This system continued, in modified form, through the first half of the twentieth century. For this reason it is misleading to view the growth of towns in Iceland as a decisive break with the past; this urbanization took place firmly within the context of pre-existing modes of existence.

Living conditions

Living conditions in towns and villages differed in certain respects from those in the country. The figures for house construction types given in chapter Three mask a difference between urban and rural areas: in the country the dominant form remained the turf farm, while it was the growth of towns that accounted for most of the increase in stone and timber construction. In addition, and as a generalization, dwellings in towns differed more in quality than those in the country.

Small houses and shacks were thrown up rapidly in the towns to cater for the stream of migrants from the country. Reykjavík took on a very mixed appearance, with the better homes of the merchants and government officials interspersed with areas of shanty towns. As we find frequently mentioned in contemporary sources, newcomers from the country, unused to any form of urbanism, often found the town strange and outlandish with its prevalence of new types of housing. To farmer Böðvar Magnússon (b. 1877), writing in his autobiography *Undir tindum* (Under the Mountain Peaks), Reykjavík appeared vast and impressive when he first saw it at the age of eleven – this at a time when the entire population numbered just 3,800! In time, and especially as we move further into the twentieth century, growing numbers of people managed to build themselves better houses and the housing stock began to improve. For the vast majority of the population, though, living conditions remained very poor. In his autobiography *Í útlegð* (In Banishment) Þorfinnur Kristjánsson (b. 1887) describes the house he grew up in in Reykjavík: 'As for the homes of ordinary people, I think it is safe to say that most were very poor. Our house could hardly have looked less prepossessing. There was no furniture other than the beds, a table and some stools. I do not remember that there were any pictures on the walls. And the same was true of most other homes I visited.'

In 1916 Guðmundur Hannesson, a doctor from Reykjavík, produced a report on housing conditions in towns. Having observed that

Middle-class homes differed significantly from working-class homes as regards design, furnishings and space. Many of these homes were fairly opulently fitted out with custom-built furniture, either produced locally or imported from England or Denmark. The interior in the picture is typical of middle-class houses in the first years of the twentieth century. The woman in the foreground is dressed in traditional Icelandic costume. The others are wearing modern clothes in line with fashions from Europe and North America.

there were no publicly available figures for the size of the average home, he extrapolated from such records as did exist and came to the following conclusion: 'The average home would then have 2–3 heated rooms and 1–2 rooms without heating, in addition to a kitchen and a larder. However it is quite clear that the vast majority of houses are considerably smaller than this, a large percentage consisting merely of one-room dwellings. It is only the better off that live in reasonable comfort.'[6] Guðmundur's report covers Reykjavík and three other villages and passes the following general comment on living standards in urban areas: 'Whether we look at the three villages or the sample of dwellings in Reykjavík, we find that almost a half of all dwellings consist of a single room and a kitchen, or less. It is obvious that such dwellings are inadequate for families to live in and it is no comfort to realize that conditions are no better in cities in other countries. Basements are rare outside Reykjavík, and there they are of very poor quality, both cold and damp.'

In an article in the newspaper *Lögrjetta* in 1906, 'Fátæku heimilin í Reykjavík' (The Poor Homes in Reykjavík), another doctor, Steingrímur

Matthíasson, gives a graphic account of the conditions in which much of the population of Reykjavík was forced to subsist. Like other family doctors, Steingrímur was well familiar with the situation at first hand from his visits to families throughout the town:

> To start with the basement slum, on entering or leaving one generally hits one's head on the doorframe. Inside it is dark and gloomy as there is no sight of the sun from one end of the year to the next except as a reflection in the windows of the house opposite. The air is damp and the walls are rotten and covered in mould. There is no proper heating, just a small stove where the food is cooked and the steam from the pot fills the room and mixes in with the foul-smelling air emanating from all the people that huddle there night and day. Ventilation is non-existent except for the draught brought in when the door is opened.

Steingrímur goes on to describe with similar outrage the attics that formed the homes of many town dwellers, before finally turning to the turf houses that still existed in some numbers in Reykjavík:

> These are unfit for human habitation and an appalling disgrace to the town. Overcrowding is no worse than in other types of houses, but there is even greater lack of light and ventilation and the earth floors and walls make these houses appreciably more wretched. In one place I happened on a cow in a side chamber off the main living room. This, it occurred to me, was how they got their heat. The air was thick with cow dung and urine and the entire house reeked of the stench of cattle. What all these houses have in common is that they have whole families, maybe as many as ten people, crammed into them, subsisting day and night in rooms that are really only big enough for two.

The situation seems to have improved little in the first decades of the twentieth century. A government official called Indriði Einarsson described conditions in Reykjavík in an article, 'Reykjavík fyrrum og nú' (Reykjavík Past and Present), in the newspaper *Ísafold* in 1919. He pointed out that house-building was lagging well behind the demand caused by the large-scale migration to the town. As a result rents were rising steeply. He also points to the potentially catastrophic consequences of poor housing, as brought home during the Spanish influenza epidemic of 1918:

> In one place three sick girls were lying in an attic. They had nothing to cover them except the iron-clad roof, and the wind

One of the major tasks facing Iceland in the twentieth century was to develop a road system. Until this time, roads as such were more or less unknown, only tracks trodden by horses and livestock over the course of the centuries. Until well into the twentieth century the Icelandic road system was seriously inadequate, and it was only in 1974 that the ring route around the country was finally completed. The last section to be opened was across the glacial outwash plains along the south coast. Prior to this, road traffic from Reykjavík to the east had to travel right the way around the north of the country.

was coming in through the nail holes in the roof. A doctor was fetched to attend to some sick people who lived in some basement rooms in one part of town. In the front room he could hardly find anywhere to put his feet because of people lying on mattresses, the floor was covered so thick. When a doctor comes to a place like this during the day the mattresses are pushed against the wall or stacked up to make some space for people to move around. If someone dies in this kind of house the body has to stay there in among the living. In many places there is water and condensation running down the basement walls. The housing situation is woefully inadequate for as many as a quarter of the population of this town.

Other than the greater use of stone and timber for construction purposes, housing conditions for the poor in towns were thus not much different from those in the country as described in chapter Three. For the first decades of the twentieth century progress was slow: even in 1928 45 per cent of dwellings in Reykjavík lacked sewers and toilets and only eleven per cent had baths. Other aspects of living standards – health and sanitation, for instance – remained strikingly similar in both towns and the country. It was only in the years following the Second World War that town and country moved decisively apart and Iceland could be said to have acquired a genuine urban culture.

One of the jobs taken by working-class women in Reykjavík in the latter part of the nineteenth century and early part of the twentieth was doing the laundry for middle-class households. The washing site was built around a hot spring a fair distance out from the centre of town. The washerwomen set off early in the morning and returned late in the evening, often – as in so many other jobs – taking their children with them.

13

The Myth of the Model Woman: Gender Roles in Urban and Rural Iceland

Women in the workforce

How did life for women differ in urban environments from rural areas? It is worth considering some statistics. According to Magnús S. Magnússon in *Iceland in Transition*, in 1901 about a quarter of the female population of Iceland between the ages of fifteen and 64 was engaged in some kind of employment other than farming.[1] For the country as a whole, including farming, the figure was 59 per cent (falling to 39 per cent by 1940). Magnús argues that the fall in the number of women in farming after 1910 does not necessarily indicate a rise in female participation in the urban workforce; it might equally suggest that increasing numbers of women were migrating to towns in order to marry rather than in search of new job opportunities. The proportion of women in the workforce in Reykjavík was higher than for the country as a whole; the main occupations were in fishing (fish processing), manufacture (weaving and clothmaking), public services (education and health) and private service, which was particularly important in Reykjavík, with many young girls from the countryside coming specifically to Reykjavík and other urban centres to work as servants in middle- and upper-class households.

The local historian Kristín Ástgeirsdóttir, working for the Department of Ethnology at the National Museum of Iceland, investigated the subject of women in domestic service in Reykjavík in the period 1909 to 1956. Her principal sources were a group of 25 women, all then living in old people's homes and selected from a sample of 200 interviewees. All had once been domestic servants in Reykjavík, mostly between the ages of sixteen and twenty. They cited basically three reasons for going into service: to leave home; to ease the burden on their own families; and to learn domestic skills and experience something new. Some mentioned the absence of other work opportunities. 'During these years work in the fish trade was unreliable and there was fierce competition for every job that came up. For the first half of this period, in winter there were simply no other jobs to be had. Domestic service was thus the first port of call for many women when they arrived in town and were establishing themselves. Few of these women had any education and this limited their chances of finding other employment in the longer term when more jobs became available. Service had the advantage that it came with room and board and job security, if all went well; set against this, wages were low, the hours long, and you were tied to one place and had to serve others'.[2] Kristín noted that most of the women she interviewed had to take other jobs over the summer to supplement their wages, for instance on farms. Most got married during their time in service.

In the article 'Bakburður kvenna í Reykjavík' (Women with Weight on their Shoulders), written in 1887 for the newspaper *Dagskrá*, a doctor from Reykjavík called Guðmundur Guðmundsson gave an account of the duties that might be expected of women in domestic service: 'It is well-known practice here for female servants, after they have finished their day's work, to have to take a big sack of dirty clothes to Laugar and spend all night there washing, then bring it home in the morning, and then sometimes have to work the whole of the next day.' Laugar here was the hot springs on the outskirts of Reykjavík where people of the town did their laundry in the open air.

In 1910 domestic servants accounted for 54.5 per cent of the total female workforce in Iceland. By 1940 this had fallen to 41 per cent. Overall, female participation in the workforce was fairly high. The kinds of work they did, however, depended on class. Women from more affluent backgrounds worked only inside the house; poorer ones had less choice in the matter. The newspapers of the time printed several vivid accounts of women at work, such as the following from *Ísafold* in 1890, called 'Eyrarvinna kvenna og aðrir vinnubragða – ósiðir' (Women's Dock Assignments and other Bad Methods of Work):

> It is a cause for thought and concern to see handsome young girls, perhaps only recently confirmed, carrying 200 pound sacks on their backs or their shoulders. Or seeing two strong men hoist a heavy bag of coal or salt onto the shoulders of a young girl to carry into the warehouse, day in day out, without rest. Her body is bent double, her feet are swollen and she often has to dip them in the sea to soothe the pain. Her body becomes stiff and misshapen and in the bloom of life, or even younger, her health is wasted and her strength withered away.

Guðmundur Guðmundsson, quoted earlier, writes in similar vein. There were particular dangers, he pointed out, for 'pregnant women and women who have just given birth, and they would hardly do this kind of work if they realized how dangerous it was for their safety and well-being.'

Employment per se is of course only half the story. Married women, although registered as housewives, often made an essential contribution to the family economy. As well as running the household, they tended livestock, or did wool working at home and sold the produce on to local merchants, or dried fish for processing companies, even in their own back yards. As described in chapter Twelve, many women left town every summer and went to the country as seasonal agricultural labourers, often taking one or more of their children with them.

In fact, women's work in towns had much in common with women's work in the country. In the years leading up to World War II, unquestionably more and more women withdrew from active contribution to the family income and concentrated their efforts on service to the family. But this did not become common until after 1940, as industry in Iceland matured and the national economy stabilized. Until well into the twentieth century the seasonal nature of the economy, particularly agriculture and fishing, demanded that women continue to be active contributors to the general workforce. Despite changes to the social fabric of Iceland in the early years of the twentieth century, the majority of women continued to approach work with the same attitudes and mentality as women in rural areas had done for centuries.

Before going further, we need to understand that there was a wide difference between the reality of gender roles in the nineteenth century and how they were customarily presented in speeches and writings of the time. If we look at popular culture in the nineteenth century from the point of view of the individual, it becomes clear that people were beguiled by the 'myth of the model woman', the image of what women were 'supposed' to be. This paradigm was employed in various ways in the second half of the nineteenth century and the early part of the twentieth for the purpose of curbing social change and popular ambitions. It rested upon the complex legally prescribed division of labour between men and women and came out most clearly in the image of the 'perfect housewife', living on a large and prosperous farm, preferably the wife of the local minister. Thus the customs and mores of the upper class shaped people's conceptions of what women were and how they ought to behave. The model assumed that a woman's place was firmly in the home, bringing up the children and running the household, and so long as they performed these tasks conscientiously the interests of the family and society were safe and secure.

The truth, as described in diaries and autobiographies of the period, was quite a different matter. Farmers and their workers approached

The advent of the trawler age had an enormous impact on living conditions in Iceland. The first trawler arrived in 1904. The new ships were much bigger and had a much higher productivity than the smaller vessels fishermen were used to and as a result generated a huge demand for labour on land for both men and women. Trawlers carried a maximum crew of 30, reduced to sixteen for half the year, i.e. each trawler provided 23 full years' work for the actual crewmembers. In addition, each trawler is estimated to have provided work for 33 more people on land in processing the catch and in maintaining and managing the ships. In total, therefore, each trawler created jobs for around 60 individuals directly. If we assume that each of these people was the bread-winner for a family of five, then each trawler supported something like 280 people. In 1910 the population of Reykjavík was 11,500 and there were six trawlers, i.e. over 10% of the population was living off the income generated from trawling. By 1917 this figure had risen to around 20%. In the first decades of the twentieth century the trawler fleet expanded rapidly, and with it Icelanders' economic reliance on the fisheries.

the tasks that needed doing irrespective of gender. The division of labour was as likely to depend every bit as much on age, physical capacity and experience.

Gender roles in theory and practice

The basis for gender roles was laid down in the law of the land, however much actual practice often ran directly counter to the spirit of this law. We must remember that women did not receive the right to vote in Iceland until the first twenty years of the twentieth century – initially in local elections, subsequently in parliamentary elections. Their social rights were similarly restricted in most areas. Such restrictions on general participation in society reinforced a specific and rigid pattern of roles that allowed for little variation. The man was the face of the household to the world outside, responsible for everything that touched the family's formal relations with the public authorities, in just about any form whatsoever. Laws dating back to the eighteenth century gave the master of the household almost unlimited power over his family and other members of the household. These laws made it the duty of the householder to enforce this power with firmness and shoulder the responsibilities it entailed without compromise: the spirit underlying this arrangement directly assumed that the well-being of society depended on householders taking this duty seriously. The threefold division of power between king, Church and householders rested upon each of these entities working efficiently and fulfilling its appointed functions. The division of roles between the sexes was thus inextricably bound up with the structure of society.

The spirit of the law was not always applied with equal rigour. People's attitudes were often governed by the tone taken in public debate in the newspapers. Though very few commentators discuss gender roles specifically, their ideas on the roles and rights of women are often latent in their attitudes to subjects like the tension between town and country, the popular desire for education, and pauperism. The debate took on an appreciably different tone in the early part of the twentieth century as the new, urban, middle-class society began to assert itself against the traditional values of the older order.

'The estate of headship of the household is the oldest and primary institution of human society', wrote the Rev. Ólafur Ólafsson in a lecture called 'Heimilislíf' (Domesticity) published in 1889. He went on: 'And we cannot imagine that this position will ever pass from being, since it is in reality not the work of man himself, rather its roots lie in human nature itself, in other words, it is the work of God; at the same time as he created mankind, he also created this estate.' Ólafur goes on to discuss a whole range of issues relating to household management and finds much to condemn in how things then were. He is fairly charitable on the subject of women's tasks and feels that women often have a heavy load to bear. It is hard for them to rise under the burdens of everyday life. But in their behaviour he finds much to criticize: 'Neither can I forbear from mentioning here that it is only natural that many house-wives fail to perform their domestic duties to the proper extent. This comes out most clearly when one examines the preparation many girls receive for the estate of housewife. With many of them, it is that they are born into squalor and poverty, grow up without discipline and care, and drink in wretchedness and slovenliness with their mother's milk.' Ólafur describes this as a vicious circle that eventually leads to perdi-tion, with women as the pawns of fate.

Despite the Rev. Ólafur's relatively positive attitude to women – his were, indeed, among the most liberal views to be expressed on the sub-ject – there is no escaping the fact that he felt women were in large part responsible for the problems he perceived all around him with the breakdown in traditional values. Others were less restrained and claimed that these problems were entirely the result of women wanting more education. Symptomatic of this discussion among many of the more affluent farmers was a lack of understanding of the mentality and con-ditions of ordinary people. Those who were most vocal in expressing their views came almost without exception from the more educated and usually more affluent section of the farming class. The debate on the problems facing agriculture was repeatedly punctuated with appeals to the 'myth of the model woman' in rural society, presented as an exemplar of how things ought to be. This whole debate, which gathered steam as the end of the century approached, was aimed, directly or indirectly, at providing a more precise definition of the position of women in national life and thus sharpening the distinction in gender roles. The migrations from country to town thus became the occasion for a new examination of the formal social conditions of men and women.

Around the turn of the century the debate took on a slightly new light, with a spate of articles representing the views of the new middle class. These views, as it happened, had much in common with those that richer farmers had been advocating in the decades immediately preceding: that a woman's place was in the home and that was an end to the matter. 'The myth of the model woman' gained new impetus. Like the representatives of traditional rural society before them, the educated middle class was anxious to impose greater discipline and control on society and sharper lines between the sexes. Only now these views were also coloured by intellectual currents that came from abroad, reflecting the attitudes of the European middle classes.

Almost by definition, the middle class was the section of society that was most influenced by the manners and behaviour of urban Europe. Educated, bourgeois in outlook, and anxious to assert its newfound influence, it sought to promote particular values designed to move society in directions that best served its own interests. One of the keypoints of these new ideas was a much clearer distinction between male and female roles than ever before. This was essentially an urban outlook: it was only in towns that a sharp demarcation between home and the workplace existed, and thus it was only in towns that such a separation of gender roles was possible.

One of the most pressing tasks facing the middle class was to impose a greater order on society, to teach people how to live in an urban environment with all the temporal and spatial restrictions that this entailed. We find articles by middle-class writers again and again advocating similar views to those previously expressed by richer farmers, laying the blame for any failure in society on a lack of enterprise and discipline among the working classes. For example, many articles appeared claiming that the greatest threat to the country lay in the popular clamour among many women pressing for better educational opportunites. Bríet Bjarnhéðinsdóttir, who is widely regarded as one of the foremost campaigners of her time for women's rights, says the following regarding women's education in a lecture called 'Sveitalíf og Reykjavíkurlíf' (Peasant life and Reykjavík life) delivered in 1894 and published the same year:

> As things now stand, what characterizes the people of the lower orders of the town, and especially women, is this unexampled mania for education that afflicts them so much that they can neither sleep nor eat. Nobody should think of blaming young girls for wanting to learn something that might be of benefit to them, intellectually or practically. But this 'education' of theirs – in inverted commas – appears to do little to educate them, to make them more sensible, better or more capable of performing their duties after than before. The result often seems to be that they think themselves too good to do any work other than some worthless frippery, which they cannot live from, or something of the sort, mainly dressmaking, which even then they have no real skill at.

According to Bríet, this so-called practical education for women led only to idleness and indiscipline. When one finds comments like these coming from a woman like Bríet Bjarnhéðinsdóttir, one can just imagine the attitudes of people who had little regard for women's contribution to society. There is no question about Bríet's deep concern for women's conditions, but initially she took fierce exception to the lack of direction she saw in their education. Up until the first decade of the twentieth century she promoted these views in a highly traditional manner in *Kvennablaðið* (The Women's Paper). Her articles appear to be aimed primarily at middle-class women readers, providing various pieces of 'sound advice' that had little to do with the great majority of working women in Iceland. Such a stance served further to reinforce the myth of the model woman. The ideology that lay behind it encouraged heads of households to assert their power and address the problems of society with ever greater inflexibility. And yet these views coming from Bríet, to start off with at least, need not surprise us: her models came from the world outside Iceland, where the women's rights movement was closely associated with the middle class and its growth.

Thóra Melsteð, one of the early advocates of improved education for women, was also true to the world-view of her class in an article, 'Um kvennlega menntun og Reykjavíkur kvennaskóla' (About the Education of Women and their Schooling in Reykjavík), published in *Ísafold* in 1897:

A well brought-up and well educated woman – married or unmarried – *who is able to fulfil her position properly*, which is: *in her own home* – will almost always win the love and respect and the rights that are due and fitting to her . . . And though above anything else the home should be her workplace – and this in truth is broad, valuable and rich in blessings – she might of course take a great part in public issues alongside her husband, even though she has no position in the community, or the right to vote, etc. only so long as first and foremost she perform her duties well within her home.

Thóra goes on to discuss the need for discipline in the bringing up of children and urges its systematic application, since 'the spirit of free will can hardly lead to good, wheresoever it reigns supreme, and he or she who has never learnt in his youth to obey will neither be able to command in later years when duty so requires and circumstance demands.'

As the economic influence of the middle class grew the range of roles open to women was greatly curtailed. Women lost many of their former industrial and productive functions and turned in ever greater numbers to bringing up their children and managing the household. In the farming community the role of child rearing had traditionally been shared among various members of the household, with the mother as just one contributor out of many. In middle-class urban homes the woman's workload shrank markedly as family sizes fell and it became commoner for homes to employ domestic help from outside, as noted earlier in this chapter. Middle-class women devoted the majority of their time to bringing up their children, together with practising recognized bourgeois accomplishments in their spare time.

A further change that can be traced to the burgeoning middle class lay in attitudes to illegitimacy. Traditionally, social control in Iceland had been relatively weak. Although not recommended – for example, illegitimate children were obviously more likely to end up on the parish – illegitimacy had always been fairly well tolerated in rural society. Unmarried mothers were regarded with some disapproval but were not subject to social ostracization and continued to be active contributors to society. Their position was of course financially precarious but any disapproval they encountered was more on social than moral grounds. Throughout the period 1830–1930 illegitimacy stood at around 15–20 per cent, considerably higher than in most countries in Europe; by way of comparison, in the same period rates hardly exceeded 10 per cent in Norway, Denmark and Sweden.[3]

With the rise of the middle class in the early years of the twentieth century there was an appreciable change in attitude; the influx of ideas from abroad and the desire to protect accumulated wealth meant that having children out of wedlock now became a social stigma and middle-class girls with illegitimate children became less marriageable. At least, this was the case among the middle classes themselves. Attempts by the authorities to curb people's sexual activities and in particular procreation outside marriage may perhaps account for a slight fall in the illegitimacy rate. But in general these changes had little effect on the behaviour and attitudes of the working class. Once again, traditional rural values were transferred into the new urban environment and illegitimacy rates remained far higher in Iceland than elsewhere in Europe and North America.

Like their counterparts around much of the world, the Icelandic middle classes were openly disparaging and critical towards the lower classes. Many of their strictures were of course beside the point due to their ignorance of the conditions under which working people actually lived. Judgement of this kind, however, went on constantly and served its purpose: by drawing attention to the failings of others, the ever-growing middle class was no less bringing itself up; such talk bolstered the self-confidence of the middle class and helped to draw a sharper line between itself and the common people and thus mark out a unique position for itself.

'The model woman' in the early twentieth century

One thing that is indisputably true is that women tended to specialize in certain kinds of work in urban areas, creating a distinct division of labour between the sexes. This division, however, was not unlike what occurred in rural areas: particular jobs might be seen primarily as the province of men or women, but the contribution of women was equally significant in both areas. As in rural areas, working patterns in towns were liable to become disrupted at regular intervals when conditions demanded that a task be done and the work would be assigned to whoever was available, male or female. In many instances this would turn into a permanent arrangement and women would become trapped, for instance, in jobs that required heavy manual exertion. In the lives of ordinary working people, the boundaries between men's work and women's work were extremely blurred.

The experiential world of the richer farmers and the spokesmen of the middle classes was projected onto the whole general populace, both in towns and in the country. Attempts were made to recast and remodel the role of women in publications aimed specifically at a female readership. This recasting went on under the terms of the middle class, guided entirely by its own values and attitudes. This tenor within the contemporary debate has had a deep effect on how modern Icelanders understand their past.

In particular, people's thinking on women's and gender issues in later times has been heavily influenced by the concept of 'the model woman' in rural society. It has often been claimed that the early years of the twentieth century saw women increasingly breaking away from the yoke of traditional gender roles and beginning to establish a position for themselves on the labour market. This seems to fly in the face of what actually happened, at least for the large majority of women in Iceland: for an ever-growing number of women the 'myth of the model woman' and the strict demarcation of gender roles turned increasingly into reality as the twentieth century progressed. Women's roles became determined by gender more than at any time before in the country's history. As I see it, in their personal lives women had traditionally had a broad scope for involvement in a range of activities and for women of the working class this scope continued on into the early part of the twentieth century, whether they liked it or not. Their power over their own actions and responsibilities were key to the welfare of the family.

Within the traditional rural society women had been subject under law to glaring inequalities that limited just about every aspect of their public lives. This inequality, as noted earlier, manifested itself in their political and economic status as well as their lack of educational opportunities. Early in the twentieth century the formal status of women began to change with the granting of increased rights. The benefits of these new rights were largely confined to women of the upper and middle classes. At the same time as women's formal rights improved, gender roles became more sharply defined. In a certain sense, the first decades of the twentieth century can be viewed as a kind of interim period so far as women were concerned. Their status – particularly the status of middle-class women – was extremely ambiguous; on the one hand they now enjoyed greater formal rights, but they were simultaneously expected to conform to prescribed and universal patterns of female behaviour. The force of the myth of the model woman had, if anything, increased.

The greater formal freedoms gained by women at the start of the twentieth century were of much less significance to women from the urban working class. Like their sisters in the farming communities, they continued to perform a vital role as providers for their families. As time passed, though, more and more working-class women opted to stay at home as their middle-class counterparts were already doing. This, however, was hardly a realistic proposition until job security had increased appreciably, and this did not occur until the 1930s and '40s at the earliest. Being a housewife thus became a mark of status. Middle-class ideas of behaviour had gained the upper hand, though without eliminating older values entirely. What is notable here, however, is that in Iceland the period in which it was the norm for women to stay at home was very short, just a few decades. This goes some way to explaining the extremely active part that women have always played in Icelandic society.

14

Death in the City

Change and continuity in the face of death

In this book I have described how people's entire personalities were often coloured by their repeated exposure to death during childhood. As we move into the twentieth century, improvements in health and changes in family structure served to modify this situation somewhat. It is worth examining how the part of death in the everyday lives of town-dwellers changed and how these changes affected the way they regarded death.

As noted in chapter Seven, infant mortality fell dramatically through the second half of the nineteenth century but at the end of the century still stood at around 11 per cent. This was clearly a significant change, bringing infant mortality eventually into line with levels found in the rest of Europe. The improvements continued through the first three decades of the twentieth century, with endemic diseases like diphtheria, typhoid, leprosy, hydatids and tetanus, which had been major killers in the nineteenth century, finally being brought under control. Professional health care began to extend to an ever-greater proportion of the population, as indicated, for example, by the increase in the number of doctors and hospitals in the early years of the twentieth century: in 1905 there were just six hospitals in the whole of Iceland, all of them fairly small; by 1915 this number had risen to nineteen and the number of beds had more than doubled. Most hospitals however remained very small and thus limited in scope. In his annual report for 1938 the director of public health, Vilmundur Jónsson, noted that of the 40 general hospitals in Iceland at the time, most contained only two to five beds. There were only nine general hospitals with over twenty beds, the largest being the National Hospital with 100 beds and an average of between 140 and 150 patients. In the whole country there were 1,100 hospital beds, or one for every hundred inhabitants of Iceland. This figure included specialist tuberculosis hospitals, leper hospitals and mental hospitals. So far as general hospitals were concerned, the number of beds rose from 60 in 1900 to 730 in 1940.

This is of course not to say that diseases and epidemics were a thing of the past, or that people ceased to live in fear of them. At the start of the twentieth century conditions of public health remained parlous as a result of poor housing, nutrition and sanitation. While medical facilities undoubtedly improved as the century progressed, ideas about health control and attitudes to death did not necessarily move forward in step with them: when somebody around them was sick, people were accustomed to just sitting and waiting for death or recovery, and it often took many years for them to accept the idea that medical help was an option. This is shown, for example, in a survey carried out by the Department of Ethnology of the National Museum of Iceland: many of the respondents confirmed that they did not seek medical advice except in cases of extreme emergency.

A fair example is the case of Sigurður Jón Guðmundsson (b. 1895) as related in his autobiography *Til sjós og lands* (On Sea and Land). Sigurður Jón was born in the fishing port of Ólafsvík on the Snæfellsnes peninsula in the west of Iceland and fostered out at the age of nine when his mother died. Around the age of his confirmation he contracted a severe chill, which developed into a high fever.

> One week passed and then another, and then more after that, and I felt worse and worse. In the end I stopped getting dressed and eating anything other than milk and it was hard keeping even that down. But although I was genuinely in such bad shape there were people in the house so hard-nosed that they thought that I was perfectly capable of getting up and working . . . Someone mentioned calling the doctor for me but this was felt to be too expensive and not worth the expense.

As far as most people were concerned, Sigurður Jón was just malingering, but he stayed in bed the whole summer. Eventually he managed to get to see a doctor, who diagnosed bronchitis and a kidney disease and ordered him to stay in bed. But his father had other ideas and, without consulting him, hired him out as a deck-hand on a fishing boat. On the boat he became extremely ill again and when he got back to land the doctor wanted to send him to hospital. Once again his father took the view that this was unnecessary and got him another job shortly afterwards. Somehow Sigurður Jón managed eventually to recover and get on with his life.

Despite the fall in child mortality, nineteenth-century attitudes to death persisted well on into the new century. Three factors in particular lay behind this continuity: memories of former times when diphtheria and death had been frequent experiences for the average family; the funeral rites, which remained essentially unchanged from one century to the next; and the country's literary and religious tradition.

Tuberculosis, Spanish flu and the tradition of mortality

The Icelandic winter-evening gatherings described in chapter Five were built heavily upon oral tradition. These gatherings continued long into the twentieth century and provided an important forum for the exchange of news and propagation of memories. Despite an increasing reliance on the written word, the oral tradition retained a powerful hold over people's thinking.

Memories, for example of the high incidence of mortality in the nineteenth century, were passed on from one generation to another and on into the twentieth century and had a profound influence on people's attitudes to death. Hulda Á. Stefánsdóttir (b. 1897) recalled in her autobiography a story her father had told frequently at home in the early years of the twentieth century. He was the headmaster of an agricultural college in the north and had moved to Akureyri in 1904. Early in his life his family had had to face the ordeal of an outbreak of diphtheria which had snatched away four of his brothers and a sister in a single night:

> It was already evening and that same day a body had been carried out into the storehouse. There were five children left, all at death's door. A little sister of my father's shared a bed with him; her name was Guðrún and she was a year younger than him. She was his favourite sister and he wanted to take care of her as best he could. In the night he felt she was getting cold and so he tried to wrap the blanket around her, but with minimal success. He himself was feeling more and more ill and was having difficulty breathing. His aunt sensed there was something wrong and came in and stuck her fingers down his throat and scraped away the phlegm that was caught there. Later he said that this had saved his life. But when she turned to little Guðrún she realized she was already dead . . . That whole night grandmother Guðrún paced the floor at the south end of the living room with a sick infant on her shoulders who died at dawn. That morning the house of Heiði was a scene of utter devastation.

Hulda goes on to say that, according to her father, her grandparents had borne their grief in silence, supported by their faith in God. She concludes her account with her personal reactions: 'Stories like this had a huge influence on us children; there was nothing that frightened us more than diphtheria.' Tragedies like these were very real to children growing up in the early twentieth century; the fact that close relatives could recall horrific scenes of this kind from their own experience must have left a lasting impression on those that heard them. The fears and terrors of one generation could be passed on to the next and add to their insecurity about themselves and the world around them.

Despite the significant improvements in healthcare Icelanders were still exposed to a range of fatal diseases. Sigurveig Guðmundsdóttir (b. 1909), from the town of Hafnarfjörður close to Reykjavík, lost her infant brother at the age of five and her father four years later. She recorded her thoughts in her autobiography *Þegar sálin fer á kreik* (When the Soul is on the Move): 'I think, too, that death was not so distant to children as it is now. Children saw adults lying on their death beds, saw them die at home and be borne out to their funerals and were there when they were buried. Beyond question this had a major impact on their attitude to death. I think we took death rather casually.'

Children's exposure to death in the early years of the twentieth century had a major impact not only on their attitude to death but also on their behaviour. In her autobiography *Í sannleika sagt* (In Truth Told), Bjarnfríður Leósdóttir (b. 1924) from Akranes on the west coast gives a detailed account of family deaths, diseases and disasters during her childhood years. In her mind, death was always just around the corner and this had a profound affect on her behaviour. She was, for example, terrified of being separated from her parents, even for a few hours, because she believed they would die if she was not there with them.

The most intractable disease of the early twentieth century and the one that took the greatest toll in human lives was tuberculosis and many of the autobiographers attest to the fear it inspired. Vilmundur Jónsson, chief medical officer for Iceland between 1931 and 1959, noted that at the turn of the century, though other endemic diseases were at last being brought under control, tuberculosis really took off as a result of increased communication between rural and urban areas and greater social interaction in general. The number of people dying from tuberculosis stood at around 200 a year through the first four decades of the twentieth century, peaking in 1930 at 232. A specialist tuberculosis sanatorium was established outside Reykjavík in 1910. By 1938 it had treated over 2,000 patients, some with histories of the disease going back over decades.[1] Tuberculosis often struck people in the prime of life and was deeply feared throughout the country, especially among the young. The writer Einar Bragi (b. 1921), who was brought up in the fishing port of Eskifjörður on the east coast, describes the dread the disease inspired in his autobiography *Af mönnum ertu kominn* (From Men are You Come):

Death to me was a constant threat throughout these years, always ready to intrude itself forcefully on my consciousness. While I was growing up tuberculosis was endemic in Eskifjörður, striking children and young people with especial virulence. This being so, it was no wonder that everyone was haunted by a single chilling question: Who will be next? When I think back to those years, I recall that it was seldom that a coastal steamer arrived without a coffin being carried down onto the quay of someone who had died at Vífilstaðir or Kristnes, depending on whether the ship was coming from the south or north. On the dock stood the close relatives, waiting for their loved one. It was a pitiful scene. Then the coffin was taken to church with the relatives following behind, broken and in silence.

Sigurveig Guðmundsdóttir was a patient at the tuberculosis hospital outside Reykjavík for four years and describes the life there and the constant nearness of death in her autobiography. When the doctors told her that she was going to be discharged she had deep reservations: 'I knew too that people were generally very fearful of patients from Vífilstaðir. Tuberculosis was a disease that everyone wanted to avoid. Who would give a person like that a job? We were all fully aware of this, and it meant there was nothing to look forward to when one left hospital.' Her misgivings were justified: on discharge she felt isolated and found people shunning her and avoiding her home.

These horrific images and fears of death received periodic reinforcement from new outbreaks of disease, mostly notably the Spanish influenza epidemic of 1918. According to the medical reports, in the first week of November 5,000 cases were reported, most of them acute. National estimates suggest that around 10,000 people in total were infected – and this despite the fact that the epidemic was successfully contained to the south and south-west of the country by isolation measures. Þórarinn Gr. Víkingur (b. 1880) happened to be in Reykjavík on a visit when the disease struck and his movements were restricted until the middle of January. He himself remained uninfected and he joined one of the groups of nursing volunteers formed when the authorities realized the magnitude of the problem. He described his first assignment in his autobiography *Komið víða við* (Here, There and Everywhere): 'The first night I was sent out to give assistance to a family I did not know. What faced me there was a pitiful sight: the housewife was dead and her husband and five-year-old son dreadfully ill. There was a middle-aged woman at death's door, in such unbearable pain she could hardly stop screaming. It was cold in the house and it was my first task to light a fire in the coal stove.'

The Spanish flu had a major impact on the community at large, as described in a series of harrowing accounts. The sufferings were undoubtedly exacerbated by the poor housing conditions in which most people lived and the extreme shortage of qualified medical care. Many homes had no fuel. Rescue workers going from house to house often encountered families where both parents had died leaving only young children alive. The overall death toll in the two months of the epidemic was around 500, of which about 260 were in Reykjavík. Páll V. G. Kolka, a medical student at the time, noted that the flu claimed many more victims later and there were others who never really recovered fully. His estimate of the death toll was a little lower than the figures given above but broadly comparable. This was out of a total population in Iceland at the end of 1917 of around 91,300.

Páll described his experiences in these few months of 1918 in his memoirs *Úr myndabók læknis* (From a Doctor's Picture Book). At the time he was a student in his third year at medical school and, as he himself says, totally unprepared for what he had to face. He was sent out on assignment to a number of little fishing villages on the south coast near to Reykjavík where the flu had struck particularly hard and his account of the magnitude of the disaster in these villages and the human tragedy he witnessed there makes moving reading.

He tells, for example, of a house he visited where a mother and three daughters lay critically ill. The only healthy person was the husband. In the end the mother and one of the daughters died more or less in Páll's arms. When Páll offered the husband his sympathy, the husband smiled through his tears and said: 'I am not afraid of the strength nor the power of death, my good doctor, and I know that this will only be a short separation.' His response reminds one strongly of those from earlier times that we met in chapters Six and Nine, from a time when people were encouraged to face death with a stoic calm and dignity, believing it was not in their power to do anything about it.

Accidents and disasters

While the Spanish flu was exceptional, it was by no means the only dramatic intrusion of death upon the consciousness of Icelanders in the early part of the twentieth century. As noted earlier, the fishing industry grew steadily in the second half of the nineteenth century and went through a boom in the early years of the twentieth. With growing numbers of men working at sea, accidents increased. For a society that was neither highly complicated nor technologically advanced, the incidence of death by industrial accident through the late nineteenth century and into the twentieth is astonishing, holding steady at an average of around a hundred

This photo, taken from the porch of Dómkirkjan, the cathedral in the centre of Reykjavík, shows the distress on the faces of the dead man's British colleagues. Thousands of foreign seamen perished around the coast of Iceland over the centuries, frequently whole crews. Their bodies were often found washed up on the shore. Funerals in Iceland were traditionally social as much as religious occasions. For example, the wake was often accompanied by heavy drinking and other refreshments. With the growing influence of middle-class values in the twentieth century, death and funerals took on the bourgeois aspects familiar throughout the Western world today – formal and distant. One unusual custom, however, remains in full force today: deaths are announced on the radio and many of the newspapers, especially the oldest, Morgunblaðið, carry long, detailed articles recounting the lives of almost everyone that dies. It is irrelevant whether the person in question was in any way famous or remarkable; everyone gets their mention. These articles therefore make excellent contemporary sources for the lives of ordinary modern-day Icelanders.

cases a year. This figure does not take account of the large number of foreigners drowned in the seas off Iceland and whose bodies were often washed up on the shores around the country. For example, from 1825 to the start of World War I, around 400 French ships and around 4,000 French fishermen were lost in Icelandic waters. This is a huge number for just one country. To this we would need to add probably even greater numbers from countries such as England, Germany and Norway, all of whom fished the waters off Iceland throughout this period.[2]

In some years deaths at sea accounted for up to two-thirds of all accidental deaths. The social consequences could be devastating. Many of the Icelandic fishing boats were manned by crews of between five and ten men, often from the same village. Losing one such boat could decimate the workforce of an entire community, leaving a high proportion of its families destitute and without a breadwinner.

Fishing 'boats' fell into three categories: those with crews of one to three, those with four to six, and those called *skip* (ships) with crews of eight or more. The beginning of the twentieth century saw the introduction of trawlers. Trawlers grew in size in the 1910s and '20s and carried crews of between 15 and 27 hands. Since the economy of most urban areas was closely connected to the sea, accidents posed a very real threat for any family whose livelihood depended directly or indirectly on fishing.

In her autobiography *Lífsjátning* (Affirmation of Life), Guðmunda Elíasdóttir (b. 1920), who came from a small fishing port in the west of Iceland, describes herself and her mother waiting anxiously for her father to return from sea after a bad storm had hit the area:

> My mother opened one of the windows in the roof and hung a lamp there. Outside it was pitch black and a howling gale. She stood there at the little window and a strange light from the lamp lit up her face, pale and drawn but at the same time set with strong and fixed lines. This small but dignified woman stared in silence at the swell and the dark ocean. Somewhere out there in that stormy sea was my father and a small crew struggling to get to land in a motor vessel called the *Egill Skallagrímsson*. My mother leaned over me and lifted me up to the window. At first I could see nothing but darkness and I screwed my eyes up whenever a gust of wind blew against the window. Then I saw a dim light in many of the houses around. There were more people than us who were waiting.

Guðmunda and her mother held vigil all through the night for news of her father but the phone never rang: 'No news came, only anxiety filled the house, and even though I did not fully understand the enormity of what had taken place I sensed the tension and solemnness all around. Then I fell asleep. The next day the pastor walked up to our house.' Her father was missing, presumed dead, and the ordeal lived with Guðmunda long into her adulthood. What she had gone through was far from exceptional among children and families who were in some way connected with fishing. The ocean gave and the ocean took away, as people said.

The mechanism of death

The entire mechanism of death, its rites and procedures, continued largely unaffected by the movement to urban areas. Funerals and burials were performed in much the same way in towns as they had been in rural areas in the previous century. According to respondents to the National Museum Department of Ethnology survey of people born around the turn of the century, most people continued to die in their own homes, with the preparations for the funeral carried out by the family. The lack of hospitals and mortuaries meant that this remained the norm through the first part of the twentieth century.

The only mortuaries in the country were at the Reykjavík cemetery and the National Hospital, and both of these were very small. In 1931 a doctor and advocate of cremation called Gunnlaugur Claessen wrote an article on funeral practices in the newspaper *Vísir*. He lamented the lack of facilities in Reykjavík for storing bodies: 'The mortuary at the cemetery is a disgrace to the parish and the town. Bodies usually have to be kept for inordinate lengths of time in people's homes and many houses are too small for this. It is to be hoped that at some time in the future it will be possible for bodies to be housed in a city mortuary. This would be a welcome relief for many homes.' Families still washed and prepared the body for the funeral in their living room and held a wake for guests. The nature of the funeral wake changed somewhat in the second decade of the twentieth century – notably the heavy drinking that had previously accompanied it fell into disfavour – but in other respects practices remained very similar. Drinking after funerals was banned following a propaganda campaign by the Church and social reformers.

Popular religious belief included the concept of a fatalistic connection between God and everyday life. One respondent to the National Museum survey mentioned above, born in 1908, made the following comment: 'People believed, and probably still believe, that death was predetermined and that if people tried to avoid it any success they had would only be short-lived.' Religious faith, in particular in so far as it deals with death, became a matter of major controversy in the first decades of the twentieth century when a spiritualist and theosophical movement sprang up, founded by a group of educated and influential figures of Reykjavík society. Broadly speaking, its roots lay in the growing urban middle class, which was searching for an individual intellectual identity in a predominantly peasant society. The historian of religion Pétur Pétursson put it thus:

> The followers of the movement started out with a set of elevated
> concepts that were able to unify otherwise disparate interests

and give their class a sense of membership in an international order and community with the middle classes of other countries. Socially, this quasi-religious movement served the interests of a social order then in formation. Fundamental to the movement was a concern for the individual and his spiritual needs and an open-minded and positive attitude towards science and progress in all areas of life, including the spiritual. Through this the individual acquired a certain ideological foothold in society, a kind of 'cultural optimism', that was essential if the bourgeoisie was to survive and prosper in this new terrain.[3]

The various groups that gathered together to explore mysticism and psychic phenomena all had a very elitist outlook. The movement never really appealed to the masses. But the interests of these societies managed to capture the attention of the public at large in other ways. The winter-evening gatherings and the work of nineteenth-century collectors had helped to preserve a vast corpus of folktales that remained extremely popular with the general public. The interests of the spiritualists fed into certain dominant themes in these tales and in Icelandic folklore in general. For instance, a very large proportion of the general population believed in supernatural beings – elves, hidden people, giants and so on – who shared the landscape with themselves. There was thus a latent occultism or mysticism that ran throughout Icelandic society (and to some extent still does). Coincidental with the new spiritualistic movement, and probably associated with it, around the turn of the century there was a great upsurge of interest in the collection of folktales and other popular lore of rural Iceland.

To give an example of the world of popular superstition in Iceland in the early years of the twentieth century we can turn again to Sigurveig Guðmundsdóttir. Sigurveig was born in 1909. As mentioned earlier in this chapter, when she was five her parents lost a baby son shortly after birth. 'It was my mother and father's belief that the disfigurement the baby suffered and its death were the revenge of an elf-woman.' While they had been building their house a rock on the plot of land had been damaged. They had tried to remove the rock but a neighbour came and told them to stop: apparently there was an elf-woman living in this rock and people who had tampered with it before had been badly injured. Sigurveig's parents had taken this warning absolutely seriously but the leader of the work gang had carried on regardless. According to Sigurveig, her mother often had supernatural experiences and talked about them frequently. It is worth noting here that, although poor, this was a relatively educated, middle-class family. Traditional folk beliefs thus received a new lease of life from the spiritualist movement with

Child-rearing practices remained primitive in Iceland until the late nineteenth century and infant mortality was high. Death was everywhere close at hand. When photography arrived in Iceland in the nineteenth century, a custom soon developed of taking death-bed photographs of those who died, especially children, to keep their memory alive. Many of the pictures of dead children have an extraordinary sense of peace and beauty. The floral decorations on one shown here also illustrate the infiltration of middle-class tastes into Icelandic society.

its focus on the connections between life and death. This, together with the obvious continuity of religious belief and practice between nineteenth-century rural society and twentieth-century urban society, served to maintain the central position of death in the world view of Icelanders despite the apparent changes in most areas of their external lives.

15
Children in Urban Areas

Children at work

From the age of five or six most children were expected to make some sort of contribution to the workforce; this was no less true in Reykjavík and the small towns and villages around the coast than had always been the case on farms. As the twentieth century progressed an appreciable difference began to materialize between Reykjavík and the rest of the country. More and more people in the capital managed to escape the endemic poverty of Iceland and join the growing middle class, and through this ceased to exploit the labour potential of their children. But for the vast majority of families in urban areas poverty remained a serious and persistent problem and child labour continued to be an essential part of the family economy.

The autobiography of Tryggvi Emilsson (b. 1902), *Fátækt fólk* (Poor People), provides a good account of a typical working day for parents and their children in the early decades of the twentieth century. Tryggvi was one of eight brothers and sisters and at this point in the narrative the family is in dire financial straits, living in a little shack called Hamarskot above the Oddeyri district of Akureyri in the north:

The autumn of 1906 arrived. My father stoked the furnaces at the fish processing plant at Oddeyri. He was up before the crack of dawn to light the fire and usually returned only late at night. If the weather was bad he would sometimes come home soaked to the skin because he had no rainwear, but this was just something that men had to put up with. They could consider themselves lucky to have a job . . .

My mother took good care of the home. She fetched the water from the well or a stream in a nearby bog and saw to the livestock and kept the house so clean that people used to remark on it. She went almost every day to buy fish for the family and

Children got used to working hard from a young age. As economic conditions improved after the middle of the twentieth century and most children started staying at school well into their teenage years, their full-time participation in the workforce was of course delayed accordingly. However, the schools were closed for more than four months each summer and during this time almost all children were expected to work. This remains the case in Iceland today, though the motivation now is not so much economic necessity as consumer aspirations. Modern Iceland is an intensely consumerist society, and youngsters seem to be prepared to go to considerable lengths to be able to dress in the 'right' clothes and provide themselves with the accessories of contemporary life.

brought it home along with other things from town. She was constantly washing and cooking. She had to take my father food twice a day at work and she sometimes used the opportunity to dry fish under the cliffs. There was no end to everything she had to do but she still found good time to care for her children.

The children followed their mother around and helped in any way they could, depending on their age. This was, in fact, the lot of many children; they travelled about with their parents, usually their mothers, while they tended the livestock or worked at drying fish for some fish processor. As soon as they were old enough to help they were expected to do so.

In many cases, in the absence of their husbands, housewives saw to all the day-to-day running of family affairs, as of course did single mothers, often with their children in tow. Þorvaldur Guðmundsson (b. 1911), the son of a single mother from Reykjavík, described her unremitting struggle to keep body and soul together in a collection of interviews published in 1985 under the title *Reykjavík bernsku minnar* (Reykjavík of my Childhood): 'She fought for her own right to exist as an independent woman, and for my existence too. She did all kinds of jobs during those years: cleaning, laundry, domestic service, gutting fish, housekeeping, milking and haymaking. The opportunities were not great. I always went around with her and started to help as soon as I was able. For example, I helped her putting the laundry through the mangle in the evenings.' Þorvaldur started to work at his mother's side in a fish plant at the age of seven, having earlier sold newspapers and delivered milk on his own.

Farming remained an important part of life in urban areas. In his autobiography *Í útlegð* (In Banishment), Þorfinnur Kristjánsson (b. 1887) describes his daily round of work in Reykjavík in the last decade of the nineteenth century: 'Housework was much the same as on a small farm: in spring, spreading dung and preparing the hayfield, levelling it and spreading seaweed, seeing to the vegetable patch – ours was rather small – and planting the seeds, shearing the sheep and sitting over them during lambing and keeping them off the hayfield. Alongside this my father went fishing for lumpfish but only to provide food for us at home. I often went with him to check the nets and enjoyed this a lot.'

By way of comparison, the following – from the autobiography of Jóhannes R. Snorrason (b. 1917), *Skrifað í skýin* (Written in the Clouds) – describes the life of children growing up in the little fishing port of Flateyri in the Westfjords some thirty years later:

> Most people in Flateyri did some farming alongside working in the fish, and this provided enough for their families to live on. Boys in Flateyri were brought up in close touch with all the jobs that went on in the family, both indoors and, more often, out: taking care of the cows and sheep, fishing for lumpfish in spring, helping with the haymaking, and in autumn it was common practice for us boys to have to chase after the sheep and herd them back if they wandered out too far along the fjord in case there was a sudden snowstorm.

The father of the writer Einar Bragi (b. 1921) was the owner and captain of a fishing boat at Eskifjörður on the east coast. Besides this the family kept a small farm, described in Einar's autobiography *Af mönnum ertu kominn* (From Men are You Come): 'Tending the small-holding was of course mostly left to my mother and us kids because my father was away from home for long periods working.' By the 1910s and '20s small-scale farms of this kind were more likely to be found in the smaller ports and villages around the country than in Reykjavík, but many of the autobiographies make clear that this sort of activity also continued in Reykjavík well into the twentieth century. It was mostly the poorer sections of society that were involved but it was also fairly common for wealthier people to maintain a plot to farm on, either for recreational purposes or to provide food for domestic use.

My own grandfather, a merchant called Helgi Magnússon, ran what the family called their 'summer farm' on the outskirts of Reykjavík in the 1920s and '30s.[1] The family lived there over the summer months and employed a farmhand to see to things in winter. The same picture emerges from the National Museum Department of Ethnology survey mentioned in the last two chapters. One respondent, born and brought up in Reykjavík, made the following comment: 'Even though it was Reykjavík, life here was very similar to in the country. It is not so long since Reykjavík was a smaller place and people had room to dry fish, grow potatoes and have fields and livestock all over the town, especially in the outskirts.'

Parents who could not find something for their children to do with them simply sent them out on their own to work. Here they were expected to keep pace with the adults. Árni Helgason (b. 1914) describes his introduction to the world of work as follows: 'I was only six or seven years old when I started helping in the baiting shed, baiting fishing lines. It was cold and hard work.' Árni believed this work was the main cause of the polio he suffered for two years between the ages of ten and twelve. 'I am convinced – though it has never been proved – that it was working in the baiting shed that did for me. As a boy I worked for hours on end baiting the lines and stacking the tubs. It was a heavy load for a child to have to bear.'

Children were sometimes expected to handle tasks that taxed their powers almost beyond endurance, simply for want of other manpower or because there was sickness in the family. Tryggvi Emilsson (b. 1902), quoted earlier in book, describes what life was like for him at home after his mother died in 1908. Within a few months of her death six of his brothers and sisters had been sent off in different directions to foster homes. Only Tryggvi, then aged six, and his sister Laufey, aged nine, remained with their father: 'Laufey had to look after the house, keep the stove burning, cook, do the washing and clean the dishes and floors. Then she had to tend the livestock, both the sheep and the cow we had bought that summer, as well as milk the cow and feed them all. I of course went along with her every step and we held hands in the dark. Then our father would come home and we would feel better, even though he was never the same again and wept every night.'

One of the respondents to the National Museum Department of Ethnology survey, born in 1896, had had a father with leprosy who had been hospitalized for several years. She described to the interviewer the workload she and her mother had had to cope with in a Reykjavík fish factory: 'During the summer months her mother worked in the fish processing plant at Kirkjusandur, and when the respondent grew older she started to work there too, along with other children. For a time they lived at Kirkjusandur in housing attached to the plant. Her mother worked in the fish from March through to autumn. In winter she was in domestic service, cleaning and doing laundry for others.' As echoed by many of the respondents, the workday lasted at least from 6 a.m. to 7 p.m. and sometimes longer.

A striking feature of the survey is the number of the respondents who specifically commented on how young they were when they started working in the fish. Many of the tasks involved were possible to do at home. For instance, in saltfish production the fish was laid out to dry in the sun on an area covered in flat stones, and then taken up and restacked in the evening. One of the respondents, from Reykjavík and born in 1891, described her early work experience to the interviewer: 'Often when there was a shortage of people to process the fish, married women and children were called on to work. She worked in the fish in spring and went out to a farm for the haymaking. One time the respondent and a friend got a job unloading coal from a ship which involved carrying the large sacks of coal on their backs. The foreman felt this was too much for them and wanted them to stop, and a few days later he found them a different job carrying timber.'

Most children had to take any work they could get – running errands, delivering parcels, chasing horses around town or minding children. Many were sent off to farms to work for four to six months a year (see chapter Twelve). It was also common for poor families from towns to foster their children out to farms for a number of years, either because of extreme poverty or in the event of the death or sickness of one of the parents, as in the case of Tryggvi Emilsson cited earlier. This of course could be deeply troubling for the children concerned.

In other cases the annual migration of large numbers of children from town to country in summer to work in the haymaking could be treated as a kind of holiday, a welcome change – as in the following, from the autobiography of Hannes Sigfússon (b. 1922) *Flökkulíf* (A Roving Life), written in 1981: 'I went to the farm as soon as school was finished, just as I was used to. It came as a relief, even though this time I would be staying with total strangers and have to work for my keep. It was not unusual in Iceland at this time, and not so unusual today either, for youngsters to be gadding about from one world to another according to the season – town and country, school and work.' Hannes was born and grew up in Reykjavík. His experience of a child's life between town and

*Many of the children in the picture bear the signs of their social background —
bowed legs, assorted and mismatched clothing — yet still have something
impressive about them. These children, from the poorest section of Reykjavík
society in the 1930s, are captured here on film showing off their Sunday best.*

country was, as he says, typical of many children of his time and. This
seasonal migration and the introduction it provided to other modes of
existence had a powerful influence on children's thinking and how they
viewed life in general and urban areas in particular. In Hannes's time and
before, it was also often essential to the family's economy.

Town children got exposure to traditional peasant society in other
ways, too. Most families living in urban areas had large numbers of
relatives still living in the country. Periodically these country cousins
would have business of some type to do in town and would almost
invariably stay with their relatives. In some cases such visits might last
for months, for instance if they were for medical treatment or school
attendance. Árni Helgason, quoted earlier in this chapter, describes such
visits from country relatives while he was a child. It must be remembered that most houses, especially in urban areas, were very small and of
poor quality. Things could become extremely cramped when there were
guests staying; in Árni's case, as many as five families, altogether 49
people, were for a time living in the two small houses side by side that his
own family occupied. 'No one was turned away. Sometimes there were
three or four to a single bed before the end of the evening but nobody
complained. In my childhood I would often wake up to find there were
a couple more sleeping there with me. It was never a problem.'

General attitudes to work in urban areas in the early years of the
twentieth century were essentially the same as the ones the migrants
had brought with them from the country. In spite of the tirades of
certain propagandists against the laxity of town life, for most families it

The new age meets the old. The boy, who clearly belongs to an older period of Icelandic history, is shortening his journey by taking a lift on this enormous vehicle brought to the country by the Allied forces in World War II. The bag and the parcel suggest he is doing his bit for 'the family economy' by running errands for some company in town. In all probability he has been sent to make a delivery somewhere outside the city limits. The picture is symbolic of the changes that occurred in Iceland with the arrival of the British and later American forces.

was a constant struggle to get by and every hour's work that could be picked was to be taken as a blessing. Páll Kristjánsson (b. 1889), a carpenter from a small town in the north and the father of seven, describes the work ethic in his own household during the 1910s and '20s in his autobiography *Það er gaman að vera gamall* (It's Fun to Be Old): 'I made it a rule that the children should start working with me as soon as they reached the proper age, especially the boys. Ásta helped her mother at home with the household and running errands. I think this is the best way to bring up children, giving them plenty to keep them busy while they are young, so long as it does not get too much for them.' We find this attitude, that work is good for children, repeated frequently in autobiographies from the late nineteenth century and early decades of the twentieth. Many of the authors describe the heavy workload that was expected of them as children, but many also express their fondness and appreciation for what they experienced during these years.

A day at home and a day in school

As in rural areas, children in towns began education at home early, essentially learning to read and write. In 1907 an act of parliament was passed making education compulsory for all children in the country between the ages of ten and fourteen. Children living in urban areas who were able to attend a formal school (which was by no means the case for all of them) were supposed to get six months' schooling a year. In rural areas children could attend so-called 'peripatetic schools' for at least two months a year. In both rural and urban areas there was still a strong emphasis on education at home before the start of formal schooling, in line with the practice of traditional peasant society. Home education was considered extremely important. Indeed, well into the twentieth century formal schooling and whether it was really good for children was the subject of keen debate; it was argued that parents would neglect to teach their own children if they knew that these children would sooner or later be able to go to school.

The form of home education changed a little in the early years of the twentieth century. Conditions of course varied from family to family and many continued to teach their own children to read and write at home. But as more and more people sought employment outside the home, especially through the winter, and had limited time to attend to their children, it became increasingly common for children to be sent out to older people in the town for tutoring. Despite the strictures of some commentators who claimed that parents were neglecting their duties, it seems that most children in urban areas continued to get a basic education that was comparable to what their peers were getting elsewhere in the country.

Another custom carried over from traditional rural society was the pastoral visit. Until well into the twentieth century – in most urban areas up to the 1930s – every household with children would receive regular visits from the parish minister to test the children on their reading, writing and Christian knowledge. As time passed, though, these functions were taken over by other institutional procedures and the importance of such visits diminished.

Urban society also took over, in somewhat modified form, the winter-evening gatherings that had characterized rural Iceland. However, the domestic wool-working – carding, spinning, knitting and weaving – that had been a major part of the nineteenth-century economy became less important as the twentieth century progressed. Since children no longer needed to work in the evenings there was less pretext for families to gather together and thus less reason for group entertainment. Even so, most families made and repaired their own clothes and this provided a forum for a continuation of the practice of reading aloud from books and hearing children saying their lessons. The literature of choice at such gatherings remained the ancient sagas.

One of the principal goals of primary education was to instil in children a sense of national identity. The whole issue of national identity, which had been one of the main planks of the independence movement from its inception in the nineteenth century, came even more strongly to the fore with the progressive moves towards national independence in 1874, 1904 and 1918. Here the sagas were regarded as a valuable tool for inculcating what was seen as 'the Icelandic way of thinking'. A number of books that were at heart simply romanticized adaptations of the sagas were produced and taught in primary schools under the guise of Icelandic history. The message they were supposed to impart to children was that it was their duty to face life head on, no matter what, with the same will and determination as the heroes of ancient times when Iceland was a land of brave people; this was an unshakeable moral imperative and an unchanging guiding principle that applied to rich and poor alike.

The Education Act of 1907, as noted, introduced compulsory education for children between the ages of ten and fourteen. Its implementation in actual practice varied somewhat around the country. These first schools were open six months a year. In most of them the school day lasted only three or four hours. However, one of the oldest public schools in the country, in the small town of Eyrarbakki on the south coast, provided 30 hours' teaching a week and included non-academic subjects such as swimming, gymnastics, singing and handicrafts. In 1925–6 children aged fourteen in Reykjavík attended school for 26 hours a week, including the non-academic subjects. However, for children in the first class it was only thirteen hours a week. The school day thus differed appreciably according to age and location. The curriculum was in many ways similar to what had traditionally been taught at home; thus it has been argued that, for the first decades of the twentieth century at least, the introduction of formal education had only a minimal impact on children's lives.

A particularly striking feature of the autobiographies that describe urban childhoods around this time is how little the authors have to say about their early school days. This indifference changes markedly in the case of those who took their education further, to the Latin School or to one of the agricultural colleges, where almost without exception the authors go into their experiences in great detail. By the age of ten many children were already so deeply integrated into the workforce and such an important part of the family economy that to them education was a matter of secondary importance. For many children in urban areas in the first half of the twentieth century, there remained a palpable separation between work time and school time.

School and work – tension and interaction

Guðlaugur Gíslasson was born in 1908 and grew up in the fishing community on Vestmannaeyjar (the Westman Islands) off the south coast. His father died when he was nine. His case provides a good illustration of the dichotomy between work and education in the life of a child of ten in the early years of the twentieth century: 'With our breadwinner no longer with us, we had as good as nothing to keep ourselves going at home. The year 1918, the last year of the First World War, was very hard in the islands, like everywhere else in the country, and people could consider themselves lucky if they had enough to keep body and soul together from one day to the next.' The local authorities became concerned about the family's welfare and the sheriff proposed splitting them up and sending the children off to foster homes: 'I remember my mother became extremely angry and told him that this would never happen as long as she had the strength to stand on her own two feet. She thanked the sheriff and told him that one way or another we would make it through the winter . . . I was very proud of my mother for standing up to him like this, even though I realized that by doing so she was putting us at the mercy of an uncertain fate.' Guðlaugur describes the constant hunger and the struggle they went through to survive the harsh winter. But, to his mind, the experience was not wasted: 'I learned a great deal from that winter. I gained an understanding of what it meant to stand on the lowest rung of poverty and the importance of facing up to hardships with only one thing in mind: to overcome them, no matter how terrible they appeared when things looked at their bleakest.'

In the spring Guðlaugur's mother got a job drying fish and he and his brother worked there with her. This kept them going until the next winter. Then he and his brother came up with a scheme for bringing in something better. They had noticed that the men unloading the boats always lost a certain number of fish into the sea and did not have time to go and retrieve them. So Guðlaugur and his brother started getting up before dawn, collecting what the fishermen had left behind and selling it on to the fishing stations. By the end of that winter they found that this had brought in the equivalent of a mate's share on a decent fishing boat. But, as Guðlaugur points out, 'we had to be sure to be back home by eight in the morning so we could wash and get changed before school started at nine.' The following summer, now aged ten, he was taken on full-time at a fish factory, largely as a result of the owner's having noticed the boys' enterprise the previous winter. The working day lasted from 7 a.m. to 7 p.m., 'like everywhere else in those days.' This job ended in autumn when school started but then he got a job in the afternoons after school as a messenger boy for the local telephone exchange.

Guðlaugur's school years continued this way, his time divided between work and school. His story provides a good indication of how children in urban areas in the early twentieth century managed to fulfil the expectations that others had of them. The message was always the same: never to surrender, always to fight and to confront one's destiny with dignity and composure. This was the lesson repeated at home, in society and even at school. Life was a challenge that had to be faced for better or worse. The ethos of the sagas became part of their daily lives, the source of their moral guidance. Another autobiographer, Árni Helgason, talks about the influence of the sagas on himself and his friends in the town where he grew up; his teacher 'put great store by honour, and how these [saga] heroes had stood by their word. They would rather die than betray someone.'

The way the sagas were read at home and how people treated them is described by Guðlaugur Rósinkranz (b. 1903) from a little fishing port on the west coast in his autobiography, *Allt var þetta indælt stríð* (It Was All Such a Lovely War): 'There were often discussions about the sagas and the characters in them. It was the personalities of the saga characters that excited most debate and people often split into opposing camps, for or against some particular character . . . People would take sides for or against them, either criticizing them or defending them . . . This often led to heated and entertaining arguments.'

In her autobiography *Í sannleika sagt* (In Truth Told) Bjarnfríður Leósdóttir (b. 1924) recalls with pleasure the family gathering around the radio shortly after the state broadcasting service was set up in 1931 and listening to a well-known personality reading nightly extracts from the sagas. The programming of the early Icelandic radio owed much to the format of the old winter-evening gatherings, replicating in modern form something very traditional in Icelandic cultural life. Here again we find the home education system retaining its influence well into the twentieth century, supplementing the deficiencies of the weak school system.

At the time of the first laws on compulsory education in 1907 there were 34 general schools in Iceland teaching 1,017 students. Over four times this number – 4,260 students – attended peripatetic schools. According to public records, in 1918 there were 6,601 children in receipt of some kind of formal education, some at established schools, others being educated at home or by peripatetic teachers. In the same year there were only approximately 382 students at the various kinds of higher schools (for example, 'youth schools' or district schools). It was thus only a relatively small proportion of children who were able to continue their education beyond their compulsory schooling. On top of this there were 502 students enrolled in various specialist schools such as the Latin School in Reykjavík (*Menntaskóli*), the commercial college, the school of midwifery, the maritime and fishing college, schools of domestic science and so on. Those who attended these schools tended to be older, generally between fifteen and 35, and of course came largely from the better-off sections of society.

The peripatetic schools continued well on into the twentieth century. In 1950 there were still 103 of them in operation, but by this time there were also 97 general schools and 35 boarding schools catering for children from the widely dispersed rural population.[2] Late in the second decade of the twentieth century a bill was passed enabling schools in urban areas to offer free education to children younger than ten. The education of younger children, however, was not formalized until 1936, when the compulsory starting age of school was lowered to seven. From this point we can say that the reforms initiated in the early years of the century had finally been brought to completion. But even at this stage the majority of children had divided priorities: work came first, school second. To them, education was more of a respite from the real business of life than a foundation for the future.

16

Monsters from the Deep and the Icelandic Way of Thinking

When British and subsequently American forces occupied Iceland in World War II, the country suddenly found itself thrust into the modern age. Massive changes occurred over a relatively short space of time. For the century prior to the Second World War, transitions in the patterns of Icelandic society had generally taken place unusually smoothly, with most Icelanders managing to retain significant features of their traditional cultural background despite the increasing migration to towns. Although these changes were fairly rapid, they did not, in many areas of society at least, happen overnight and the disruption to established patterns was generally fairly limited until well after the middle of the twentieth century.

To give an idea of how Iceland faced up to increasing contact with the modern world, I intend in this chapter to present a couple of unusual examples that I believe shed a revealing light on Icelandic society in the middle and later years of the twentieth century. There is plenty of evidence to suggest that old ways died hard and that much social behaviour still went on largely along traditional lines. However strange the stories told here, and the pictures that accompany them, they say a great deal about Icelanders and Icelandic society in the twentieth century.

Dermochelys coriacea

On 2 October 1963 an article appeared in *Morgunblaðið*, the country's widest-circulation daily paper of the time, about an unusual incident that had taken place at the little port of Hólmavík in Strandasýsla, on the east side of the Westfjord peninsula. The article opened thus:

> When one of the rowing boats was coming in to land around midday today, the people discovered a giant turtle floating just to the landward side of the island of Grímsey in Steingrímsfjörður.

The boat is called the Hrefna, skippered by Einar Hansen. This appears to be the first animal of its kind to have been found in Iceland. The turtle is 157 cm in length, over 50 cm thick, and rather wider from flipper to flipper than it is long. It weighs well over 300 kilograms.

The report goes on to say that the turtle – a leatherback – was dead but undamaged on discovery. We are given its generic name, *Dermochelys coriacea*, and told that such creatures can grow up to 600 kilograms in weight and that this is the largest species of the order *Testudines* (tortoises and turtles) still walking the earth. It is said that such animals have been found along the coasts of Europe but that this is very rare. Náttúrugripasafnið (The Icelandic Museum of Natural History) has been advised and its representatives have expressed interest in the find.

Morgunblaðið was not the only newspaper to report this singular occurrence. The whole of the rest of the national press vied to produce articles. This was before the time of television in Iceland; television started only in 1966 and for many years the only station in the country, Ríkissjónvarp (National Television), did not broadcast on Thursdays and went off air for the whole of the month of July each year, an arrangement that lasted until 1986. Before this time news was in the sole hands of the newspapers and radio. The state-run Ríkisútvarp, inaugurated in 1930, was, up until the 1980s, the only radio station in the country (other than the English-language American forces radio).

One of the papers obtained an interview with the captain of the boat. He mentioned that fishing had generally been slack that whole summer and autumn. On the way home from a fishing expedition he had noticed something odd floating in the water. 'Blow me, if that isn't a turtle here in Steingrímsfjörður', said Einar Hansen to himself, adding to the reporter from the newspaper *Þjóðviljinn*, 'And so it turned out. We fixed it to the side of the boat and were an hour getting it back to port.' It was reported that Einar was of Norwegian origin but had lived in Iceland since 1930. In the twinkling of an eye, Einar became a national celebrity and tales of the find graced the pages of all the papers in the country. In the interviews with Einar it came out that in his younger days he had been on fishing expeditions down the coast of Africa and had often seen turtles swimming in the sea, and that was how he had realized immediately what was going on.

The media made a lot out of the story in various ways. For example, the newspaper *Vísir* visited a boy in Reykjavík who kept two little terrapins to get some idea of what kind of creatures they were talking about. The headline over the article read 'They are clean and unassuming.' In an interview with a pet-shop owner it emerged that it was easy to buy little terrapins in Reykjavík, but only smaller kinds. It was illegal to bring bigger ones into the country because of the risk of infection. Even today it is forbidden to import live animals to Iceland unless they spend several months in quarantine on a particular island off the north coast. The shopkeeper added that since the Hólmavík find there had been a huge increase in trade in his shop and all kinds of interest in tortoises and the like. The journalist ended his article in *Alþýðublaðið*, 3 October 1963, with these words:

> Children get immense pleasure from animals of every kind and beyond all dispute it is extremely healthy for them to have contact with animals. As one might expect, town children have only limited exposure to animals, and so it would be good if as many parents as possible let their children have some sort of pet around the house, as the benefit to their development is of almost inestimable value.

Along with all these stories in the papers there were pictures of the finders themselves, Einar and his son Sigurður, a young lad then still in his teens. Over the next few days naturalists came to the definitive conclusion that this was indeed a leatherback turtle. Apparently it was put in a freezer at the Hólmavík fish plant and immediately on 3 October it was reported that the people of Hólmavík had a mind to put the animal on display in Reykjavík. Doubts were raised about whether displaying the animal was a good idea as this would involve a considerable risk of it being damaged. How could one make sure the flesh was kept fresh and unspoilt? The chairman of the Hólmavík parish council was quoted in the papers as giving thought to what was best to do with the beast and requesting advice on this.

During all the humming and hawing about the best way to display the animal, the people of Hólmavík and their little town off the beaten track found themselves at the focus of national attention. The animal was photographed backwards and forwards and in various positions. The first picture taken shows the turtle on the foreshore, on a kind of tarpaulin, being dragged in to land. In the background one can see the houses of Hólmavík – a small enough place, numbering 420 inhabitants at the time, though this was more than at any earlier time in its history. Most of the houses are squat *timburhús*, timber-frame constructions clad with corrugated iron – hardly very prepossessing, but then this was a little fishing village whose inhabitants subsisted on the uncertain produce of the sea. The houses look rather run-down, as do the jetty and the boat bobbing at its end. One or two of the houses look rather more prepossessing, evidence that some the villagers were doing better

than others. In most respects, Hólmavík was like many other fishing ports at the time: a small population with very basic infrastructure, with most dwellings in a poor condition, often limited work opportunities and low wages. As one can see in the picture, the boat that brought the catch to land was tiny by any kind of modern standards.

Once the turtle had been landed the bystanders got an opportunity to admire this wonder of the deep. What on earth is going on there? the boy standing and watching from some distance off might be thinking. The other boys who have dared to come closer are wearing the typical clothes of boys at the time: knitted sweaters, old trousers and the

rubber shoes that were popular in those days. (It has been said that rubber was the most beneficial of all things new to reach Icelandic society, especially when Wellington boots were first imported around 1920 and Icelandic workmen and seamen no longer had to suffer wet feet every day of their working lives.)

It looks very much as if something has been hooked into the animal's eye and used to drag it up the beach. People are clustered round the creature on all sides, trying to work out what kind of marvel this can be. Lying there just above the tideline is a real giant tortoise, something the people of Hólmavík had obviously never seen before. It was imperative to get it up off the shore and into some safe place of storage. Many hands make light work, and the animal holds the people's undivided attention. The pictures tell us a great deal about Hólmavík and the people who lived there in the years around 1960.

Obviously the thing to do is to sit on the creature's back and have your picture taken. You can almost make out a strong similarity of expression on the faces of both animal and captor, each seemingly grinning from ear to ear. One can see from the fisherman's rough hands that a seaman's life at the time was no bed of roses.

Once the animal has been got onto the trolley there is no holding back. First some pictures are taken: one from the side, with the turtle lying flat on the trolley. In the distance you can make out a young boy looking at it. Just behind the boy stands a Willys jeep, which would have come to Iceland during the Second World War. The Willys jeep made

its mark on the Icelandic landscape in the years after the middle of the twentieth century. The picture is emblematic for showing three types of vehicle that were ubiquitous in Iceland at the time: first the trolley, an indispensable feature of life in all villages and country areas; second the jeep; and third the Volkswagen Beetle visible in the distance. These were all conveyances that Icelanders took to their bosom when the modern age finally made inroads into the country. The interesting thing is that these are all twentieth-century articles; even the trolley was largely unknown in Iceland earlier. The first motor car arrived in Iceland in 1904 but it was a long time before cars became in any way a common

sight. The boy quite probably went everywhere on foot, like everyone else of his age, unless he was lucky enough to own a bicycle. But this was rare among ordinary working people.

Next the animal's jaws are wedged open with a wooden block and some more pictures taken. In the first, there are children who appear to be interested in the beast; one of them is reaching his hand out to touch it. Others look on while the two captors, father Einar and son Sigurður, stand on guard. It is worth noting the woollen sweaters and the variety of their patterns; this was the traditional everyday dress of people of all ages from the Icelandic working class at the time, as it had

been for centuries. The other picture shows the father and son relaxing, clearly well pleased with the outcome of the day.

As is apparent from many of the pictures, the snows had plainly already arrived in Hólmavík that day in early October. The roads are unmetalled dirt tracks. The whole place looks rather run-down. But here in this little society, something newsworthy had happened. Even in Hólmavík, times were changing.

Pivotal moments

On 3 September 1919, many years before the turtle turned up at Hólmavík, Elka Björnsdóttir, a working woman from Reykjavík, looked out of her window and described what met her eye in her diary:

> Just now I saw out of my window a thing that has never been seen in Iceland before, and 20 or 25 years ago, or even later, few would have imagined would ever happen to mankind, and least of all here: there were men flying in the air. In honesty, I did not actually see any person, just the wings and the machine itself moving past there, and so gracefully too, with all kinds of sweeps and gentle turns, like when some skilful bird in flight is playing in the air.[1]

In many ways it is fair to call the twentieth century the age of progress and technology. Both, however, were relatively slow in coming to Iceland, but still had a great influence on how people thought about life. Moments like the one Elka Björnsdóttir experienced clearly changed people's perceptions of their world.

Throughout the country there were individuals who had received an education and perhaps understood better than the common masses the opportunities the new times had to offer. These opportunities were most obvious in connection with fishing and processing the produce of the sea. But similar things happened in other areas of life. At this point in the country's history Reykjavík was indisputably the nexus of science and learning, the place that people intent on becoming part of modern society inevitably looked to. The present was in Reykjavík, exactly as the working woman suggested in her diary, and it was there that everyone headed who felt in any way part of the new age.

As soon as it was brought to land, the turtle was hauled on its wagon up to the pastor's house to get some kind of ruling on what manner of marvel this might be. By good fortune, the minister was well-off and educated enough to have an encyclopedia in his house and it was consequently he who was likeliest to be able to pass judgement on the matter. It was a big group of people that set off for the manse. The minister greeted them and looked up the animal in his book. From this point on they had some idea of what they were dealing with and it was possible to lay plans for the future. The next step was straight down to the freezing plant where the animal was housed to start off with.

The next few days were spent in a lot of head-scratching about the best way of making something out of the beast. Náttúrugripasafnið (The Icelandic Museum of Natural History) in Reykjavík was ready to pay one or two thousand krónur for it; Einar Hansen wanted 10,000. Ways were canvassed of having the animal put on display more widely. One way or another, it had to be got to Reykjavík. In the newspaper *Vísir* on 12 October it was reported that there had been problems finding a suitable place to exhibit the animal in the capital: 'Hans Sigurðsson, chairman of the Hólmavík parish council, told Vísir recently that the people of Hólmavík had still not given up all hope. But it would be very unfortunate if plans to display the creature just dragged on and on, as people's interest in seeing it might wane. In addition, the road south might get closed if the snows arrive. The turtle is still in the freezing plant of the Co-operative Society of Hólmavík.' It is clear that the entire population of Hólmavík had united around this affair from the very first minute. It brought the town together and everyone was determined to see it through to the bitter end. Reykjavík was a station on the journey that had to be reached to get the most out of the attention the turtle had engendered.

As mentioned, the people of Hólmavík were afraid that the town might be shut off before long by snow, making it impossible to move the animal away. The Icelandic road system at the time left a great deal to be desired, and this hindered all communication between different parts of the country. As one can see from many of the pictures, it was an inhospitable landscape, with snow on the hills and a generally grey and forbidding look to everything.

Over the next days the captain of the boat, Einar Hansen, set off for Reykjavík taking the animal with him. On the way he stopped at Akranes, a little port fifteen miles across the bay from Reykjavík. *Morgunblaðið* carried the following report on 20 October:

The famous leatherback turtle that was found in Steingríms-fjörður was shown here in town at the H. B. & Co. freezing plant on Thursday evening from 8–10 p.m. There was a large attendance, 5 kr. for children and 10 kr. for adults. The headmaster of the primary school gave children who wanted to see the marvel time off school from 1–2 p.m. yesterday. The turtle is a hulking thing, frozen solid with a gaping snout, small and large teeth, snaggle-toothed even. I reckon there must be a hundred of them, said one boy. No, interrupted another, fifty or so. The tongue is crinkled, like a rasp, with projections on it.

It said in the paper that Einar had taken the turtle to Reykjavík the day before and that it was going to be shown there. In another paper Einar was reported as wanting to try to recoup some of the costs of moving and storing the turtle, and this was why he was charging to see it; the idea was not to make a profit from it but simply to give people a chance of seeing this wonder of nature. Another paper reported that something like 400 to 500 people had come to see it at Akranes, a very high percentage of the town's population.

The turtle appears to have caused a sensation in Reykjavík. It was only shown for one day and a large crowd gathered at the place where it was to be shown. Estimates spoke of around 3,000 people paying to see it on that single day. The papers competed to describe the exhibition. In *Morgunblaðið*, 22 October, the captain Einar Hansen was once again asked to describe how the discovery had happened. He mentioned that the doctor in Hólmavík had been fetched to examine the animal and had pronounced it only recently dead. As with the pastor, the village intelligentsia had been called on for their opinions on this miracle and its place in the world.

Many years later, in 1984, an article appeared about the Hólmavík turtle in *Náttúrufræðingurinn* (The Naturalist). Here it is described as having weighed 370–80 kilograms, and as being 203 cm in length, 240 cm across (including flippers) and up to 50 cm thick at the greatest point. The article mentions that it was bought for 10,000 krónur with a subsidy from the Ministry of Education and Culture to be put on display at the Museum of Natural History, where it can still be seen today. A cast was later taken of the animal. The article includes various other stories about sightings of 'sea monsters' in the seas around Iceland. There is much to suggest that these have been animals such as turtles or giant squids but there is no way of knowing for sure. All proof is lacking.

Undesirable aliens

For most of its history Icelandic society has been remarkably homogeneous. The population has not only been small – only a little over 40,000 in the second half of the eighteenth century and around 300,000 at the beginning of the twenty-first – but also largely uniform in its outlook and origins. There had always been the occasional foreigner who took up residence in Iceland, especially for the purposes of business or trade, but this group was until very recently small and quickly assimilated into

Icelandic society. However, the occupation by British and American troops during the Second World War initiated a change in society that altered the way Icelanders viewed the world outside their country. Within little more than a year, between 1940 and 1941, the population of Reykjavík doubled, mostly owing to the influx of both young British servicemen and new arrivals from elsewhere in Iceland who were coming to the capital to take advantage of the work opportunities the army brought with it. Society seemed to have been turned upside down in the blink of an eye and the authorities resorted to various measures to 'protect' the local inhabitants from outside influences. In particular, young women who consorted with the soldiers were moved out of town and deposited in rural areas around the country, for their own good and for the good of the nation, as it was put. Prior to their banishment they were subjected to intimate medical examinations to see whether they had been infected by any diseases that might be traced to the occupying forces.

In the public debate around this matter the perfectly common noun, *ástand*, literally meaning just 'situation, condition, state', took on a new and specialized sense to denote the 'improper' fraternization with British or American servicemen by a fair number of Icelandic women. The usage had deeply pejorative overtones. Women who were 'in the situation' were vilified and labelled as traitors to the Icelandic race and the purity of the nation. They were 'tainted' and thus a danger to society.

So bitter was the animosity among the authorities and many men as a result of this new situation that the government set up a 'Situation Committee' to come up with proposals about how best to prevent the miscegenation of the two groups. The Chief Medical Officer, Vilmundur Jónsson, believed there was a danger of the nation simply 'losing its identity' if events were allowed to pass unchecked. Particularly prominent in the debate were the voices of doctors and nursing staff, almost to a man, it seems, decrying the danger that Icelandic women were putting themselves into by associating with soldiers. People even went so far as to talk about an epidemic that needed to be resisted at all costs.

The 'Situation Committee', which comprised three members, all men, produced a report that provoked much talk in the media. In it it was said that the police had the names of 500 women who they had reason to believe had had intimate relations with British soldiers. It was noted that 150 of these were of 'very low moral standing'. The chief of police himself believed that they had only managed to identify a fraction of those women who had been associating with men from the occupying forces. Altogether, estimates put the numbers involved as high as 2,500, or around 20 per cent of the entire female population of Reykjavík. As Bára Baldursdóttir, the historian who has studied this episode in

Icelandic history in greatest detail, notes, the committee pointed out that only a part of this group had actually been selling their bodies; this, they opined, was probably because 'Icelandic women were not clear about the difference between a prostitute and a respectable woman. The subtext was that a substantial portion of the women involved were misinformed tarts who did not have the intelligence to get paid for services rendered.'[2]

The measures taken in the wake of this report were characterized by a strong fear of everything that was new, different or alien. 'The nation's youth' (chiefly women) had to be protected and the best way of doing this was to send a proportion of them out of town, as mentioned previously. Laws were brought in that gave wide-ranging powers of intrusion into people's daily lives. For example, measures were introduced that allowed for the monitoring of young people and their behaviour up to the age of twenty. A special court was established to deal with such problems as might arise. Large numbers of young women were ordered to leave town and live on farms or in homes well away from contact with foreigners. 'Allegations of immorality were readily corroborated by a certificate from a gynaecologist to the effect that the girls in question had had sexual relations', as Bára Baldurs-dóttir notes. In addition, all these girls were made to undergo an intelligence test before they were sent away. Under the terms of the new act, suspected women were subjected to interrogations that could last for many hours: 'The youth enforcement service was a kind of moral secret police, conducting spying activities on girls suspected of close relations with servicemen. To this effect witnesses were often called from among the girls' friends and relatives, as well as neighbours and work colleagues.' What strikes one is the single-mindedness of the authorities in their operations, probably much in line with the measures taken by the authorities in many smaller societies that have had to deal with comparable circumstances.

Later on, the Icelandic state went so far as to ask the American army to agree not to station any black men at the Keflavík airbase! The historian Valur Ingimundarson describes relations between the Icelanders and the US military at the time as follows:

> This debate was then linked in with the claim that Icelandic women needed 'protecting' from foreign servicemen, particularly if they were black . . . It is quite true that no restrictions were placed on coloured people visiting Iceland. But nevertheless it was the aim of the government right from the Second World War up to the first half of the 1960s that there should be no black soldiers in Iceland . . . It was felt that the nation's interests would be best served if miscegenation, i.e. relations

between black men and Icelandic women, could be avoided. That this was public policy was never acknowledged openly. What occurred was an attempt to silence a particular truth, to hold aloft myths of tolerance and open-mindedness and then to deny having been in agreement with the policy when the truth eventually came out at the end of the 1960s.[3]

Valur of course draws attention to the fact that, from earliest times, Iceland had been an isolated country. Stronger and more frequent links with the world outside brought to the fore attitudes that could be traced either to this insularity or to simple racial prejudice.

Anomalous situations of a similar kind were to materialize in other areas of Icelanders' dealings with the world outside over the ensuing decades. Figures from the official establishment were constantly up in arms about the dangers posed to Icelandic culture and the Icelandic language by the arrival of people and things from abroad that excited public interest and attention. The general public, however, did not always go along with this. People were frequently inspired by simple curiosity to take an interest in things that were new and unusual – no matter whether this was a matter of giant turtles, foreign soldiers, whales or the polar bears that periodically turned up on the shores of Iceland, carried across from Greenland on ice floes. The degree of interest engendered was often enough to justify accusations of the Icelanders being obsessed with novelty to an almost unique degree.

Among the recurrent issues on the agenda for public debate in the second half of the twentieth century were, for example, matters like the official bans on the sale of beer and the keeping of dogs in Reykjavík, each of which was eventually revoked during the 1980s after decades of huff and puff (beer in 1986, dogs in 1988, under certain conditions). The ban on dogs meant that the mayor of Reykjavík had to live in constant trepidation of receiving letters like the following, composed in mock official style, from one of the country's leading modern poets and his wife:

Gunnar Thoroddsen, mayor.

It is the origin of this matter, that we the undersigned elderly couple, resident at Fossvogsblettur 45 off Sléttuvegur in Reykjavík, have for the past two years kept a certain female dog, red in colour and somewhat advanced in years. To us it is well known that such action is in breach of the laws and regulations of this the municipality of which we are members. Be that as it may, we have, as so often happens, formed a certain familiarity and even attachment to this pitiable creature, and it with us, in so far as we can ascertain.

It has now these last days been brought forcefully to our notice that higher powers are minded to take decisive action against this female dog, and so far as we can see matters have now come to a pass. We therefore request of you, most honourable mayor, whether you might, through the power invested in you by your position and yet more so from the kindness of your heart, allow us such exemption from the letter of the law that we may give shelter to this beast for as long as her life and health shall prevail. We wish here to state unequivocally that the bitch is unassuming and home-loving, to a degree one might call exceptional nowadays. She is also remarkably inoffensive in herself and we deem it the greatest fault of her character how great are the signs of friendship she is willing to bestow on all and sundry, known and unknown alike. But perhaps she knows better than we what is right and proper to do in such matters, and so this should not be held against her.

With friendship and regard,
Reykjavík 18/1/1957
Steinn Steinarr and Ásthildur Björnsdóttir[4]

Foreigners visiting Iceland repeatedly expressed bafflement at what on earth could lie behind bans and proscriptions of this kind, and there were few Icelanders indeed who were able to supply them with a coherent answer.

The concerns of the authorities were always the same, founded on a fear that Icelandic society would be unable to withstand the strain put on it by influences from outside. The reactions this provoked could be unpredictable. Thus, pressure from abroad – for instance for an end to commercial whaling – has been likely to provoke a jingoistic response and a point-blank refusal to countenance any foreign interference in the country's affairs. At such times Icelanders find themselves under huge social pressure to stand together: the country's independence must be protected at all costs.

In other areas, though, ever-increasing access to the world outside Iceland – the effects of various foreign cultural innovations – had a huge influence on people's attitudes to life in the postwar years, especially among the young. It made little difference whether it was music, dance, fashion or general lifestyle, the youth of Iceland proved a captive audience. The ruling forces often looked on askance, taking the view that the land stood on the brink of perdition in the face of such 'spectres', and radical measures were not infrequently imposed to protect values that were felt to be under threat, such as the Icelandic language. When the US defence force started television broadcasting at the Keflavík airbase in 1954, for example, there was a lot of talk about the harmful effects this might have on Icelandic society. The material could be picked up in communities close to the base, for instance in the town of Keflavík. When the state television broadcasting service opened in 1966 ways were found to prevent the forces' television from reaching out beyond the perimeter of the base. The main argument was that a domestic, national television station should not need to compete with American light entertainment; this could only have a detrimental effect on the shaping of Icelandic culture.

As a further example of the kinds of hard measures taken by the authorities to counter external 'stimuli' and maintain traditional Icelandic customs, until almost the end of the twentieth century foreigners who took Icelandic citizenship were required by law to give up their birth names and adopt Icelandic ones. Previously, in 1925, Icelandic families had been forbidden to adopt surnames as this was felt to be directly contrary to established Icelandic linguistic usage. This law remains in full force today.

Most of these attempts to 'protect' the nation and Icelandic nationality, particularly in matters of culture, eventually proved futile and were abandoned. Innovations of various kinds became almost an automatic part of Icelandic culture, especially in the later years of the century. Little by little, Icelandic culture became simultaneously local and global, succeeding in many ways in retaining a unique identity of its own while marking out for itself an intelligible position among the community of nations.

17

Selective Modernization and Capitalist Euphoria

The history of Iceland in the twentieth century can be divided, without serious oversimplification, into two periods: before and after 1940. Up to 1940 Iceland is best viewed as an essentially agrarian and to some extent an insular society; the country had undergone a number of significant changes in the latter part of the nineteenth century and earlier part of the twentieth, but these had caused little fundamental disruption to people's existing cultural outlook and ways of thinking. Society was grounded on the traditional peasant values of thrift and financial restraint, combined with a conservatism of attitude in matters such as culture, class structure, human relations and living standards. The great change came with Iceland's enforced emergence onto the international scene when the country was occupied by British forces in 1940 to secure Allied control of the North Atlantic in World War II. The Americans took over from the British in 1941. In 1946 the government of the new republic signed a defence agreement with the USA ratifying a continued American military presence on Icelandic soil. This agreement proved highly controversial and split the nation into bitterly opposing political camps. In 1949 Iceland became one of the founder signatories of the NATO Treaty, again against a background of fierce political controversy at home.

The latter part of the century was a time of rapid change in all areas of society. In the years after the war commerce and growing contact with the outside world came to have an ever-increasing impact on material and economic conditions in Iceland. Alongside this there were profound changes in cultural outlook. Once again, however, this did not involve a complete and unconditional rejection of the traditional values of agricultural society, which continued to play an important part in people's lives and perceptions until well into the second half of the century. Despite the rudimentary infrastructure and the fragility of the formal institutions of state, Iceland's cultural heritage remained strong, unified and largely intact.

The Second World War brought in a new world in Iceland. To quote a delivery-man from Reykjavík: 'Before the occupation you knew everyone, even the cars by the sound of their engines. There was an unhurried feel to life in town. Then the army arrived, and everything looked different. The old times were gone and they never came back.' (Quoted in Þór Whitehead, Ísland í hershöndum.) Both the British and American services put up rows of prefabs clad in corrugated iron for use as stores and as living quarters for their troops. At the end of the war these buildings were left behind and occupied by Icelanders to plug the great housing shortage that accompanied the large-scale migration to the city. As places to live they were cold and uncomfortable but these prefab slum districts remained a feature of the city as late as the 1960s.

Strands of memory

In trying to gain an insight into the development of Icelandic society in recent times it is instructive to consider the country from the point of view of 'cultural memory': what people remembered from the past and how this coloured their perceptions of themselves and the world they lived in. Looking at the nineteenth century, we can discern significant differences between conditions in Iceland and what we find in most of the rest of Europe. If we consider the three different forms of cultural memory – collective memory, historical memory and individual memory – there are good reasons to believe that the first of these, collective memory, was exceptionally weak in Icelandic peasant society.[1] As a result of the geographical conditions in the country, with almost no urban centres and settlement widely scattered on farms with considerable distances between them, it was difficult for groups to coalesce with firm enough bonds for them to be able to share their memories and hold them in common. Even the group best placed to sustain its collective memory – the educated – was dispersed among the common people with no central focus. Any earlier links that ministers of the church or government officials might have forged during their schooling and education were extremely weak compared to their links with the agricultural community among whom they lived and whose thoughts and activities they shared. As a result the collective memory – the shared world-view and experience of a relatively small group of people as passed on from one generation the next – was so tenuous that 'extra space' opened up to be filled by the other forms of memory.

Consequently people had much greater scope to create and shape their own individual memories than in most other parts of Europe. The strength of the individual memory manifests itself in a wide variety of ways in Icelandic society, but perhaps most notably in the massive outpouring of written material by ordinary working-class peasants in the eighteenth and nineteenth centuries, as discussed particularly in chapters Eight and Eleven. In these writings people found an opportunity to create a world of ideas that had a considerable influence on how they coped with the situations they faced in their daily lives. The effects of this process fed through to the wider context of power and politics, and through this ordinary people were also able to influence the way that the historical memory was shaped and the form it took. The strength of the historical memory thus increased steadily through the period, especially when compared to the rather weak position it occupied in many other nineteenth-century societies.

The wide scope open to individual Icelanders to shape their own memories was inextricably linked with a burgeoning of the historical memory, built upon people's interpretation of the country's ancient past. In the nineteenth century both of these forms of memory were nourished by the rhetoric of the leaders of the independence movement with its compelling emotional appeal to the idea of Iceland as a sovereign democratic state. The literature of medieval Iceland, and above all the sagas, was consciously employed to create a national historical memory and a perception of the values that were felt worth fighting for. Written and manuscript culture took a central place in the intellectual and political case for independence. The leader of the movement, Jón Sigurðsson, an archivist and historian by profession, applied his specialist knowledge to argue that Iceland had in fact never lawfully surrendered its national independence in medieval times, and that therefore the Norwegians and subsequently Danes had no claim over the country. There was thus an intimate connection between social and political aspirations, individual memory – the fates of the saga characters projected into the lives of their nineteenth-century readers – and historical memory. Forming part of the creation of individual memory, the new historical memory became a part of everyone's lives, something every Icelander needed to assimilate and come to terms with. This perhaps goes some way to explaining why autobiographies and other personal writings became such a ubiquitous form of self-expression in Iceland compared to other parts of Europe.

The need for self-expression has varied according to society, class and gender. In agrarian societies of the eighteenth, nineteenth and twentieth centuries, where time moved slowly to the rhythm of the seasons, those who were growing up could get by on standardized images gleaned from their immediate environments, for example from religion, literature and everyday life. In nineteenth-century Iceland we have clear evidence of young people from the working class turning with enthusiasm to the opportunities on offer to express what they thought about their lives and existence in written form, based on their own personal experience. Society was evidently changing. The heritage of the Enlightenment had trickled down to the lowest stratum of society. The ordinary people of Iceland, who were almost without exception able to read and in most cases also to write, especially the men, appear to have had a deep desire to embrace whatever knowledge they could find. We see this, for instance, in the importance that so many Icelanders of the time seem to have ascribed to weighing and measuring just about anything they could see or touch in their environments. Farm buildings, hay meadows and sheep pens were assessed and measured and precise figures recorded for the milk yields of cows and ewes. All this was done in order to obtain a firmer handle on the uncertainties of life. The people of the nineteenth century were in fact beginning to discover, in ever-increasing measure, that it was possible to influence the course of their own lives through organized and systematic action.

In this, the diaries became an important tool in the hands of motivated individuals intent on facing up to the future. With time, ever more people came to use diaries as a means of reflecting on their position in the world. The authors approached their writing slowly; but with the clear intention of giving shape to their own existences. The new Icelander was emerging, an individual grounded in the old culture but keen to take on the challenges of the future with an open mind.

It is one thing to express one's ideas in the privacy of one's own diary, another to offer them for general circulation. The twentieth century was a time of increased specialization; society was becoming more varied and complex than it had ever been before. The self-expression of ordinary people, it was widely felt, required specialist support from writers who actually told their stories if it was to be considered relevant to others. There was a rich demand for such writings. Democracy required access to public opinion, that as many people as possible might be able to have their say on the issues of the day. The age of the published book had arrived and the individual became marketed for what it could contribute to the sense of national identity. As a result, the autobiographical form came to appeal to ever more writers and we begin to hear a richer variety of voices than before. Women, for example, started to bring their life stories to a wider reading public. In the vast majority of cases 'the production of memories' followed the prescribed nationalist formula that shaped people's attitudes to life through much of the twentieth century. In a sense, though, Icelandic culture had created a greater freedom for people to shape their own private worlds, which eventually became an important constituent in the shaping of the nation's historical memory.

In recent years the world has seen what has been called a 'culture of confession'. This phenomenon supplanted what may be called the 'culture of testimony', the mode of self-expression described above that dominated public expression in Iceland in the first half of the twentieth century. This culture of testimony was based first and foremost on accounts of events that had contributed to the general shaping of Icelandic society and that detailed the parts played by individual contributors in this process. This testimony served to reinforce the overall picture by presenting the lives of those who, directly or indirectly, had had input into the events that had shaped the current state of society. Thus the autobiographies of Icelanders of the nineteenth century and first half of the twentieth are permeated with the testimony of people who took part in 'building' the country, the newly free land that had thrown off the shackles of foreign domination. Each 'victory', great or small, was rehearsed in detail, each step registered on the country's road to independence. This culture of testimony was a tool that proved extremely useful in promoting nationalistic perspectives and thus contributing to the unity of the nation.

In this sense, the autobiographies written in the spirit of the culture of testimony can be seen as political writing. They were part of the Icelanders' struggle for national independence, a device intended to boost the morale and self-confidence of a people setting out into the unknown that inevitably came with political autonomy. They contributed to the shaping of the country's historical memory. These sources, which I have used and quoted unsparingly through this book, were thus an element in the general renewal of society as a whole. Individual people felt impelled to step out into the spotlight to describe how they had lived and worked and, by doing so, help to lay the foundation for a stronger and better society through their day-to-day actions and their sense of responsibility.

With the advent of the new mode of expression, the culture of confession, came a change of perspective. People from all walks of life came forward in the present to tell their stories, but they were no longer motivated by the precepts of nationalism. The stories they had to tell were presented on their own terms, without any apparent connection to movements that might call for such texts. The culture of confession did not of course operate *in vacuo*, completely isolated from the forces and values of society. Expression of this type had links to countless informal influences and institutions that operate within society, but it was difficult to control such expression and channel it in particular directions. This created a certain fragmentation within the cultural space that, in the final decades of the twentieth century, left society wide open to outside influences.

Iceland at the end of the millennium

Most Icelanders seem to have derived enormous strength from their shared cultural background, centred on their common language, eleven hundred years of recorded history, and a strong tradition of literature and literacy. The cultivation of literature and poetry, which often demanded the systematic application of abstract concepts, proved exceptionally useful to many people when faced with the new, industrialized world of the twentieth century. The Icelanders appear to have found the leap from the turf cottages of the nineteenth century to the steam trawlers and mechanized technology of the modern age comparatively easy, and accomplished the adjustments needed without losing their links to the past. This attribute – the readiness to embrace the new while holding on to customs and attitudes developed over the centuries – has left its mark on the country's culture and economy and undoubtedly helped it to establish its position among the community of nations during the course of the twentieth century.

The immediate postwar years were a time of deep and rapid change in Iceland. Prices and inflation were high. Between 1948 and 1953 the country received $38 million in US aid under the Marshall Plan. Much of the money was used to set up factories with the aim of strengthening the industrial base, which was rudimentary, highly dependent on a single industry, and technologically backward. Some was also directed into developing the country's hydroelectric resources. The importance of fishing increased steadily. Here, as indeed throughout industry, the main resource and the chief motivating factor remained manpower. The period was characterized by strict import and exchange controls. Official policy was governed by the traditional virtue of financial prudence, although waste and corruption were rife under cover of the state-operated procurement system, through which people with links to powerful political parties enjoyed preferential treatment at the expense of the general public.

Iceland did not succeed in extricating itself fully from its financial and commercial constraints until the mid- to late 1950s. Until the late 1980s the economy remained seriously over-reliant on a single industry, fishing, and subject to cyclical fluctuation. All businesses in the country were constantly at the mercy of inflation. However, in the 1990s membership of the European Economic Area helped to stabilize Iceland's links with its major trading partners and put its economy on a more structured footing. It is only from this point that the country can be said to have embraced modernization totally and almost unconditionally in all areas of society – except the political. The old party system remained in full force, distorting relations between private individuals and the state and acting as a conduit for channelling favours to members and friends of the parties in power.

Throughout the country's history the division of labour between men and women has been fluid and women have traditionally occupied a major part in the workforce. In the years after 1930 a significant middle class began to develop and many women gave up outside employment and retired into the home, their roles now being defined by managing the household purse and bringing up the children. Working-class families, however, still had to rely on female labour. During the second half of the twentieth century women became an increasingly important factor economically and in all areas of work and industry and by the last decades of the century had achieved comparable professional, educational and, to some extent, political status to men.

The years after the Second World War saw an influx of new cultural influences, most notably 'pop culture' from Europe and America. Films, music, art, dance and other recreational activities originating outside Iceland swept through the country like wildfire, exerting a considerable influence on the country's sensitive culture. These external pressures were met with stern resistance in certain quarters and, as discussed in the previous chapter, concerted attempts were made to exclude material from abroad that was considered culturally 'undesirable'. This cultural tension makes the period since the Second World War in Iceland interesting: on the one hand, many Icelanders took an avid interest in the latest trends and fashions in the world outside; on the other, officially at least, nationalistic conservative forces still retained considerable influence over society up to the end of the century, and here it made no difference what political party was in power at the time, right or left.

Icelandic insularity manifested itself in other ways. From the late 1960s onwards there was a fundamental shift in political attitudes in

Reykjavík expanded rapidly after the Second World War. Government policy aimed to provide as many people as possible with their own homes and there was a massive boom in construction. Whole districts seemed to sprout up overnight. People's material resources obviously differed and many Icelanders were tempted to move into their houses before they were fully completed. Often people lived for years in houses that were still under construction, as in the picture above. The woman leaving the apartment block here has probably had to put up with living like this for several years, not just in her own home but throughout the district.

most countries of Europe and North America. Minority groups started to reject traditional political structures and demand that their voices be heard. The civil rights movement in the USA, the rise of the women's and peace movements and student revolts around the world led to further challenges to conventional politics by ethnic and environmental

Despite the controversy surrounding the continued American military presence in Iceland after the Second World War, strong links often built up between the servicemen and Icelandic families. It is at this point that one might say that Iceland had truly entered the modern age.

groups such as the Greens and opponents of nuclear power. These challenges undermined the nationalistic dialectic of the Cold War period. Concepts of national unity began to crumble. But while all this was going on, the Icelandic public for the most part had its mind on other matters. These movements largely passed Iceland by and Icelanders continued to approach the issues of the modern age on the basis of the old values of nationalism.

Two things in particular served to make nationalism a much more potent force in Iceland than in most other parts of the world. First, there were the so-called Cod Wars with Britain, occasioned by Iceland's extension of the fishing limits around its shores. This took place in a number of stages, starting in 1952 when territorial waters were extended to four miles, then in 1958 to twelve miles, in 1971 to 50 miles and finally in 1975 to 200 miles. On each occasion there were months of tension between Britain and Iceland and naval encounters between British warships and trawlers and small Icelandic gunboats. At such times the whole nation stood together, united by a common purpose; there were no significant dissenting voices. The Cod Wars were followed with keen interest both at home and abroad. Icelanders who had been involved in the struggle were treated as national heroes. Each of the Cod Wars finished with Iceland victorious and the fishing limits were eventually established internationally at 200 miles.

Ostensibly, Iceland's justification for the extension of its territorial waters was based on conservational grounds: to preserve fish stocks in the face of increased encroachment by foreign fishing vessels. However, there can be little doubt that economic factors also played a large part in it; continued prosperity at home could only be ensured by imposing a monopoly on the fishing grounds, some of which were among the richest on earth. Earnings from the fisheries had increased immensely during the course of the twentieth century. In the event, all other countries – some of which had been fishing these grounds for centuries – were forced to withdraw without any form of redress.

Secondly, politics in Iceland were dominated by an internal issue that divided the nation into two opposing camps, the American military base at Keflavík and Iceland's membership of NATO. The arguments used on both sides were first and foremost nationalistic. Those who opposed a US presence on Icelandic soil did so on the grounds of national sovereignty: it was seen as selling the country's right to self-determination, selling the country and its people. Those who supported the military, a considerably larger group than the first, maintained that this was a necessary measure to defend the country against potential attack by foreign powers, primarily the Soviet Union. In other words, both sides presented their arguments in terms of national values and interests. The debate was heated and bitter and continued over the course of several decades. Meanwhile, other points of views that had come to the fore in the world outside passed by largely unnoticed.

Icelanders' reactions in their disputes with foreign nations – in the Cod Wars and over the Keflavík base – suggest an extremely brittle self-image, a hangover from the country's colonial past. Any altercation with another country has been liable to produce a swift and uncompromising nationalistic response motivated by the Icelanders' sensitivity about the smallness of their own country. The popular perception has been one of 'plucky little Iceland'. As mentioned in chapter Sixteen, a telling case in point has been Iceland's long and continuing refusal to cease whaling activities in open defiance of international agreements on the protection of whale stocks. Here again, for most of this dispute opinion in Iceland has been more or less united, an unanimity that has only begun to break down in recent years. One might say that for Icelanders it is a matter of pride. The pressure of public opinion leaves no room for other points of view. Iceland is not going to bow to ideas from outside!

This nationalistic closing of ranks in the face of important international issues meant that Iceland lagged several decades behind political

trends elsewhere in the world. This political conservatism and isolationism was eventually to have catastrophic consequences for the country
and its development.

The new economy

In the last two decades of the twentieth century the international political scene that had lasted since the Second World War changed beyond
recognition. The fall of the Berlin Wall on 9 November 1989 can be
seen as a symbolic watershed. The period of constraints and 'stability' in
matters of ideology was over. The ruling spirit now was one of untrammelled diversity. The 'centre' crumbled away in the pace of the modern
age and onto the scene stepped countless groups, large and small, from
the fringes of society – individuals who had hitherto been paid little or
no attention. Opinions were aired on the unlikeliest subjects, with every
expectation that they would be given a hearing. The culture of confession was on prime time. What characterized these upheavals above
anything else was speed – the media, information technology, telecom-
munications, the internet, migration, all were phenomena that served
to leave white, middle-class, middle-aged males disorientated and
perplexed. The ruling forces in the world lost their foothold and the
decentralization of power became a reality. The globalization of
ideas, trade and commerce changed people's understanding, at least in
Western countries, of what life was all about.

The 1990s were a time of rapid and fundamental change in Iceland.
The traditional industries, agriculture and fishing, lost their status as
the main occupations. Jobs in the service sector multiplied, with three
out of every four Icelanders working in this area by the end of the century. The changes took place within a comparatively few years and had
major implications for the whole of society. Certain factors played a
decisive role in these changes. 1) A quota system was introduced in
fishing. As a result, the number of companies operating in the sector
fell and the profits of those that remained rose steeply. Fewer and fewer
workers meant greater per capita yields, but the wealth produced came
to be concentrated in the hands of a small number of interests. The new
arrangement created considerable social friction, many feeling that a
valuable resource that by rights belonged to the nation had been
handed over to a select group of wealthy businessmen. 2) Cheap
imports of food from other parts of the world made Icelandic farming
increasingly uncompetitive. In order to survive, Icelandic farms were
forced to expand and introduce intensive programmes of mechanization. Many farmers who were unable to meet these demands were forced
out of business. 3) The changes in fishing and agriculture led to major

During the 1950s and '60s Reykjavík took on more of the air of a modern urban society. Schools were built and the school system was brought into something much like its present form. Childhood and youth became ever more divorced from the world of adulthood. Child labour fell rapidly in these years, though many children were still sent out into the country to work over the summer. The picture here is from the 'West End' of Reykjavík, one of the districts that grew up during the 1930s and '40s.

changes in settlement patterns. Reykjavík was where the work was and more and more people moved from the rural areas and small ports and settled in the capital. The Reykjavík metropolitan area grew out of all recognition and is now home to two-thirds of the country's population. 4) Jobs in other areas such as manufacturing declined as companies turned to ever more sophisticated technological solutions. There was, however, one major exception. Governments had followed a policy of promoting heavy industry in Iceland, specifically the harnessing the country's hydroelectric resources with the aim of attracting international companies with high-energy demands to Iceland, particularly in the area of aluminium and other metal refining. This sector therefore flourished. However, these massive industrial projects attracted growing opposition from environmental campaigners and conservationist attitudes started to attract more and more support. 5) High educational levels and high career expectations among Icelanders created a shortage of labour in lower-paid, low-prestige jobs such as construction and the service sector. To compensate, Iceland loosened its restrictions on work and residence permits and there was an influx of migrants, most notably from Eastern Europe and the Far East (Thailand, Malaysia, the Philippines, etc.). This has had profound effects on Icelandic society that many native Icelanders have still not adjusted to. 6) The greatest changes were concentrated in sectors requiring high levels of skills and training such as education, technology, computing and especially finance, where the number of jobs increased markedly.

The educational revolution after around 1970 had enormous consequences for Icelandic society in the final years of the century. A major part in this revolution was the establishment of *fjölbrautaskólar*, multidisciplinary secondary schools that offered courses in all areas of education and industry and from which students matriculated aged about twenty with the right to go on to higher education. Prior to this, the number of students attaining matriculation level each year had numbered in tens, or later hundreds. Following the reforms, thousands of students flocked into university, not only at home in Iceland but all around the world. This skills revolution called for changes to the financing of higher level study. In the early 1980s the *Lánasjóður íslenskra námsmanna* (Icelandic Student Loan Fund) was restructured, allowing young students to further their education in all directions, irrespective of family income or social position.

Another important step came around 1990 with the establishment in its present form of the Icelandic Centre for Research, charged with overseeing the allocation of funds for academic research in Iceland. This made it possible for the large group of scholars and scientists who had gone abroad to work and study to return home, even after many years at universities and other institutions outside Iceland. A very large percentage of the people in question accepted the opportunity. As a result there was a flourishing of scholarly activity of a kind never before seen in Iceland. Apart from any consequences for cultural and academic life in Iceland, the development of the educational system led to widespread changes in industry, with industry in Iceland becoming more varied and diversified, as well as more stable and dynamic.

The growing importance of science and new technologies to the industrial landscape of Iceland in the last years of the twentieth century can be exemplified by the company deCode genetics, established in 1996. The company was set up with the ambitious aim of mapping the Icelandic genome. Genealogy and family history have been something

In the early modern period, particularly in the first half of the eighteenth century, much of Iceland's precious medieval manuscript heritage was collected and shipped abroad in an effort to save it from total destruction. The leading figure in this movement was Árni Magnússon, the founder of modern saga studies and professor at the University of Copenhagen. When the Icelanders gained their independence in 1944, one of their first demands was that these manuscripts be returned. After years of wrangling, the matter went before the courts in Denmark, which ruled that the bulk of the manuscripts should be sent home. In 1971 a Danish frigate arrived bearing the first consignment. Thousands of Icelanders made their way down to the harbour where a solemn handing-over ceremony took place. Children were given time off school and the whole country watched on proudly as Iceland's most remarkable contribution to world culture was restored to its country of origin. This gesture of goodwill cemented friendly relations between the two countries, a happy ending to centuries of distrust and resentment.

of a ruling passion among Icelanders over the centuries and vast quantities of demographic material have been amassed, making it possible to trace family relationships several centuries back in time. The company planned to make use of this unique fund of material, backed up, it was hoped, by access to personal medical records.

The idea was that by collating these records it might be possible to identify the causes of a host of common genetic diseases. The founder of the company was a bioscientist by the name of Kári Stefánsson who had worked for several years at a number of internationally regarded scientific institutions in the USA, most recently as a professor at Harvard. Two things proved crucial to the commercial prospects of the plan. First, Kári enlisted the support of Iceland's best-known genealogist,

The medieval literature has been an almost overwhelming presence in Icelandic culture and society. In some ways the prestige of the literature can be seen as having stunted the development of other art forms. Even in the twentieth century, when music, pictorial art and other art forms started to emerge as independent entities, one is still often aware of the weight of the literature on the work produced. The sculpture shown above is a case in point. The picture shows the modernist sculptor Ásmundur Sveinsson (1893–1982) standing beside his piece called Sonatorrek. The name, meaning something like 'unrequitable loss of sons', is the title of the most famous poem of the Saga Age, the moving elegy by the tenth-century skald and saga hero Egill Skallgrímsson in memory of two of his sons. Many other artists have based their works around stories and motifs from the ancient literature, reinterpreting them for the modern age. This has only changed significantly in recent years, with nature now replacing the past as the leading theme and Icelandic artists looking more towards international currents for their interpretations and techniques.

Friðrík Skúlason, who also ran an IT firm specializing in computer system security. On the side he had made some headway in developing a program designed to store and process the various sources of information relevant to genealogical studies. Second, the then government of Iceland was prepared to support deCode by allowing it access to various types of information held in personal medical records. The company was then to have sole commercial rights over the database generated from this information for a period of up to twelve years.

The project provoked fierce controversy and attracted international attention. It was seen as a daring and futuristic experiment, almost like something out of science fiction. In particular, considerable reservations were expressed about the proposal to introduce a new law on medical records granting the company access to sensitive personal data. At the outset it was decided that the company would be allowed unlimited use of people's records without their specific consent, on condition that secure encryption procedures were in place to ensure that the information could not be traced back to the individual. In response to public concern, provision was made for opt-outs; that is, people could apply individually for material relating to themselves to be excluded from the database. The matter was fiercely contested and for a time raised considerable disquiet. Many felt that the proposal constituted an invasion of personal privacy. An enormously high-powered research community swiftly built up around the company, providing an immense shot in the arm to intellectual life in Iceland. The company attracted an influx of highly qualified foreign scientists, as well as many Icelanders who had been living abroad but used the opportunity to return home and take up posts with deCode.

For reasons that remain unclear, the much-debated genetic database was never completed. The company is still in operation, though its commercial results so far have not lived up to the hopes expressed by its advocates at the outset.

The project has, however, produced one very interesting spin-off. Unlike its genetic counterpart, the genealogical database was not only completed but, in a sense, bequeathed to the nation. At the end of 2001 a version was posted on the web under the name *Íslendingabók* (The Book of Icelanders).[2] Public access made it possible for any Icelander to trace their relatives and family tree back over several centuries. The reaction was extraordinary: the site immediately attracted more hits than any other in Iceland and by now it is reckoned to have been visited by something like two-thirds of the entire nation – testament, if any were needed, of the Icelanders' abiding fascination with personal history, made possible by this collaboration between modern genetics and traditional genealogy.

As the century closed, the country appeared set for a bright future. All the main institutions of society appeared to be in good working order and the country enjoyed a high level of education and technological sophistication. Only later did it emerge that this stability was a mirage; there were dangers lurking beneath the surface, first and foremost because the political system had failed to keep pace with the general direction in which Icelandic society was moving.

Political culture

When we speak of political culture, what we mean is the knowledge that people build up of the politics of their community and people's attitudes toward them, a knowledge that each individual develops in his own way and assimilates into his own personal experience. Icelanders at the end of the twentieth century were well positioned to undertake this task as a result of the generally high level of education and wide experience of living and moving in a modern international environment. The problem was that the ruling forces in Iceland, backed up by the somewhat outmoded political system, excluded people who were perfectly well prepared for the modern age through both education and experience. Appointments to positions of influence were made on the basis of the interests of the political parties, who had reached a cosy mutual arrangement under which power was carved up among themselves. This applied especially to the parties that had been longest in power. An established arrangement known as *helmingaskipti* (50/50 split) meant that the parties within a governing coalition – all governments in Iceland being coalitions – divided official posts and control of institutions between themselves. Party representatives were given seats on the boards and management committees of institutions and publicly owned companies, without necessarily having any relevant qualifications or competence. Meanwhile, highly qualified professionals were often overlooked and sidelined simply because they lacked the right party card. The most obvious example of this 'jobs for the boys' culture is that former party leaders have successively, at the end of their parliamentary careers, appointed themselves governor of the *Seðlabanki* (Central Bank of Iceland). Throughout the period there has been a string of highly qualified Icelandic economists working at many of the best universities and financial institutions of the Western world, but it was very rarely felt worth turning to them for their opinions and expertise.

The political culture of Iceland, as it stood at the end of the twentieth century, was the product of a long tradition going back to the origins of the party system in the first half of the century, at the time when Icelanders were increasingly taking charge of their own internal affairs but were still subjects of the Danish crown. As described earlier in this book, Icelandic society at the time was still very simple and unsophisticated; the population was excellently educated for a society that did not require great formal education. In order to fill official positions, the authorities often had recourse to approaching individuals who were known personally to the leaders of the political parties and who they believed capable of taking on demanding tasks. What such men had to offer – and it was always men – was first and foremost connections to the highest people in the land at any given time. This arrangement was quite probably necessary when the party system first came into being, but it was plainly an open invitation to nepotism and corruption – a political corruption that thrived under the patronage of those who held the reins of public power. As the century moved forward and the nation acquired greater and more varied experience and education, this system came to be blatantly at odds with the way the country was developing in other respects. Assets and positions of enormous value were frequently handed over to party minions, people whose only qualification was that they enjoyed the favour of the party leaders.

The means employed by the constitutional political authorities to ensure and maintain their stranglehold was to manipulate the operation of the nominal three-way separation of power between judiciary, legislature and executive. Little by little in the second half of the twentieth century, the executive, ruling under the protection of the legislature, acquired absolute control over both the legislature and the judiciary. Parliament was run to suit the interests of the executive (the leaders of the parties in government). Party magnates were repeatedly discovered to have been making determined attempts to interfere in the natural course of appointments to the judiciary, preferring their own people to candidates from within the legal system. Slowly but surely the political philosophy of those with the authority to decide such matters came to revolve around building up as much power for themselves as they could get away with. Their motto seemed to be: if it isn't actually illegal, then it is fair game! The ethics, customs and practices of the constitutional state were forced to yield to the ideology of the ruling elite.

This situation continued in full force despite the progressive liberalization of other areas of society. For most of the period the political system was inextricably intertwined with business and commerce. Customarily here there were two groupings jockeying for position. On one side there was Samvinnuhreyfingin (The Icelandic Co-operative Movement), which ran a wide range of business and industrial operations throughout the country and benefited from its close links with Framsóknarflokkurinn (The Progressive Party). Despite usually receiving only 15–20 per cent of the votes, this party generally formed part of any ruling coalition, among other reasons because of an electoral bias in favour of rural areas. On the other side there was business and private enterprise. These interests were represented by Sjálfstæðisflokkurinn (The Independence Party), which stood for market capitalism and generally received the support of something over 35 per cent of the nation. These two parties, for example, shared all business contacts with the US airbase at Keflavík. The range of activities in question here was enormous, and open only to the Co-operative Movement and companies with links to the Independence Party.

The Co-operative empire collapsed at the end of the 1980s. But by this time the lending institutions had introduced a system of price indexation of loans, meaning that now all commerce was operating on a level playing field. Prior to this, the Co-operative Movement had profited by having almost unlimited access to loan capital through 'its men' in the banking system, which was mostly under state control and run by representatives of the parties. Aside from this, the Movement owned its own bank. At times of over 50 per cent inflation, as was often the case in Iceland in the postwar period – throughout the years 1973–83 – and with loans non index-linked, credit was a highly lucrative business – for the creditor!

When Iceland joined the European Economic Area in 1994 it was forced to accept European Union rules on general trading practices. This created a decisive break in the linkage between politics and business in the country. But the parties in power still had a trick up their sleeves. Around the turn of the century, the government embarked on a major programme of privatization of many of the companies in state ownership, notably the large national banks. If anyone thought that preferment of party contacts was a thing of the past, they were soon to be disabused. The banks and other valuable assets were sold off 'on favourable terms' to parties approved of by those in power at the time. The government, a coalition of the Independence Party and the Progressive Party, arranged the sell-off in such a way as to prevent the banks from passing either into widely distributed ownership among the general public or into foreign hands. This turned out to be a fatal mistake that a few years later was to drag commerce in Iceland into the gutter of greed and folly. At the same time, the teeth were deliberately extracted from the regulatory institutions such as the Financial Supervisory Authority and the Competition and Fair Trade Authority whose job it was to ensure compliance with fair and natural trading standards.

While all was going swimmingly in the final years of the twentieth century, Iceland's success seemed like something out of a fairy tale. Companies and institutions grew rapidly, producing large and quick profits. Many of them moved their operations abroad to compete on global markets. The feeling was that Iceland was too small for the talents of its entrepreneurs, a feeling encapsulated in the word *útrás*, an outrush or letting off of steam, used to denote the Icelandic 'assault' on foreign markets, and spoken in almost reverential terms. Some of these entrepreneurs built up fortunes the like of which had never before been seen in the country. For ordinary people, average incomes rose steeply. Official spokesmen travelled the world, extolling the excellence of Icelandic society in extravagant terms and speaking of 'the Icelandic wonder': the success this little country had achieved was incredible, and in so short a time, carving out a position for itself among the richest nations on earth. The Icelanders were coming and there was no holding them back. All paths lay open. The nation ended the century in a euphoria of victory. The miracle had come to pass. The remote colony had, in just a few decades, attained a place at the high table of the community of nations.

*During the 1990s Iceland gained an international reputation for being 'cool'.
This, and the high profile of Icelandic businessmen expanding into international markets, created almost a state of euphoria within Icelandic society.
The mood even extended to the sporting arena. After years of being 'plucky
losers' Iceland produced a string of successful handballers and in the 2008
Olympics, rather to everyone's surprise, the national team won the silver medal
in the men's handball event. This performance was greeted as confirmation
of the excellence of Icelandic society. Tens of thousands of fans came out to
welcome the team home at a special ceremony in the centre of Reykjavík.*

18

Black-out

A sense of inferiority

On 3 May 2005 the president of Iceland, Ólafur Ragnar Grímsson, delivered a speech to the Walbrook Club in London under the title 'How to Succeed in Modern Business: Lessons from the Icelandic Voyage'. The speech began as follows:

> Recently, I have often found myself cornered at various functions, especially here in London, and pressured to explain how and why daring Icelandic entrepreneurs are succeeding where others hesitate or fail, to reveal the secret behind the success they have achieved.
>
> It is of course tempting to let it remain a mystery, to allow the British business world to be perplexed. This mystery would give my Icelandic friends a clear advantage, a fascinating competitive edge – but when my friend Lord Palumbo asked me to speak on this subject at the distinguished Walbrook Club, I could not decline the challenge.
>
> It is indeed an interesting question how our small nation has in recent years been able to win so many victories on the competitive British, European and global markets, especially because for centuries we were literally the poorest nation in Europe, a community of farmers and fishermen who saw Hull and Grimsby as the main focus of their attention, a nation that only a few decades ago desperately needed to extend its fishing limit in order to survive, first to 12 miles, then to 50 and finally to 200 miles. Each time Britain sent the Navy to stop us but each time we won – the only nation on earth to defeat the British Navy, not once but three times. With this unique track record, it is no wonder that young entrepreneurial Vikings have arrived in London full of confidence and ready to take on the world![1]

After this prologue, the president went on to address the subject of how businessmen around the world could take best advantage of the opportunities open to them. It helped to approach every project in the spirit that lay in the Icelandic national soul. Size did not matter. Even little nations could conquer big ones, as exemplified by the successes achieved by many Icelandic entrepreneurs: 'Of course, many factors have contributed to the success of this voyage, but I am convinced that our business culture, our approach, our way of thinking and our behaviour patterns, rooted in our traditions and national identity, have played a crucial role. All of these are elements that challenge the prevailing theories taught in respected business schools and observed in practice by many of the big American and British corporations.' Here what we seem to be hearing is the voice of Dr Ólafur Ragnar Grímsson, the social scientist, setting the new business conditions in the world in a relevant context. Before his stint as a member of parliament and the leader of the Socialist Party, Ólafur Ragnar was in fact a professor of political sciences at the University of Iceland. Such has been the success of Icelandic entrepreneurs, he seems to be saying, that the business education and culture of the usa and the uk is in need of a comprehensive overhaul to make it more in line with Icelandic business models!

Towards the end of the speech the president delivered some thoughts on the importance of creativity in Icelandic culture:

> And finally, there is creativity, rooted in the old Icelandic culture which respected the talents of individuals who could compose poetry or tell stories, who were creative participants in companionship with others. These attitudes have been passed onto the business community, as is demonstrated by the Icelandic term used to describe a pioneer or an entrepreneur – 'athafnaskáld', which means literally 'a poet of enterprise'. Admiration for creative people has been transplanted from ancient times into the new global age, and originality has turned out to be a decisive resource in the global market.

Here the president's train of thought makes a great logical leap between the old world of medieval Icelandic culture and the new world of global capitalism. The connection between the two is, one might feel, somewhat tenuous, but no more so than the kinds of things that were heard from many other figures of the Icelandic establishment who found themselves called upon to sing the praises of the country and its people on formal occasions.

A little under a year after this the president delivered a similar speech in Iceland to an open meeting of the Icelandic Historical Association.

He listed ten reasons for the extraordinary successes achieved by Icelandic entrepreneurs in foreign markets. Each of these reasons was neatly set within a historical context, as follows: a) the work ethic – a heritage from traditional rural society, where conditions dictated that jobs be done strictly as they became necessary; b) a focus on results rather than process – not 'How can this be done?' but 'When can you get it be done by?'; c) calculated risk-taking – as bred into Icelandic seamen faced with the vagaries of the weather; d) a minimum of bureaucracy and red tape, the benefit of living in a small community; e) mutual personal trust – 'My word is my bond. You don't have to have everything down in writing. "We" all know each other and trust each other'; f) ease in forming close-knit collaborative groups to work together towards a common goal; g) the Icelandic style of entrepreneurship, in which the management is visible and works alongside the team; h) the Viking heritage of enterprise, adventure and discovery; i) the value placed on personal reputation – '"We" set our reputations higher than people in bigger countries. We understand that our personal reputation reflects on our national reputation'; j) an emphasis on creativity.

What makes this litany interesting is that it was presented absolutely straight-faced to a gathering of professional Icelandic historians, people who more than anyone else ought to have some idea about Iceland in a historical context.

Having sat through this lecture, I posted an article the same day on the web journal *Kistan.is* under the title '"Við" erum frábær!' ('"We" are amazing!'). In it I tried to consider what it was that really lay behind the way the president was talking about these Icelandic businessmen who had moved their operations overseas. The historical arguments he had put forward had little basis in reality; they were spin, woven out of a gossamer of empty rhetoric. So there must be something else. My article ended thus:

> At this lecture at midday today, while the president was listing the qualities he felt he perceived in the Icelandic way of doing things . . . I started to wonder how much of this reasoning – that we hear so frequently from figures from the establishment, and indeed also from people in the media – might be put down to an inferiority complex. So far as I can see, this factor overshadowed almost everything else in Ólafur Ragnar Grímsson's lunchtime talk to the Icelandic Historical Association today.[2]

Exactly the same could be said of the London speech in 2005; throughout, it gives an impression of bluff and bluster indicative of a sense of inadequacy. Having celebrated the achievements of Icelandic entrepreneurs so far, the president ended his speech with this promise to the assembled guests: 'You ain't seen nothing yet!'

Over the course of his presidency, Ólafur Ragnar Grímsson delivered a great many such speeches to audiences at home and abroad, expatiating on qualities that he felt to be especially Icelandic and traceable back to the country's history. He cast his net wide in search of comparisons, as in the following, from an interview in the *Observer*, 20 November 2005: 'When we look at Renaissance Florence, Renaissance Venice and even classical Rome and classical Athens, they were all about the same size as Iceland is now. It is an important lesson of history that small creative communities can do extraordinary things.' It was presumably comparisons of this kind that led the historian Sigrún Pálsdóttir to write an article on the Icelandic inferiority complex for the *Lesbók* supplement of the newspaper *Morgunblaðið* on 4 March 2006, under the title '101 árs gamalt íslenskt mont' (101-year-old Icelandic Bombast). In it she speculated on whether Icelandic self-glorification might not count as a part of the country's cultural heritage, since the kinds of extravagant claims the president seemed so fond of making for Icelandic business have a long history behind them in Iceland. Foreign visitors to the country, for instance, report similar things in the speeches of national leaders and the opinions of Icelandic peasants over the last three or four centuries. What strikes one is how tenacious these national illusions are, especially in view of the work of historians of later times, who have one after another shown reasons for thinking, for example, that the vaunted solidarity and honesty of Icelanders towards each other is built on wishful thinking rather than having any basis in fact. On the contrary, the history of Iceland – as of any other country – is one of clashes and conflicts of interest. Sigrún goes on to consider how this Icelandic tradition of self-satisfaction came about and how it developed. After presenting several examples in support of her case, she comes to the following conclusion:

> If we judge things by the history of the official reception and celebratory speech, this is incontrovertible proof that Icelandic self-praise is a valuable cultural heritage, something that we need to protect and preserve. And this in return provides us with justification for the pronouncements of this particular school of history: just as the Viking nature can be used to justify Icelandic neo-capitalist business practices, we can use the bragging of Icelandic peasants to justify smugness and complacency over the strength of our position in the world, now and in the future. But only, of course, so long as we do not care how it sounds in the ears of the world around us.

In another article in the *Lesbók* supplement of *Morgunblaðið* on 15 November 2008, 'Hvernig erum við?' (What Do We Embody?), a third historian, Sumarliði Ísleifsson, looked into the historical background behind the kinds of arguments the president was so fond of parading. He drew attention to Icelanders' extreme sensitivity to what people say about them and their country, especially when it is a foreigner speaking and the comments can be seen as negative in any way. In such circumstances, the response is often powerful and vehement. The whole subject of the excellence of the Icelandic people took on a new dimension when race became a major issue among European intellectuals in the early part of the twentieth century. Well-regarded Icelanders claimed to find 'innate' qualities in their fellow countrymen that explained their superiority to other peoples. One of these men, Guðmundur Finnbogason, director of Landsbókasafn Íslands (The National Library of Iceland), described the national character thus: 'Gifted, polished and courteous, scholarly, gracious and poetic, hospitable, cheerful, robust, skilled with their hands, upright and candid.' Sumarliði pointed out that Guðmundur Finnbogason was by no means alone in expressing such views, views that find an explanation in the prevailing spirit of the interwar years. This spirit appealed strongly to a nation with a poor self-image, people who needed to talk themselves up to bolster their own self-confidence.

Not all Icelanders of former times have been subject to this same sense of inferiority combined with self-assertive belligerence. As discussed earlier in this book, many were very cautious about the demand for national sovereignty in the nineteenth century and early years of the twentieth. There was a great deal of scepticism about the country's ability to stand on its own two feet and fend for itself. We perhaps see this doubt most clearly reflected in the countless newspaper articles from the time urging Icelanders to shoulder the responsibility that came with national independence with determination and common sense. There was a strong emphasis on moderation and caution in the building up of the public sector, for instance the school system. The economy, in the opinion of many, stood on weak ground and it was uncertain whether the country would be able to sustain major financial obligations.

It needs repeating that the country at this time suffered from low self-esteem as a former colonial subject, and that this sense of self-doubt betrayed itself in different ways. Around 2000 this inferiority complex took an entirely new turn in the pronouncements of luminaries such as the national president. The determination to talk the country up proved contagious, and soon prominent figures from business, politics, the sciences and the arts could be seen, whether appropriate or not, queuing up to hold forth on the excellence of the Icelandic people, often with an intensity that took one's breath away. One can safely say that in the vast majority of cases this was all just empty talk, entirely devoid of substance – nothing more than a manifestation of a state of mind that bore every sign of an acute and deep-seated sense of inadequacy.

Peace, strength and freedom

In the first years of the twenty-first century the hullabaloo about the wonders of Iceland got completely out of hand. The few dissenting voices that were raised expressing reservations about this or that aspect of life in Iceland were shouted down as not just unwelcome but downright dangerous. National interests were at stake! If such comments came from anyone from outside the country the reaction was likely to be particularly violent. A telling example occurred in the case of the Kárahnjúkavirkjun, an enormous hydroelectric project in the highlands of the east of Iceland that received governmental approval in 2002. This decision proved highly controversial and provoked fierce protests from people who opposed the scheme on a number of grounds. When certain foreign environmental campaigners joined the Kárahnjúkar protests, the authorities reacted with unaccustomed force. In the event, the country's image abroad was felt to have suffered, particularly the idea of Iceland as a land that was clean and unspoilt.

Early in 2008 a report came out, commissioned by the government under the leadership of the then prime minister Geir H. Haarde. The report bore the title *Iceland's Image: Strength, Status, Direction*. The committee behind it comprised a group of influential figures from Icelandic society, backed up by an army of 130 researchers and consultants called in to assist in the production. The remit was to define how Icelanders viewed themselves and how they were viewed by others, with the objective of making the greatest possible capital out of this image. The final report was released to a fanfare of considerable attention and gratification, not least because, describing the Icelanders and their activities, it was full of terms like 'adaptability', 'perseverance', 'creativity', 'unshakeable optimism', 'resourcefulness', 'achieving the impossible', 'high-powered job creation', 'freedom of expression', 'security and freedom of action', 'individuality and intolerance of restrictions', 'boldness and spontaneity', 'natural strength'. Despite widespread satisfaction at the high marks awarded, there were people who could make no sense out of all the ballyhoo brought together there. 'Peace, strength and freedom' were words that rang out as a rallying call at the heart of the project but in fact sounded more like slogans from a car advertisement. The idea was to use the material to launch promotional campaigns on the international front, to present Iceland to the world in the proper

The Icelanders have generally had the reputation of being a peaceable nation. In the autumn of 2008, when the country's economic, political and banking systems collapsed around them, the people of the country were shaken from their apathy and poured onto the streets brandishing pots and pans – hence the name, 'the Kitchen Implement Revolution' – and drove from power the impotent and inept politicians and officials who were held responsible for the disaster. Anger ran very deep, producing responses unlike anything seen in the country since the anti-NATO riot of 1949. The victory was only temporary and the 'system' remained in place and largely unchanged: new individuals now occupied the seats, but politics went on in much the same way as before.

spirit. In an interview with *Viðskiptablaðið* on 8 April 2008, marking the publication of the report, the prime minister said: 'If people lose out due to misconceptions about the country, this can affect the whole population. The image needs to be such that it can withstand setbacks.'

The board of the Icelandic Historical Association felt impelled to voice its objections to this report, particularly on the grounds of its uncritical use of hackneyed factoids about the country. For instance, it presented the hoary old legend about the first settlers in the ninth century being driven to Iceland by a yearning for freedom, and went on to ascribe Iceland's current success to regaining its 'freedom' in the twentieth century. The report was thus propagating the myth that the nation's sense of liberty had lain entirely dormant through the colonial period until blossoming suddenly with independence, that its rise to affluence and international standing had occurred only because the native population had been allowed to decide things for themselves, all in perfect peace and harmony. For indeed, according to the report, the Icelanders were

The European Union appears to be an option that Icelandic politicians can no longer ignore. Icelandic nationalism has often taken the form of isolationism and until the autumn of 2008 there was a general consensus among most Icelandic politicians that moves towards closer European integration were largely irrelevant so far as Iceland was concerned. Ordinary Icelanders were given little say in the matter and the politicians seem to have consciously kept them in the dark about what closer links with Europe might mean. It was all simply not an issue. The arguments against entry into the EU have a strongly nationalistic flavour: Iceland for Icelanders! Our country will not be 'sold'! The question now is whether the economic collapse of autumn 2008 will force those in authority to abandon their nationalist dogma. According to this, Iceland is a rock in the North Atlantic that will brave the storms of the present moment in the same spirit as the independence heroes of the nineteenth century braved the wrath of the Danish colonial overlords. The statue of the leader of the independence movement, Jón Sigurðsson, stands proudly in splendid isolation on its plinth outside the parliament building (Alþingishúsið). But what direction does the future hold for the little boy cycling past him? Iceland? Europe? America?

'an industrious and proud nation, shaped by the struggle for life in an unforgiving land'. So far as the Icelandic Historical Association was concerned, much of this was unsupported hogwash, a million miles from the tensions and conflicts of interests among disparate groups that constitute the realities of human history.

As mentioned previously, many Icelanders were only too happy to swallow this flattering image of themselves whole and lined up to wave the flag for themselves and their country at meetings and gatherings around the world. People who were unhappy with all the uncritical talk about the country, its people and its history tried to draw attention to how tenuous it was. An exhibition put on in the north at Listasafnið á Akureyri (Akureyri Art Museum) in the spring of 2008 held up a satirical light to the prevailing mood. The title of the exhibition, 'Bæ Bæ Ísland', was pure English, interpretable alternatively as 'Bye-bye Iceland' or 'Buy Buy Iceland', in either case a sideswipe at the current state of the nation: the country had been bought up, sold off, and was on its way out. The name of course implied a certain romantic view of the country, that once upon a time it had existed in a void without the intrusion of external forces. Within this naive perspective the exhibition directed its criticism at the central ideas of the people who had held power in Iceland over the previous decades about how the country should order its affairs – a childlike faith in untrammelled market forces.

In a broad and varied catalogue that went with the exhibition there was a piece about a bit of graffiti that had been seen painted in a prominent place in the town in 2002, bearing the words: 'Akureyri sucks so big time!' We can perhaps extend the sentiments of the graffitist to Icelandic society as a whole as it rushed blindly towards the total breakdown of the bankrupt ideas that had shaped the thinking of an entire generation.

Confluence of meanings – a wasteland with words

Iceland is in some senses a wasteland. One can, if one wishes, see some kind of reflection of the physical surroundings in the Icelanders' cultural obsession with literacy, an urge to impose order on the desolation of the Icelandic landscape, to build a wasteland with words. But wastelands can come in other forms. In October 2008 the population of Iceland sat helplessly as the country's entire financial, banking and political systems collapsed around them in the course of a few days.

Iceland is blessed with an impressive natural beauty. It is a land of towering mountains and headlong valleys. It is easy to be captivated by the sheer power of the landscape. The magic of the barren sands, glaciers, surging torrents and grassy hillsides touches all who see them. In the land have lived people who have had to grapple as best they could with these surroundings. At times they have done this with an eye to creating harmony between themselves and nature, using the land with respect and moderation; at others they seem to have been set on exploiting and abusing its fragile qualities.

Little by little modern living has erased people's links with nature and made them ever greater strangers to their own country. The values that replaced these links and came to be held in highest regard took no account of the history of the generations. This was perhaps in many ways inevitable as Iceland became an increasingly mechanized and urban society. The land was seen at a remove through the windscreen of a car and appeared intimidating, even hostile. It was as if men had wanted to bend it to their own wills, gain complete control over the laws of nature, so that nothing need surprise them ever again.

The people that governed Iceland over the last decades of the twentieth century had little interest in the traditions and customs of their forefathers, except when it came to making fine speeches for formal occasions. The whole picture has become distorted: all points of reference have been cut away from their origins. A rift has built up between the land and its people – at least, a significant section of society seems perfectly happy to leave behind a trail of scorched earth wherever it sets its foot. Alongside this there has been a careful fostering of the cult of 'great men', the veneration of the leaders of the nation now and in the past. The public is fed glossy images of men who have aspired to guide the nation and various subtle tricks of propaganda are employed to convince them of their genuineness. Thus the public authorities have been ever-ready to put on festivals in celebration of 'Icelandic culture', to fund historical publications about people and situations that suited their agenda (as, for example, in the lavish overview of a thousand years of Christianity in Iceland, published in the year 2000),[3] and to organize events whose only purpose has been to raise the profile of particular individuals as representatives of influential groups and political interests within Icelandic society. Rather than protest at these fossilized images of the past that are brandished aloft for the benefit of certain parties and individuals, a very large part of Icelandic society has been only too happy to jump on the bandwagon and act as willing participants in all the hype. The sad result has been that dissenting voices among the scientific and educated community have been stifled by a community of interests between the authorities and the universities, where it seems to be everyone's dream to pontificate at length about the 'loves and fates' of the great men of politics.

While all this was going on, Iceland lay in the hands of what I call 'the failed generation' – the people who came to power under the cover of an outdated party system and eventually drove the country into bankruptcy. Such was the sad fate of the group of politicians and business leaders who claimed to be guiding the country but lacked the interest and application to understand their own times, a time of great change in which the values of the Cold War were forced to yield to a new and different world. Those who sat in government during the 1990s were still entrenched in the old politics and many appeared blind to the new currents that were sweeping the world. When Davíð Oddsson, prime minister between 1991 and 2004 and at the time governor

BLACK - OUT

COLOURS:
ICELANDIC 1050 - Y10R
ICELANDIC 6010 - R90B

The national symbol – Black-out – as interpreted by the conceptual artist Birgir Andrésson (1955–2007).

of the Central Bank of Iceland, was asked in 2006 in an interview with the magazine *Veggfróður* what thing he would most like to be without, he replied the telephone, and added: 'But I'm useless with computers, so I could quite easily do without them. I have had such good support over the years that I've never had to learn how to use them properly . . . The emails that people think I ought to see have to go through the system here and I get them printed out on paper.' It is worth remembering that Davíð was prime minister at the time when the computer and internet revolution was sweeping the world. So perhaps it is fair to say that the great invention of 'the failed generation' was, as Davíð suggests, the mobile phone, and that was as far as it went. And so the world passed them by without them even noticing what was happening.

When the country collectively fell over the brink in the autumn of 2008, many wondered how this could have happened. For others the course that events had taken came as no surprise; if not entirely predictable in how it happened, there were many who had had the feeling that Iceland was heading for dangerous waters and that this was the inevitable payoff of an obsolete political system and the way that it operated.

With the collapse of its financial and political institutions, the fragile self-image of the former colonial nation shattered and disintegrated. The country was thrust back into the twentieth century, back to the time when as a young nation it struggled with the great questions that came with the establishment of the republic on 17 June 1944: How does a nation come into being? And what kind of country do we want to be? These are presumably the same questions that will occupy the minds of the people of Iceland in the years and decades to come.

REFERENCES

Introduction: Blind Spots in History

1 National and University Library of Iceland (*LBS*) 2503 4to, *Dagbók Níelsar Jónssonar* [Diary of Níels Jónsson], 13 July 1893.
2 *Dagbók Níelsar Jónssona*, 2 February 1894.
3 *LBS óskráð*, uncatalogued letter, Níels Jónsson to Guðrúnar Bjarnadóttir, written at Tindur, 3 March 1892.
4 Sigurður Gylfi Magnússon, *Menntun, ást og sorg: einsögurannsókn á íslensku sveitasamfélagi 19. og 20. aldar*, Sagnfræðirannsóknir 13 (Reykjavík, 1997).

1 Modern Times: Society, Work and Demography

1 Sigurður Þórarinsson, 'Population Changes in Iceland', *Geographical Review*, 3 (1961), pp. 519–20; Pétur Pétursson, *Church and Social Change: A Study of the Secularization Process in Iceland, 1830–1930* (Vanersborg, 1983), p. 22.
2 Sigurður Nordal, *Icelandic Culture*, trans. Vilhjálmur T. Bjarnar (Ithaca, NY, 1990), p. 53.
3 See Harald Sigurðsson, *Ísland í skrifum erlendra manna um þjóðlíf og náttúru landsins* [Ritskrá: Writings of Foreigners Relating to the Nature and People of Iceland: A Bibliography] (Reykjavík, 1991).
4 Guðmundur Hálfdanarson, 'Old Provinces, Modern Nations: Political Responses to State Integration in Late Nineteenth and Early Twentieth-Century Iceland and Brittany', PhD dissertation, Cornell University, 1991, p. 40. See also an important work by Eggert Ólafsson, *Traveles in Iceland: performed by order of his Danish Majestry. Containing observations on the manners and customs of the inhabitants, a description of the lakes, rivers, glaciers, hot-springs, and volcanoes; of the various kinds of earths, stones, fossils and petrifactions; as well as of the animals, insects, fishes, &c* (London, 1805).
5 Uno von Troil, *Letters on Iceland: Containing Observations on the Civil, Literary, Ecclesastical, and Natural History; Antiquities, Volcanos, Basaltes, Hot Springs; Customs, Dress, Manners of the Inhabitants, &c.* (London, 1780), pp. 24–5.
6 John F. West, ed., *The Journals of the Stanley Expedition to the Faroe Islands and Iceland in 1789*, vol. II: *Diary of Isaac S. Benners* (Tórshavn, 1975), p. 93.
7 Guðmundur Jónsson and Magnús S. Magnússon, eds, *Hagskinna: sögulegar hagtölur um Ísland* (Reykjavík, 1997), pp. 52–63.
8 Gísli Ágúst Gunnlaugsson, *Family and Household in Iceland 1801–1930: Studies*

in the Relationship between Demographic and Socio-Economic Development, Social Legislation and Family and Household Structures (Uppsala, 1988), pp. 27–9.

9 Sigurður Gylfi Magnússon, *Menntun, ást og sorg: einsögurannsókn á íslensku sveitasamfélagi 19. og 20. aldar*, Sagnfræðirannsóknir, 13 (Reykjavík, 1997), pp. 171–214. See also Ólöf Garðarsdóttir, *Saving the Child: Regional, Cultural and Social Aspects of the Infant Mortality Decline in Iceland, 1770–1920* (Umeå, 2002).

10 For a discussion of Icelandic emigration to North America, see Sigurður Gylfi Magnússon, 'The Continuity of Everyday Life: Popular Culture in Iceland 1850–1940', PhD dissertation, Carnegie Mellon University, 1993, pp. 45–89; Davíð Ólafsson and Sigurður Gylfi Magnússon, eds, *Burt – og meir en bæjarleið: dagbækur og persónuleg skrif Vesturheimsfara á síðari hluta 19. aldar*, Sýnisbók íslenskrar alþýðumenningar, 5 (Reykjavík, 2001).

11 For these changes in Icelandic society, see Sigurður Gylfi Magnússon, 'From Children's Point of View: Childhood in Nineteenth-century Iceland', *Journal of Social History*, XXIX (Winter 1995), pp. 295–323.

12 Björn Lárusson, *The Old Icelandic Land Registers* (Lund, 1967), pp. 71–82. See also Gísli Ágúst Gunnlaugsson, *Family and Household*, p. 32.

13 Magnús S. Magnússon, *Iceland in Transition: Labor and Socio-Economic Change before 1940* (Lund, 1985), p. 28. See also Gísli Ágúst Gunnlaugsson, *Family and Household*, p. 32.

14 Gísli Ágúst Gunnlaugsson, *Ómagar og utangarðsfólk: fátækramál Reykjavíkur 1786–1907* (Reykjavík, 1982); Sigurður Gylfi Magnússon, *Menntun, ást og sorg*, pp. 87–120.

15 Magnús S. Magnússon, *Iceland in Transition*, p. 32.

16 Gísli Ágúst Gunnlaugsson, *Family and Household*, p. 33.

17 Ibid., pp. 33–4.

18 Magnús S. Magnússon, *Iceland in Transition*, p. 52.

19 Gísli Gunnarsson, *Monopoly Trade and Economic Stagnation: Studies in the Foreign Trade of Iceland, 1602–1787* (Lund, 1983).

2 People and Politics

1 Guðmundur Hálfdanarson, 'Old Provinces, Modern Nations: Political Responses to State Integration in Late Nineteenth and Early Twentieth-Century Iceland and Brittany', PhD dissertation, Cornell University, 1991, p. 52. See also for references on people in power: Guðmundur Hálfdanarson, *Historical Dictionary of Iceland*, 2nd edn (London, 2008).

2 Pétur Pétursson, *Church and Social Change: A Study of the Secularization Process in Iceland, 1830–1930* (Vanersborg, 1983), p. 42.

3 Guðmundur Hálfdanarson, *Old Provinces, Modern Nations*, pp. 54–5.

4 Pétur Pétursson, *Church and Social Change*, p. 42.

5 Guðmundur Hálfdanarson, *Old Provinces, Modern Nations*, p. 55.

6 Ibid., p. 277.

7 See Sigurður Gylfi Magnússon, *Menntun, ást og sorg: Einsögurannsókn á íslensku sveitasamfélagi 19. og 20. aldar*, Sagnfræðirannsóknir, 13 (Reykjavík, 1997), pp. 113–20; Guðmundur Hálfdanarson, *Old Provinces, Modern Nations*, p. 54.

8 Guðmundur Hálfdanarson, 'Íslensk þjóðfélagsþróun á 19. öld', in *Íslensk þjóðfélagsþróun 1880–1990. Ritgerðir*, ed, Guðmundur Hálfdanarsón og Svarur Kristjánsson (Reykjavík, 1993), p. 33.

9 Sigurður Gylfi Magnússon, *Menntun, ást og sorg*, pp. 113–20; Guðmundur

Hálfdanarson, *Old Provinces, Modern Nations*, pp. 92–134. See also a great reference work: Árni Daníel Júlíusson and Jón Ólafur Ísberg, eds, *Íslandssagan í máli og myndum* (Reykjavík, 2005).

10 Gísli Ágúst Gunnlaugsson, *Family and Household in Iceland 1801–1930: Studies in the Relationship between Demographic and Socio-economic Development, Social Legislation and Family and Household Structures* (Uppsala, 1988), pp. 128–53.

11 Gísli Ágúst Gunnlaugsson, *Family and Household*, p. 112.

12 See Loftur Guttormsson, *Bernska, ungdómur og uppeldi á einveldisöld: Tilraun til félagslegrar og lýðfræðilegrar greiningar* (Reykjavík, 1993), pp. 70 and 77.

13 Gísli Ágúst Gunnlaugsson, *Family and Household*, p. 64.

14 Ibid., p. 95.

15 Ibid., p. 127.

3 The Feeling of Swallowing a Hunchback: Material Culture

1 John F. West, ed., *Journals of the Stanley Expedition*, vol III: *Diary of John Baine* (Tórshavn, 1976), pp. 100–1.

2 Hörður Ágústsson, 'Íslenski torfbærinn', in *Íslensk Þjóðmenning I: Uppruni og umhverfi*, ed. Frosti F. Jóhannsson (Reykjavík, 1987), pp. 297–8. See also Hörður Ágústsson, *Íslensk bygginararfleifð* (Reykjavík, 2000), vol. I–II.

3 Guðmundur Jónsson and Magnús S. Magnússon, eds, *Hagskinna: Icelandic Historical Statistics* (Reykjavík, 1997), p. 373.

4 Guðmundur Hannesson, 'Húsagerð á Íslandi', in *Iðnsaga Íslands*, ed. Guðmundur Finnbogason (Reykjavík, 1943), vol. I, p. 193.

5 Þorvaldur Thoroddsen, *Hugleiðingar um aldamótin: Tveir fyrirlestrar eftir Þorvald Thoroddsen* (offprint from *Andvara*, XXVI) (Reykjavík, 1901), p. 29.

6 Halldór Laxness, 'Um þrifnað á Íslandi', *Iðunn,* XII (1928), pp. 310–33; Halldór Laxness, 'Raflýsing sveitanna', *Halldór Laxness: af menníngarástandi* (Reykjavík, 1986), pp. 128–43.

7 *Þjóðskjalasafn Íslands,* Skjalasafn landlæknis: Ársskýrslur lækna DI & II: 1901: Reykjavík-Siglufjarðar: Jón Blöndal, Borgarfjarðarhérað, 1901.

8 *LBS* 1673 4to, *Uppskriftabók Halldórs Jónssonar: Í tómstundum* [Notebook of Halldór Jónsson: Leisure Time].

9 *Þjóðskjalasafn Íslands,* Skjalasafn landlæknis: Ársskýrslur lækna DI & II: 1907: Reykjavík-Standahérað: Sigurður Sigurðsson, Dalahérað, 1907.

10 *Þjóðskjalasafn Íslands,* Skjalasafn landlæknis: Ársskýrslur lækna DI & II: 1899: 1–13, Læknahéruð: Davíð Scheving Thorsteinsson, 4. læknishéraði 1899.

11 Jón Ólafur Ísberg, *Líf og lækningar: íslensk heilbrigðissaga* (Reykjavík, 2005), p. 80.

12 Lárus H. Blöndal and Vilmundur Jónsson, *Læknar á Íslandi,* 2nd edn (Reykjavík, 1970), vol. I, pp. 68–72.

13 Vilmundur Jónsson, 'Health in Iceland: A Survey on Public Health Organization and Health Conditions in Iceland', *Heilbrigðisskýslur 1938* (Reykjavík, 1940), pp. 181–2.

14 Sveinbjörn Rafnsson, 'Um mataræði Íslendinga á 18. öld', *Saga*, XXI (1983), pp. 73–87.

4 Icelandic Connections: The Lure of the New World

1 Hans Norman and Harald Runblom, *Transatlantic Connections: Nordic Migration to the New World after 1800* (Oslo, 1987), pp. 17–24. See also an important work by Helgi Skúli Kjartansson, 'Emigrant Fares and Emigration from Iceland to North America, 1874–1893', *The Scandinavian Economic Review*, 28 (1980), pp. 1–19.

2 Júníus H. Kristinsson, *Vesturfaraskrá 1870–1914* (Reykjavík, 1983).

3 Sveinbjörn Rafnsson, 'Formáli', in ibid., p. ix.

4 *LBS* 2222 4to, *Dagbók Magnúsar Hj. Magnússonar* [Diary of Magnús Hj. Magnússon], September 1904.

5 Anna Agnarsdóttir, 'Er Íslandssagan einangruð?', *Saga*, xxiii (1995), pp. 68–76.

6 Quoted in Arnór Sigurjónsson, *Einars saga Ásmundssonar. Fyrra bindi. Bóndinn í Nesi* (Reykjavík, 1957), p. 333.

7 Ibid., p. 348.

8 Ibid., pp. 348–9.

9 Hjörtur Pálsson, *Alaskaför Jóns Ólafssonar 1874*, Sagnfræðirannsóknir, 4 (Reykjavík, 1975).

10 Jón Ólafsson, *Eitt orð af viti um vesturfara og Vesturheimsferðir: svar og ávarp til Bjarna ritstjóra Jónssonar upp á allan þann ósannindaþvætting, óhróður og óráðs-bull, sem útbreitt er í og með „Ísafold": Benedikt Gröndal afklæddr, hirtr og settr í gapastokk* (Reykjavík, 1888).

5 Tactics for Emotional Survival: Education, Work and Entertainment

1 Pétur Pétursson, *Church and Social Change: A Study of the Secularization Process in Iceland, 1830–1930* (Vanersborg, 1983), p. 56. Descriptions of these gatherings are very common in the autobiographies.

2 Magnús Helgason, *Skólaræður og önnur erindi: Uppeldis- og heimilishættir í Birtingarholti fyrir 70 árum* (Reykjavík, 1934), pp. 2, 4.

3 See, for example, Loftur Guttormsson, 'The Development of Popular Religious Literacy in the Seventeenth and the Eighteenth Centuries', *Scandinavian Journal of History*, xv (1990), pp. 7–35.

4 Jón Ólafsson, 'Jón Ólafsson', in *Brautryðjendur, þrjár sjálfsævisögur: Páll Melsteð, Tryggvi Gunnarsson, Jón Ólafsson*, ed. Vilhjálmur Þ. Gíslason (Reykjavík, 1950), pp. 175–6.

5 Pétur Pétursson, *Church and Social Change*, p. 53.

6 See Sigurður Gylfi Magnússon, 'From Children's Point of View: Childhood in Nineteenth-century Iceland', *Journal of Social History*, xxix (Winter 1995), pp. 307–17.

7 Loftur Guttormsson, 'Læsi', in *Íslensk þjóðmenning VI: Munnmenntir og bókmenning*, ed. Frosti F. Jóhannesson (Reykjavík, 1987), p. 133.

8 Sigfús Blöndal, *Endurminningar* (Reykjavík, 1960), pp. 40–41.

9 Sigurður Nordal, 'Literary Heritage', in *Iceland 1986*, ed. Jóhannes Nordal and Valdimar Kristinsson (Reykjavík, 1987), p. 76.

10 Gunnar Benediktsson describes this interest in poetry in his autobiography, *Stiklað á stóru: Frá bernsku til brauðleysis* (Reykjavík, 1976); Gunnar claims to have copied out 650 hymns and poems during the period of his childhood.

11 Guðmundur Finnbogason, *Íslendingar*, p. 195.

6 Death and Daily Life

1 Eggert Ólafsson and Bjarni Pálsson, trans. Steindór Steindórsson, *Ferðabók Eggerts Ólafssonar og Bjarna Pálssonar um ferðir þeirra á Íslandi árin 1752–1757* (Reykjavík, 1974), pp. 264–5.

2 Guðmundur Jónsson and Magnús S. Magnússon, eds, *Hagskinna: Icelandic Historical Statistics* (Reykjavík, 1997), pp. 182–7.

3 *Þjóðskjalasafn Íslands*, Skjalasafn landlæknis: Ársskýrslur lækna DI & II. 1898. Reykjavík-Siglufjarðar: Jón Blöndal, Borgarfjarðarhérað, 1901.

4 *Þjóðskjalasafn Íslands*, Skjalasafn landlæknis: Ársskýrslur lækna DI & II. 1907. Reykjavík-Strandahérað: Guðmundur Scheving Bjarnason, Strandahérað, 1907.

5 *Þjóðskjalasafn Íslands*, Skjalasafn landlæknis: Ársskýrslur lækna DI & II. 1900. Reykjavík-Siglufjarðar: Jón Blöndal, Borgarfjarðarhérað, 1900.

6 *Þjóðskjalasafn Íslands*, Skjalasafn landlæknis: Ársskýrslur lækna DI & II. 1907. Reykjavík-Strandahérað: Sigurður Sigurðsson, Dalahérað, 1907.

7 Guðmundur Hannesson, *Heilbrigðisskýrslur 1911–1920: samið hefur eptir skýrslum hjeraðslækna: Landlæknirinn á Íslandi* (Reykjavík, 1922), pp. xcix–c.

8 *Lbs óskráð*, uncatalogued letter, Elín Samúelsdóttir to Níels Jónsson, written at Miðdalsgröf, 9 November 1914. Passages quoted in the following are from this letter. Elín's son, Samúel Halldórsson, died on 22 October 1914 and was buried on 28 October.

9 On the treatment of children put out to foster, see Gísli Ágúst Gunnlaugsson, '"Everyone's Been Good To Me, Especially the Dogs": Foster-Children and Young Paupers in Nineteenth-Century Southern Iceland', *Journal of Social History*, XXVII (Winter 1993), pp. 341–58.

10 Halldór Laxness, *Brekkukotsannáll* (Reykjavík, 1957), p. 7.

11 *LBS* 1673 4to, Halldór Jónsson, *Í tómstundum* [Notebook of Halldór Jónsson].

12 Ibid.

13 *LBS*, 4257 4to, letter from Benedikt Gröndal to Árni Helgason, written Reykjavík, 8 August 1851.

7 Childhood, Youth and the Formation of the Individual

1 Sigurður Gylfi Magnússon, 'From Children's Point of View: Childhood in Nineteenth-century Iceland', *Journal of Social History*, XXIX (Winter 1995), pp. 295–323.

8 A True Passion: Writing as Personal Expression

1 Halldór Jónsson's diaries and related material are preserved in the manuscript section of the National and University Library of Iceland, shelf mark *LBS* 2503–50 4to, etc. These sources are quoted hereafter in this chapter without further reference.

2 Klaus-Joachim Lorenzen-Schmidt and Bjørn Poulsen, eds, *Writing Peasants: Studies on Peasant Literacy in Early Modern Northern Europe* (Århus, 2002).

3 *LBS* 2503–50 4to, *Dagbók Níelsar Jónssonar* [Diary of Níels Jónsson].

4 Þórbergur Þórðarson, 'Lifnaðarhættir í Reykjavík á síðari helmingi 19. aldar', *Landnám Ingólfs: Safn til sögu þess: Ýmsar ritgerir*, vol. II (Reykjavík, 1936–40), p. 149.

9 The Shaping of Modern Man

1 *LBS* 1673 4to, *Uppskriftabók Halldórs Jónssonar: Í tómstundum* [Notebook of Halldór Jónsson: Leisure time].

10 The Middle Ages and Beyond: A Cultural Foundation

1 Daisy Neijmann, ed., *A History of Icelandic Literature*, Histories of Scandinavian Literature, vol. v (Lincoln, NE, and London, 2006).

2 Heather O'Donoghue, *Old Norse–Icelandic Literature: A Short Introduction* (Oxford, 2004), pp. 22–3. The sagas of Icelanders are translated in Viðar Hreinsson, ed., *The Complete Sagas of Icelanders*, 5 vols (Reykjavík, 1997). This edition also includes the short stories in saga style known as *þættir* ('tales').

3 Viðar Hreinsson, *Complete Sagas of Icelanders*, III, pp. 30–31.

4 See Torfi Tulinius, *The Matter of the North: The Rise of Literary Fiction in Thirteenth-century Iceland* (Odense, 2002).

5 Jesse Byock, *Viking Age Iceland* (London, 2001), pp. 63–4.

6 Axel Kristinsson, 'Lords and Literature: The Icelandic Sagas as Political and Social Instruments', *Scandinavian Journal of History*, XXVIII (2003), pp. 1–17.

7 *Lögbók Íslendinga* (Hólar, 1578). The book appears to have been printed at the request of lawman Jón Jónsson.

8 Már Jónsson, 'Inngangur', in *Jónsbók: Lögbók Íslendinga hver sampykkt var á Alpingi 1281 og endurnýjuð um miðja 14. öld en fyrst prentuð árið 1578*, Sýnisbók íslenskrar alþýðumenningar, 8 (Reykjavík, 2004), pp. 24–7.

9 See, for instance, Davíð Ólafsson, 'Wordmongers: Post-medieval Scribal Culture and the Case of Sighvatur Grímsson', PhD thesis, University of St Andrews, 2008.

10 Gunnar Karlsson, *Iceland's 1100 Years: The History of a Marginal Society* (Reykjavík, 2000).

11 Dame Bertha Phillpotts, ed. and trans., *The Life of the Icelander, Jón Ólafsson, Traveller to India, Written by Himself and Completed about 1661 AD, with a Continuation by Another Hand up to his Death in 1679*, 2 vols (London, 1923–32).

12 Guðbrandur Jónsson, ed., *Ævisaga síra Jóns Steingrímssonar eftir sjálfan hann*, 2nd edn (Reykjavík, 1945), p. ix.

11 The Barefoot Historians and the 'People's Press'

1 Pétur Pétursson, *Church and Social Change: A Study of the Secularization Process in Iceland, 1830–1930* (Vanersborg, 1983), pp. 54–5.

2 The term 'barefoot historians' is taken from German historical usage, where it is used for the pioneers of *Alltagsgeschichte*, 'everyday life history', many of them non-professional historians. See Alf Lüdtke, 'Introduction: What is the History of Everyday Life and Who are its Practitioners?', in *The History of Everyday Life: Reconstructing Historical Experiences and Ways of Life*, ed. Alf Lüdtke, trans. William Templer (Princeton, NJ, 1995), p. 29.

3 *LBS* 1673 4to, *Dagbók Magnúsar Hj. Magnússonar* [Diary of Magnús Hj. Magnússon], 28 February 1899.

4 Davíð Ólafsson, 'Wordmongers: Post-medieval Scribal Culture and the Case of Sighvatur Grímsson', PhD thesis, University of St Andrews, 2008. See also another important work: Matthew Driscoll, *The Unwashed Children of Eve: The*

Production, Dissemination and Reception of Popular Literature in Post-Reformation Iceland (Enfield Lock, 1997).

5 Kristmundur Bjarnason, 'Alþýðufræðsla í Skagafirði fram undir síðustu aldamót: Nokkrar athuganir', in *Gefið og þegið: Afmælisrit til heiðurs Brodda Jóhannessyni sjötugum* (Reykjavík, 1986), p. 227.

12 Urban Living: Industry, Labour and Living Conditions

1 Helgi Skúli Kjartansson, 'Fólksflutningar til Reykjavíkur 1850–1930', in *Safn til sögu Reykjavíkur: Reykjavík í 1100 ár* (Reykjavík, 1974), pp. 256–7; Guðmundur Jónsson and Magnús S. Magnússon, eds, *Hagskinna: Icelandic Historical Statistics* (Reykjavík, 2007), pp. 85–9.

2 Gísli Ágúst Gunnlaugsson, *Family and Household in Iceland 1801–1930: Studies in the Relationship between Demographic and Socio-Economic Development, Social Legislation and Family and Household Structures* (Uppsala, 1988), p. 139.

3 Jón Gunnar Grjetarsson, 'Upphaf og þróun stéttskipts samfélags á Íslandi', in *Íslensk þjóðfélagsþróun 1880–1940: Ritgerðir*, ed. Guðmundur Hálfdanarson and Svanur Kristjánsson (Reykjavík, 1993), p. 245.

4 Magnús S. Magnússon, *Iceland in Transition: Labor and Socio-economic Change before 1940* (Lund, 1985), pp. 104–6.

5 Gísli Ágúst Gunnlaugsson, *Family and Household*, pp. 143–69.

6 Guðmundur Hannesson, 'Um skipulag bæja', *Fylgirit með ársskýrslu Háskóla Íslands* (Reykjavík, 1916), p. 14.

13 The Myth of the Model Woman: Gender Roles in Urban and Rural Iceland

1 Magnús S. Magnússon, *Iceland in Transition: Labor and Socio-economic Change before 1940* (Lund, 1985), p. 108.

2 Kristín Ástgeirsdóttir, 'Konur í vist í þéttbýli 1909–1956', unpublished paper for the Department of Ethnology, National Museum of Iceland, p. 2.

3 Gísli Ágúst Gunnlaugsson, *Family and Household in Iceland 1801–1930: Studies in the Relationship between Demographic and Socio-economic Development, Social Legislation and Family and Household Structures* (Uppsala, 1988), pp. 115–16.

14 Death in the City

1 Vilmundur Jónsson, 'Health in Iceland: A Survey on Public Health Organization and Health Conditions in Iceland', *Heilbrigðisskýrslur 1938* (Reykjavík, 1940), pp. 183–4.

2 Guðmundur Jónsson and Magnús S. Magnússon, eds, *Hagskinna: Icelandic Historical Statistics* (Reykjavík, 1997), p. 195; Elín Pálmadóttir, *Fransí biskví: Frönsku Íslandssjómennirnir* (Reykjavík, 1989), p. 12.

3 Pétur Pétursson, 'Trúarlegar hreyfingar í Reykjavík tvo fyrstu áratugi 20. aldar: Þriðji hluti: Spíritisminn og dultrúarhreyfingin', *Saga*, XXII (1984), p. 171.

15 Children in Urban Areas

1 Sigurður Gylfi Magnússon, *Lífshættir í Reykjavík 1930–1940*, Sagnfræðirannsóknir 7 (Reykjavík, 1985), pp. 65–92.
2 Guðmundur Jónsson and Magnús S. Magnússon, eds, *Hagskinna: Icelandic Historical Statistics* (Reykjavík, 2007), pp. 846–7.

16 Monsters from the Deep and the Icelandic Way of Thinking

1 *LBS* 2234–7 8to, *Dagbók Elku Björnsdóttur* [Diary of Elka Björnsdóttir].
2 Bára Baldursdóttir, 'Kynlegt stríð: Íslenskar konur í orðræðu síðari heimsstyrjaldar', *2. íslenska söguþingið, 30. maí–1. júní 2002: Ráðstefnurit* 1 (Reykjavík, 2002), p. 71.
3 Valur Ingimundarson, 'Sögulegt minni og pólitískt vald: Herinn og (kven)þjóðin á kaldastríðstímanum', *2. íslenska söguþingið, 30. maí–1. júní 2002: Ráðstefnurit* 11 (Reykjavík, 2002), pp. 343–4.
4 Steinn Steinarr, *Við opinn glugga: Laust mál* (Reykjavík, 1961), pp. 97–8.

17 Selective Modernization and Capitalist Euphoria

1 On memory in Iceland, see Sigurður Gylfi Magnússon, *Fortíðardraumar: Sjálfsbókmenntir á Íslandi*, Sýnisbók íslenskrar alþýðumenningar, 9 (Reykjavík, 2004); Sigurður Gylfi Magnússon, *Sjálfssögur: Minni, minningar og saga*, Sýnisbók íslenskrar alþýðumenningar, 11 (Reykjavík, 2005). See also Guðmundur Hálfdanarson, 'Þingvellir: An Icelandic "lieu de memoire"', *History and Memory*, XII (2000), pp. 4–29.
2 See www.islendingabok.is. The name is taken from Ari the Learned's twelfth-century history of Iceland.

18 Black-out

1 The full text is available at http://english.forseti.is/media/files/05.05.03.Walbrook.Club.pdf.
2 See http://kistan.is/Default.asp?Sid_Id=28002&tre_rod=002|&tId=2&FRE_ID=39395&Meira=1.
3 Hjalti Hugason, ed., *Kristni á Íslandi* (Reykjavík, 2002), in four volumes and running to almost 1,700 pages.

SELECT BIBLIOGRAPHY

Benediktsson, Hreinn, *The First Grammatical Treatise* (Reykjavík, 1972)

Byock, Jesse L., *Medieval Iceland: Society, Sagas, and Power* (Berkeley, CA, 1988)

—, *Viking Age Iceland* (London, 2001)

Dennis, Andrew, Peter Foote, Richard Perkins, eds and trans., *Laws of Early Iceland.
Grágás. The Codex Regius of Grágás with material from other manuscripts*, I
(Winnipeg, 1980)

Driscoll, Matthew, *The Unwashed Children of Eve: The Production, Dissemination and
Reception of Popular Literature in Post-Reformation Iceland* (Enfield Lock, 1997)

Garðarsdóttir, Ólöf, *Saving the Child: Regional, Cultural and Social Aspects of the
Infant Mortality Decline in Iceland, 1770–1920* (Umeå, 2002)

Gunnarsson, Gísli, *Monopoly Trade and Economic Stagnation: Studies in the Foreign
Trade of Iceland, 1602–1787* (Lund, 1983)

Gunnlaugsson, Gísli Ágúst, '"Everyone's Been Good to Me, Especially the Dogs":
Foster-children and Young Paupers in Nineteenth-Century Southern Iceland',
Journal of Social History, XXVII (Winter, 1993), pp. 341–58

—, *Family and Household in Iceland 1801–1930: Studies in the Relationship between
Demographic and Socio-Economic Development, Social Legislation and Family and
Household Structures* (Uppsala, 1988)

Guttormsson, Loftur, 'The Development of Popular Religious Literacy in the
Seventeenth and the Eighteenth Centuries', *Scandinavian Journal of History*, XV
(1990), pp. 7–35

Hastrup, Kirsten, *Nature and Policy in Iceland 1400–1800: An Anthropological Analysis
of History and Mentality* (Oxford, 1990)

Hreinsson, Viðar, ed., *The Complete Sagas of Icelanders Including 49 Tales*, I–V
(Reykjavík, 1997)

Hálfdanarson, Guðmundur, *Historical Dictionary of Iceland*, European Historical
Dictionaries, XXIV 2nd edn (London, 2008)

—, 'Old Provinces, Modern Nations: Political Responses to State Integration in Late
Nineteenth and Early Twentieth-Century Iceland and Brittany', PhD dissertation, Cornell University, 1991

—, 'Þingvellir: An Icelandic "Lieu de Memoire"', *History and Memory*, XII (2000),
pp. 4–29

Jochens, Jenny, *Women in Old Norse Society* (Ithaca, NY, 1995)

Jónsson, Guðmundur, and Magnús S. Magnússon, eds, *Hagskinna: sögulegar hagtölur
um Ísland* (Reykjavík, 1997), pp. 52–63

Jónsson, Vilmundur, 'Health in Iceland: A Survey on Public Health Organization
  and Health Conditions in Iceland', *Heilbrigðisskýslur 1938* (Reykjavík, 1940)
Karlsson, Gunnar, *Iceland's 1100 Years: The History of a Marginial Society* (Reykjavik,
  2000)
Kjartansson, Helgi Skúli, 'Icelandic Emigration', *European Expansion and Migration.
  Essays on the International Migration from Africa, Asia, and Europe*, ed. P. C.
  Emmer and M. Mörner (New York, 1992), pp. 105–19
—, 'Emigrant Fares and Emigration from Iceland to North America, 1874–1893',
  The Scandinavian Economic Review, 28 (1980), pp 1–19
Kristmundsdóttir, Sigríður Dúna, 'Outside, Muted, and Different: Icelandic
  Women's Movements and their Notions of Authority and Cultural
  Separateness', *The Anthropology of Iceland*, ed. E. Paul Durrenberger and Gísli
  Pálsson (Iowa City, IA, 1989), pp. 80–97
Lárusson, Björn, *The Old Icelandic Land Registers* (Lund, 1967)
Lorenzen-Schmidt, Klaus-Joachim, and Bjørn Poulsen, eds, *Writing Peasants: Studies
  on Peasant Literacy in Early Modern Northern Europe* (Århus, 2002)
Magnússon, Magnús S., *Iceland in Transition: Labor and Socio-Economic Change before
  1940* (Lund, 1985)
Magnússon, Sigurður Gylfi, 'The Continuity of Everyday Life: Popular Culture in
  Iceland 1850–1940', PhD dissertation, Carnegie Mellon University, 1993
—, 'From Children's Point of View: Childhood in Nineteenth Century Iceland',
  Journal of Social History, XXIX (Winter 1995), pp. 295–323
Miller, William Ian, *Bloodtaking and Peacemaking: Feud, Law, and Society in Saga
  Iceland* (Chicago, 1990)
Neijmann, Daisy, ed, *A History of Icelandic Literature*. Histories of Scandinavian
  Literature, v (Lincoln, NE, and London, 2006)
Nordal, Sigurður, 'Literary Heritage', in *Iceland 1986*, eds. Jóhannes Nordal and
  Valdimar Kristinsson (Reykjavík, 1987), pp. 65–83
—, *Icelandic Culture*, trans. Vilhjálmur T. Bjarnar (Ithaca, NY, 1990)
Norman, Hans, and Harald Runblom, *Transatlantic Connections: Nordic Migration to
  the New World after 1800* (Oslo, 1987)
Ólafsson, Davíð, 'Wordmongers: Post-medieval Scribal Culture and the Case of
  Sighvatur Grímsson', PhD thesis, University of St Andrews, 2008
Ólafsson, Eggert, *Travels in Iceland: performed by order of his Danish Majesty.
  Containing observations on the manners and customs of the inhabitants, a description
  of the lakes, rivers, glaciers, hot-springs, and volcanoes; of the various kinds of earths,
  stones, fossils and petrifactions; as well as of the animals, insects, fishes, &c* (London,
  1805)
Ólafsson, Stefán, *The Making of the Icelandic Welfare State: A Scandinavian Comparism*
  (Reykjavík, 1989)
Pétursson, Pétur, *Church and Social Change: A Study of the Secularization Process in
  Iceland, 1830–1930* (Vanersborg, 1983)
Sigurðsson, Harald, *Ísland í skrifum erlendra manna um þjóðlíf og náttúru landsins.
  Ritskrá. Writings of Foreigners Relating to the Nature and People of Iceland. A
  Bibliography* (Reykjavík, 1991)
Tulinius, Torfi, *The Mattere of the North: The Rise of Literary Fiction in Thirteenth-
  Century Iceland* (Odense, 2002)

PHOTOGRAPHIC ACKNOWLEDGEMENTS

I wish to take this opportunity to express my gratitude to all those who have helped me in collecting, or giving their permission to reproduce, the photographs and other illustrative material used in this book. The photographs come from both private and public collections. First mention should go to Gísli Helgason, Head of Research and Documentation at the Reykjavík Museum of Photography (Ljósmyndasafn Reykjavíkur), which is the source of most of the photographs in the book. Gísli provided me with invaluable assistance in sifting through and selecting from the enormous collection of material under his charge. My thanks go also to Inga Lára Baldvinsdóttir, Photograph Collections Manager of the National Museum of Iceland (Þjóðminjasafn Íslands); Tómas Ponzi, of the Reykjavík Academy; Sigríður Backmann, historian at the Reykjavík Academy; Eggert Þór Bernharðsson, senior lecturer at the History Department of the University of Iceland; Helgi Bragason, photographer at the National Library of Iceland (Landsbókasafn Íslands); Sigurgeir Steingrímsson, senior research lecturer, and Rósa Þorsteinsdóttir, research lecturer, of the Árni Magnússon Institute at the University of Iceland; Guðfinna Ragnarsdóttir, of the Junior College in Reykjavík (Menntaskólinn í Reykjavík); Arnaldur Freyr Birgisson, son of the late Birgir Andrésson, artist; Ingólfur Júlíusson, photographer at the Reykjavík Academy; and my friend Jón Jónsson, cultural director for the Vestfirðir (Westfjord) region, who drew my attention to the Hólmavík turtle photographs that form the basis of a 'picture essay' in chapter Sixteen. The help and guidance provided by these people and their institutions have been of incalculable value and I offer them all my warmest thanks.

The list below (with page citations) provides details of the photographs used in this book, their provenance, who took them and their period or date, where such information is available.

6 *Map of Iceland*
National Land Survey of Iceland (Landmælingar Íslands).

9 *One of Níels Jónsson's love letters to Guðrún Bjarnadóttir*
National Library of Iceland. Photographer: Helgi Bragason.

25 *Farm work*
Reykjavík Museum of Photography (TRÓ 62). Photographer: Trausti Ólafsson.

29 *Eight-oar fishing boat and crew*
Frank Ponzi, *Howell's Iceland: 1890–1901* (Reykjavík, 2004), p. 34.

41 *Peasant family at the farm of Neðri-Háls, southwest Iceland, Sunday, 11 June 1882*
Frank Ponzi, *Iceland – The Dire Years: 1882–1888* (Reykjavík, 1995), p. 143.

42 *Round-up at Hafravatnsrétt in the hills outside Reykjavík*
Reykjavík Museum of Photography (MAÓ 430). Photographer: Magnús Ólafsson.

52 *Peat-cutting*
Reykjavík Museum of Photography (PSÖ 43). Photographer: Peter Söraa.

57 *Poverty and disease*
National Museum of Iceland. Graphic based on a drawing by Auguste Mayer from 1836 of a woman with leprosy.

66 *Horses being sent for export*
Reykjavík Museum of Photography (KAN 002 135). Photographer: Karl Christian Nielsen.

86 *Main room of a traditional Icelandic farmhouse*
Reykjavík Museum of Photography (EFT 1664). Photographer: Bárður Sigurðsson.

98 *Children in the country*
Frank Ponzi, *Iceland – The Dire Years: 1882–1888* (Reykjavík, 1995), p. 75.

117 *Work, education and entertainment. The people of Hegranes farm by Lake Mývatn in Þingeyjarsýsla, around 1920*
Akureyri Museum (*Minjasafnið á Akureyri*). Photographer: Bárður Sigurðsson.

119 *Confirmation*
Frank Ponzi, *Iceland – The Dire Years: 1882–1888* (Reykjavík, 1995), p. 149.

127 *Manuscript remains of Halldór and Níels Jónsson*
National Library of Iceland. Photographer: Helgi Bragason.

129 *Haymaking*
Reykjavík Museum of Photography (TRÓ 61). Photographer: Trausti Ólafsson.

136 *Itinerant workers: 'Love' Brandur and 'Rat' Petersen*
Private collection of Sigurður Gylfi Magnússon. Reproduced in Sigurður Gylfi Magnússon, *Snöggir blettir* (Reykjavík, 2004), pp. 17 and 33. Photographers unknown.

145 *Four older workmen in town*
Reykjavík Museum of Photography (KAN 002 167). Photographer: Karl Christian Nielsen.

148 *Medieval manuscripts from the Árnastofnun collection*
Árni Magnússon Institute for Icelandic Studies. Photographer: Jóhanna Ólafsdóttir.

171 *Cross-country postal service*
Reykjavík Museum of Photography (MAÓ 821). Photographer: Magnús Ólafsson.

179 *Women gutting fish under the open skies*
Reykjavík Museum of Photography (PAÓ 2). Photographer: Pétur A. Ólafsson.

182 A *middle-class interior of the early twentieth century*
Reykjavík Museum of Photography (MAÓ 1542). Photographer: Magnús Ólafsson.

184 *Road-building*
Reykjavík Museum of Photography (KAN 109). Photographer: Karl Christian Nielsen.

186 *Outdoor washing site at Laugadalur in Reykjavík*
Reykjavík Museum of Photography (MAÓ 106). Photographer: Magnús Ólafsson.

190 *Trawlermen at sea*
Reykjavík Museum of Photography (MAÓ 864a). Photographer: Magnús Ólafsson.

204 *Funeral of a British seaman, late 1920s*
Reykjavík Museum of Photography (MAÓ 265). Photographer: Magnús Ólafsson.

208 *A dead infant*
Reykjavík Museum of Photography (MAÓ 1801). Photographer: Magnús Ólafsson.

INDEX